T0229586

Information and Communication Technologies in Healthcare

Information and Communication Technologies in Healthcare

Edited by
Stephan Jones and Frank M. Groom

CRC Press
Taylor & Francis Group
Boca Raton   London   New York

CRC Press is an imprint of the
Taylor & Francis Group, an **informa** business
AN AUERBACH BOOK

CRC Press
Taylor & Francis Group
6000 Broken Sound Parkway NW, Suite 300
Boca Raton, FL 33487-2742

Version Date: 20110817

International Standard Book Number: 978-1-4398-5413-6 (Hardback)

Visit the Taylor & Francis Web site at
http://www.taylorandfrancis.com

and the CRC Press Web site at
http://www.crcpress.com

Contents

Contributors

Gabriel G. Brotman
Northwestern University
Evanston, Illinois

Stuart N. Brotman, J.D.
Harvard Law School
President
Brotman Communications
Harvard Law School Faculty
Cambridge, Massachusetts

Lori A. Byers, Ph.D.
College of Communication,
    Information, and Media
Ball State University
Muncie, Indiana

Chad Cagnolatti
Impact Advisors, LLC
Naperville, Illinois

Jane Ellery, Ph.D.
College of Applied Science and
    Technology
Ball State University
Muncie, Indiana

Peter J. Ellery, Ph.D.
College of Architecture &
    Planning
Ball State University
Muncie, Indiana

Robert Faix
Impact Advisors, LLC
Naperville, Illinois

Carl Fleming
Impact Advisors LLC
Naperville, Illinois

David Flynn
Impact Advisors, LLC
Naperville, Illinois

Jay E. Gillette, Ph.D.
Center for Information and
    Communication Sciences
Ball State University
Muncie, Indiana

Frank M. Groom, Ph.D.
Center for Information and
    Communication Sciences
Ball State University
Muncie, Indiana

Todd Hollowell, Vice President
Impact Advisors LLC
Naperville, Illinois

Jared B. Linder, MS, PMP
Indiana University School of
    Informatics
Indianapolis, Indiana
and
Center for Information and
    Communication Sciences
Ball State University
Muncie, Indiana

Laura L. S. O'Hara, Ph.D.
Department of Communication
    Studies
Ball State University
Muncie, Indiana

Jennifer E. Paul
Harvard Law School
Cambridge, Massachusetts

Sydney Morris
Center for Information &
    Communication Sciences
Ball State University
Muncie, Indiana

Carolyn K. Shue, Ph.D.
Department of Communication
    Studies
Ball State University
Muncie, Indiana

Chelsey Sigler
Ball State University
Muncie, Indiana

Lou Ann Stroup
Ball State University
Muncie, Indiana

Kent Supancik
Ball State University
Muncie, Indiana

Colleen Willis
Center for Information &
    Communication Sciences
Ball State University
Muncie, Indiana

Dave Yoder
Information Systems
Indiana Organ Procurement
    Organization
Indianapolis, Indiana

1

HEALTHCARE SYSTEMS

Introduction

FRANK M. GROOM, PH.D.

Contents

As the population ages, the economy struggles, and healthcare costs soar, the focus of the nation and the Healthcare Industry is on determining the means to reduce costs and make the delivery process more effective. Systems experts are like carpenters in their view of these problems. To a carpenter, every information problem appears solvable with nails and a hammer (or screws and screwdriver, or at least a little carpenter's hide or wood glue). To information technology people, solutions frequently involve collecting data into a repository and then making it searchable, understandable, and relatable.

In this book, we approach the healthcare industry and its problems from an Information Systems prospective and attempt to determine how to create a helpful and holistic Medical Records System as a core component to be employed in addressing a wide range of healthcare issues. A basic principle we flow is that data should be captured only once, stored in a repository, and then made available throughout the medical system for all medical purposes.

Such a Medical Records System Data Repository starts with a record created by a patient's physician. Furthermore, additional records of request are sent by the patient's physician for any tests and procedures that the physician determines must be undertaken and any specialists to whom the patient is referred. For an efficient systems process, a patient's information file from that physician's office should initially be forwarded into a common record-keeping system. All further information from other healthcare providers can subsequently be entered into a common file and updated with hospital, specialist, and further diagnostic and performed procedures. Any additional patient, symptom, and planned procedures can be inserted in an existing medical record that has previously been standardized, edited, and vetted for completeness by an initial medical provider and need not be re-entered at each subsequent registration time.

For each patient, from the time of physician prescribing a medication or ordering a set of tests, specialist evaluations, or full hospitalization, an Electronic Case Report (ECR) should be prepared and stored in a common repository. This ECR should then follow the patient throughout the healthcare process, office to office, doctor to doctor, with information accumulating as the process proceeds. The updated ECR should be stored in the central Health Care Data Repository (HCDR) (Figure 1.1) as the patient proceeds through each step of

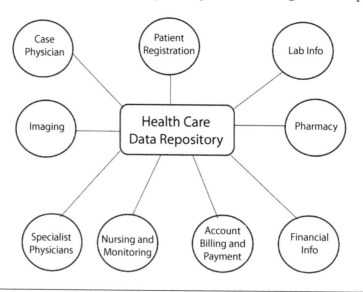

Figure 1.1   Health Care Data Repository: system sub-components.

the medical process. Providers access a common patient ECR record, and subsequently update it with the additional information gathered from that stage's processes. The accumulated set of patient information always remains in the central (HCDR) storage.

Central Data Repositories

Initial versions of such a central repository are currently deployed in a number of specialized centers. As an example of such a repository, the Clinical Data Repository/Health Data Repository (CHDR)2 is a joint initiative between the Department of Veterans Affairs (VA) and the Department of Defense (DoD). Another example is AHLTA (Armed Forces Health Longitudinal Technology Application), an enterprisewide medical and dental information management system that provides secure online access to Military Health System (MHS) beneficiary records. To achieve computable interoperability, both agencies standardize their data for each given clinical domain (pharmacy, allergy, etc.) and exchange the standardized data through a common interface.

Thus, the CHDR repository consists of an interface between the DoD's Clinical Data Repository (CHDR), the AHLTA repository, the DoD's electronic health record, and the VA's Health Data Repository (HDR). The CHDR is thus a Cross-Government Department Data Repository that enables the bi-directional exchange of patient, pharmacy and medication, and allergy data. Furthermore, common usage of the CHDR enhances decision support by permitting data from VA and DoD repositories to be cross-referenced for drug-to-drug interactions and drug-allergy effects.

The CHDR is an important step forward toward system and provider interoperability and represents a departure from a "viewable" data approach. Instead of healthcare providers merely being empowered to a have a common view of the patient data, the data is only entered and stored once and does not merely appear the same to all providers but is in fact only a single common record in a common file. By employing an agreed-upon "vocabulary" for their data and thus a common procedure naming convention, the VA and the DoD have standardized their data so that they can to use each other's data in decision support applications and in making medical decisions and reaching common medical conclusions.

Another Data Repository System, Microsoft's Azyxxi Data Repository, was developed by a group of doctors and initially used in Washington Hospital Center's emergency department beginning in 1996. Microsoft subsequently purchased the system from these doctors. The University of Washington currently employs the system, now called the Azyxxi Data Repository system, to centralize all information associated with their Pain Control Clinic. The Azyxxi Data Repository system has since been deployed at six other hospitals, among which are Georgetown University Hospital and the MedStar Health group, a nonprofit network in the Baltimore-Washington region.

In addition to storing basic patient information, the Azyxxi software and associate Data Repository system is designed to retrieve and quickly display information from many sources, including scanned documents, EKGs, x-rays, MRI scans, angiograms, and ultrasound images (Figure 1.2). Essentially, the Azyxxi Data Repository is an advanced multimedia, object-oriented database system with user-oriented interfaces, displays, and search engines.

There are several more established suppliers of clinical information technology systems, including Cerner, Epic, G.E., Eclypsis, and others.

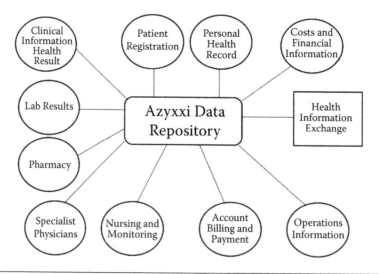

Figure 1.2 Information available in Microsoft's Azyxxi healthcare repository.

Figure 1.3 Data verification and correction processes.

A current list of software vendors providing healthcare data repository software systems is available by means of Google search or Wikipedia.

Data Information Entry, Verification, and Correction

Although a common, central repository is critical, additional sub-systems are required for each of the groups and organizations that will use data in the repository. A standardized report system should be created with a format and vocabulary that is understood by all information users. Furthermore, a patient data verification process should be conducted whenever a patient has any medical procedure performed. Additionally, an overall information quality assurance procedure should be performed against the stored data on a regular basis (Figure 1.3).

Regional Sharing of Information

It is important that all medical facilities in a region have access to a commonly stored and shared information set. This commonality ensures that a least cost data acquisition, verification, and storage processes are employed for all users in a given area without duplication, variation, or proprietary restrictions. Such an example is contained in Figure 1.4 from the West Coast.

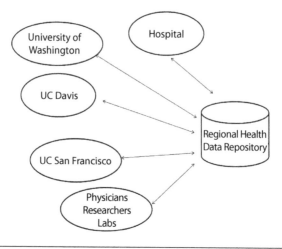

Figure 1.4   Regional employment of a common healthcare repository.

Data Privacy and Protection

When multiple people within a physician's office, hospital, support facility, and imaging and laboratory sites have access to a common shared Health Care Record System, many opportunities exist for misuse of the data by people with malicious or inappropriate intent. Federal and state laws have been enacted to enforce the privacy of such records. The operators of a common Health Care Records System must carefully follow such regulations. These measures include restriction as to access, both at the device and at the system level. These may include encrypting the data, employing and frequently changing passwords, requiring the use of authentication and certification systems, employing tracking systems, and the maintenance of a support team that is trained and experienced with the system and the deployed technologies.

Open Systems

Medical Information Systems have been plagued by a number of issues. They have frequently been built by small companies with limited financial stability. They tend to be designed for a specific specialized need and limited user group. They frequently have been developed with a proprietary programming system, deployed to operate on proprietary hardware and software, and based upon a limited data management and storage system.

This proprietary situation may be difficult to address. For example, the various scanning and imaging devices that exist may produce records of results that are in a proprietary format associated with the hardware deployed. That imaging information could possibly limit the ability to directly enter the resulting data into a central repository system written with standard C, C++, COBOL, or other commonly used software, or with an operating system of Unix, Linux, Windows®, MVS (IBM's Multiple Virtual Storage now called Z/OS), VM (IBM's Virtual Machine now called Z/VM), or other generally deployed operating systems. As a result, an organization that employs such systems frequently has had difficulty connecting one system with another and sharing data across the systems. A major step in enabling interactivity between systems is to deploy them with common, industry-supported naming conventions and to use open systems (operating systems, programming languages, and, where possible, web-technology). Linux operating systems, hypertext markup, HTTP transport, and other extended web/Internet protocols enable simple interaction and joint usage, as well as convenient information browsing.

Compliance

A perfect Health Care Information Data Repository of itself will not be satisfactory if a major area is not covered—that of compliance. It starts with the patient who must correctly and routinely follow medical, personal, and situation prescriptions from the attending physician or technician. Furthermore, the doctors themselves must follow generally established procedures and prescribe appropriate and standard medicines and behavior for the patient. To maintain compliance, the pharmacist must deliver the prescribed medicines while simultaneously checking the validity of the dosage and medicines prescribed. Hospitals and other facilities must also follow standard procedures and approaches. In support of this, pharmaceutical companies must comply with FDA and healthcare industry standards of practice and not suggest inappropriate use of their drugs, such as suggesting the "off-label" use of their drugs for other diseases or purposes. Thus, compliance with national standard practice cuts across all participants in the healthcare field.

Conclusion

A common Health Care Data Repository is the core component of a Healthcare System. For such a common system, assurances of accuracy, standard procedures and practices, validation of data, sharing of information, and protection against misinformation and misuse of medications and procedures can be controlled. This book assumes that a common data repository system is at the heart of a healthy healthcare system.

Areas Covered by This Book

- Healthcare technology
- Healthcare data standards
- Healthcare information exchange
- Legal and regulatory issues
- Electronic medical records
- Usability by patients and physicians
- Security and privacy
- Healthcare facility planning
- Emerging media and healthcare
- Case study

Bibliography

3M Clinical Data Repository/3M™ Clinical Data Repository, 3M Health Information Systems.

Department of Veterans Affairs (VA) and Department of Defense (DoD), Clinical Data Repository/Health Data Repository (CHDR).

Foly, Mary Jo, Microsoft to Offer Health Care Software, ZDNet, February 26, 2007.

IBM, Health Care Definitions.

Lohr, Steve, Microsoft to offer health care software, *New York Times*, July 26, 2006.

Wikipedia, List of open source healthcare software.

2

Technology as a Catalyst for Health Enhancement

JANE ELLERY, PH.D. AND
PETER J. ELLERY, PH.D.

Contents

Introduction

Emerging technologies can go a long way toward enhancing quality of life and improving well-being. These same technologies also can be a key contributor to stress and frustration. The specific aim of this chapter is to present a framework for developers to use while designing and developing health information and communication technologies. This framework can support a level of thinking that has the potential to maximize health enhancements and minimize frustrations. To do this we will:

- Discuss the "technology-centered/user-centered" design continuum,
- Introduce Salutogenesis and the related concepts of Generalized Resistance Resources and Deficits,
- Highlight the Institute of Medicine's healthcare system redesign recommendations, and
- Offer a "thinking" strategy for use in information and communication technology design.

A brief background for each of these areas will be presented, followed by a synthesis of ideas and recommendations for practitioners.

Techno-Centric, User-Centric, and Everything Between

Whether considering human-computer interaction, website user interface, knowledge management, or health informatics, the processes embraced by academics and practitioners alike are very valuable. Innovation emerges when designers and developers focus on new technologies, when consumers develop new ways to use existing technologies, when academics discuss human-environment interactions, and in all of the spaces in between.

During the Health and Science Communications Association's 2009 conference, David Poteet, President of New City Media, reminded the audience that the "strategic value of user experiences lies in its power to help you make smart decisions as you pursue a vision" (http://www.hesca.org/stlouis/?page_id=5, accessed October 11, 2010). Making often expensive technology decisions without considering fundamental human and usability factors represents severe oversight and lack of planning on the part of decision makers.

Poteet explored questions of usability and emphasized the need for flexibility and technology tailored to the needs of the users, asserting that it "depends on the goals of the organization creating the site and what the users are trying to accomplish" (http://www.hesca.org/stlouis/?page_id=5, accessed October 11, 2010). Remaining mindful of the users is crucial to successfully designing and launching health-related technologies. Interface design without the user in mind leads to a waste of human and financial resources.

User-centered design (UCD) proactively involves end users throughout the design, development, and implementation of technology to ensure an intuitive interface and a high level of usability. Usability is "the measure of the ease with which a system can be learned and used, including its safety, effectiveness, and efficiency" (Dabbs, 2009, p. 176). Involving end users in user-centered design reduces development time (Mayhew, 1994).

Some experts suggest several analyses must take place when designing and re-designing healthcare interfaces. These analyses include

- A user analysis to examine user characteristics,
- An environmental analysis to examine social, cultural, and physical structures,
- A task analysis to investigate the nature of the users' goals and specific tasks,
- A more complex functional analysis examining structural and cognitive issues, and
- A representational analysis to provide the best visual information display, and an analysis of the users' specific tasks and goals (Johnson, Johnson, & Zhang, 2005).

In short, thorough analysis of the user and the context is necessary for successful design and implementation of healthcare technologies. A diverse team and open, collaborative discussions are critical in assuring that user experience informs smart decision making. How to structure conversations to value both the goals of the organization and the expected outcomes for the individual being exposed to the technology is difficult. Using Antonovsky's Sense of Coherence (SOC) construct encourages the adoption of practices that focus on the *human-information interaction* with the technology considered a catalyst or artifact of that interaction. This approach has the potential to support the robustness of existing practice and can help transform decision-making efforts.

Salutogenesis and Sense of Coherence

Aaron Antonovsky's work related to Salutogenesis and SOC provide the foundation for the information presented in this chapter. One of Antonovsky's general arguments is that we should be focusing on health as a resource for living rather than as the outcome for our interventions (Antonovsky, 1996). His paper entitled "A Sociological Critique of the 'Well-being' Movement" (Antonovsky, 1994) offered a framework to explain the emergence and maintenance of a strong SOC:

> The framework was built in terms of systems theory and its core idea, information processing. In brief, the individual is seen (1) as a system linked to/isolated from suprasystems, (2) from which information/noise is received, (3) whose messages are internally integrated/undeciphered

by the individual, (4) who sends information/noise to the suprasystem, (5) which provides feedback to/ignores the message. A strong sense of coherence, I maintain, is determined by the extent to which a person is linked to suprasystems from which information is received, who is capable of integrating it and transmitting information to the suprasystems, which provides feedback. (Antonovsky, 1994, p. 7)

Central to this concept is the development and maintenance of resources that enable an individual to have a higher quality of health and life. These resources, often referred to as Generalized Resistance Resources (GRRs), provide an individual with the ability to deal with stressors and situations that can impair quality of life and health (Antonovsky, 1987). These GRRs can be personal (e.g., skills to interact with technologies, general knowledge or intelligence, individual genetic traits, social supports, and personal ties) as well as environmental (e.g., technology interfaces, work environment layout, access to transportation, and geographical location), and can be both material and nonmaterial in nature (e.g., time and knowledge represent nonmaterial GRRs, whereas food and hardware are material GRRs).

GRRs provide an individual with the attributes and skills needed to successfully comprehend, manage, and find meaningfulness in life. Antonovsky refers to the terms "meaningful," "manageable," and "comprehensible" collectively as an individual's Sense of Coherence (SOC) and suggests that Salutogenesis is a problem-solving, life-orientation concept that describes the interaction between people and the structures of society.

For individuals to accept, adapt to, and ultimately adopt new technologies, these technologies must be presented in a meaningful, manageable, and comprehensible manner. This means that individuals who are required to engage in the use of these new technologies must have the GRRs needed to successfully transition to them. If they have the GRRs, or the GRRs are built into the environment in a way that minimizes effort, then the transition to the new technology should be met with very few problems. If the necessary GRRs are not present or, in turn, are provided in a way that is not readily usable, then using the new technology will be stressful to the individual involved. This leads to reluctance by individuals to engage in using the new technology and lengthens the adaptation and adoption time frame.

GRRs that are needed by an individual to successfully accomplish a task, but that are not available to them, are referred to as Generalized Resistance Deficiencies (GRDs). The presence and availability of GRRs increase the likelihood of both the acceptance and adoption of a new technology, while GRDs are the basis for problems experienced by the user during transition to the new technology and form the foundation for lack of acceptance and the resistance that users exhibit toward the new technology.

Application of GRRs and GRDs to Healthcare Technology

Consider the implementation of a local government health information website for lower socioeconomic groups within the community. From a health information distribution perspective, the use of a website would appear to be a viable and economically efficient government strategy. The health information being distributed could be kept current by the information technology staff employed within the local government, the information provided could be specifically tailored to the health issues being experienced in the community, the costs associated with printing and mailing health information would be reduced, and the community could access the health information they needed, whenever they needed it, from one central health information source. From this perspective, the use of web-based technology appears to benefit everyone. So, why aren't initiatives like this one as effective in practice as they are in theory?

Consider the user of this information—the individual from a lower socioeconomic region in the community. What GRRs do they possess that enable them to readily accept, adapt, and adopt this approach to getting their health information? Do these individuals from lower socioeconomic areas within the community normally have a computer that would allow them to access this information? Do they have Internet access or the software needed to view this information? Are they knowledgeable on the use of both the hardware and the software needed to access and view the information they seek? These are just some of the environmental GRRs that must be considered when looking to implement a program such as this.

Personal GRRs should also be considered. For example, is the health information presented through the website in a way that is readily understood by the target group? Is the reading level appropriate and the information culturally sensitive? Is getting health information from a website something that individuals from lower socioeconomic areas do, or have they historically sought out their doctor or health practitioner when searching for information on their health and well-being? Is the information offered through the site meaningful to the user? Is the information they seek readily available, or is it buried beneath layers of links? Does it answer all the questions they are seeking answers to and provide opportunities for referral and assistance when information is not found? Most of all, does the information provided impact the user's life in a significantly meaningful way?

Addressing GRDs through Technology Design

Using a salutogenic approach allows those who create and design technology to better understand the individual who will be using it and becomes a first step in the development of a technology that addresses the individual user's needs. As such, evaluating the potential user audience to determine the GRRs and GRDs they currently possess is essential if the technology is to be accepted and adopted by the user. It should be noted that the presence of GRDs does not necessarily make the introduction of a new technology destined for failure. It simply increases the likelihood that using the new technology will not provide a strong SOC for the user and result in a reluctance to continue using it.

In many cases however, GRDs can be compensated for by providing personalized resources to the user. For example, consider the local government health information website discussed in the section above. One approach might be to give the individuals within the community the computers or Internet access they need if they do not have them. Another option that has been utilized is to provide the libraries and health centers within the community with these tools, especially if these are places the community readily recognizes as being health information resource sites.

GRDs can also be minimized through the technology interface. Users wishing to read, or download and print copies of health information documents they access on the local government health website may need to also have software on their computer such as Adobe Acrobat Reader®. Selecting the most appropriate file format for your population will increase the likelihood that a document can be printed. Adobe Acrobat Reader has become a relatively standard tool to use for his purpose, but is it the tool of choice for your user? At the very least, providing a link to these downloadable documents that allows the user to access and obtain a copy of the needed software is one way of minimizing a GRD and, in turn, enabling the user to continue experiencing success in using the technology.

GRDs can also be compensated for by offering multiple versions of the same technology. Text-only versions of the website could be created for those individuals with limited web browsers or those individuals with visual impairments who use text readers with their computers. Information might be offered on the website in both text and video formats, thus enabling users to view the information in a way that is most meaningful to and manageable for them. Any text information provided on the website could also be written at a reading level (4th to 8th grade) that makes comprehending the complex medical information more likely to occur in low-literacy populations. Each of these strategic approaches helps compensate for GRDs that might exist in users of new technology.

With this background in GRRs and GRDs, recommendations from several industry groups can be better understood and integrated into the design of successful technology for the transmission of health information. In the next section, identifying opportunities to develop technologies that support individuals with health decision-making while compensating for healthcare related GRDs is discussed.

A New Health System for the Twenty-First Century

Focusing on user-centered usability (which in healthcare terms may be referred to as patient-centered usability, because the patient is the user) while designing and developing healthcare technologies can help individuals feel more coherent when making decisions about their health and well-being. The Institute of Medicine's 2001 report *Crossing the Quality Chasm: A New Health System for the 21st Century* (IOM, 2001) offers a strategy for reinventing the healthcare system that includes aims for improvement, rules for redesign, and opportunities for changing the healthcare environment. This report provides a framework for addressing healthcare technology and user-centered usability.

While many reports related to technology and healthcare have emerged over the past decade, the content of the IOM report still provides an important foundation for thinking about technology as a catalyst for health enhancement. The IOM report's six specific aims for improvement focus on the expectation that the healthcare system be safe, effective, patient centered, timely, efficient, and equitable. The focus here will be on patient-centeredness or care in which patient preferences, needs, and values guide all clinical and technology-based decision making.

Patient-centered care will be difficult to achieve without information and communication technology facilitating both human-information and human-human interactions as they relate to patients, providers, clinical findings, practice evidence, and health information. *Crossing the Quality Chasm* (IOM, 2001) offers "Ten Rules for Redesign" to encourage innovation and inform change:

1. *Care is based on continuous healing relationships.* Patients should receive care whenever they need it and in many forms, not just face-to-face visits. This implies that the healthcare system must be responsive at all times, and access to care should be provided over the Internet, by telephone, and by other means in addition to in-person visits.

2. *Care is customized according to patient needs and values.* The system should be designed to meet the most common types of needs, but should have the capability to respond to individual patient choices and preferences.

3. *The patient is the source of control.* Patients should be given the necessary information and opportunity to exercise the degree of control they choose over healthcare decisions that affect them. The system should be able to accommodate differences in patient preferences and encourage shared decision making.

4. *Knowledge is shared and information flows freely.* Patients should have unfettered access to their own medical information and to clinical knowledge. Clinicians and patients should communicate effectively and share information.

5. *Decision making is evidence-based.* Patients should receive care based on the best available scientific knowledge. Care should not vary illogically from clinician to clinician or from place to place.

6. *Safety is a system property.* Patients should be safe from injury caused by the care system. Reducing risk and ensuring safety require greater attention to systems that help prevent and mitigate errors.

7. *Transparency is necessary.* The system should make available to patients and their families information that enables them to make informed decisions when selecting a health plan, hospital, or clinical practice, or when choosing among alternative treatments. This should include information describing the system's performance on safety, evidence-based practice, and patient satisfaction.

8. *Needs are anticipated.* The system should anticipate patient needs, rather than simply react to events.

9. *Waste is continuously decreased.* The system should not waste resources or patient time.

10. *Cooperation among clinicians is a priority.* Clinicians and institutions should actively collaborate and communicate to ensure an appropriate exchange of information and coordination of care. (IOM, 2001, p. 3–4).

These rules provide a framework for sharing ideas for technologies that can serve as catalysts for health enhancement:

- *Care is based on continuous healing relationships.* Ideas:
  - Online social support groups facilitate relationship building among individual with rare disorders.
  - Disease-specific care portals coordinate the interaction between patients and reputable information from both archived and live sources.
  - Art expression websites allow forums for patients to share their life stories and personal health successes, giving voice to both health and illness narratives and opening up opportunities for healing and personal growth.
- *Care is customized according to patient needs and values.* Ideas:
  - Query-driven web design tailors message delivery to meet the patients' levels of readiness for change.
  - Reminder systems can be established for individuals, customizing notification messages to be delivered through multiple channels; reputable information portals offer

users customizable access to information from multiple sources, including (but not limited to) health information.

- Life coaches reach users electronically and help connect them to appropriate resources.

- *The patient is the source of control.* Ideas:
  - Web interface customization allows individuals to select resources that conform to their health, environmental, and spiritual expectations.
  - Online, searchable databases from trusted sources contain quality information about service providers and health systems.
  - Medically based social network sites allow patients to discuss options and ideas before making a decision related to their medical care.

- *Knowledge is shared and information flows freely.* Ideas:
  - Internet/wireless facilitation of tele-health discussions between physicians and patients; patient access to electronic medical records.
  - Electronic medical information homes allow patients to control access to their medical information.

- *Decision making is evidence-based.* Ideas:
  - Professional discussion forums allow care providers to exchange ideas as they work to move from patient-focused to patient-centered care.
  - Online, searchable repositories of evidence-based findings; continuing education portals allow medical provider to engage in meaningful professional development opportunities.

- *Safety is a system property.* Ideas:
  - Electronic medical records with built-in safety checks related to medical procedure interactions and other medical errors.
  - Medical risk-management online discussion forums and support groups for hospital safety professionals.
  - Embedding and encryption to ensure the security of personal health information.

- *Transparency is necessary.* Ideas:
  - Patient access to searchable databases containing quality information about service providers and health systems.

- Personal health information and electronic medical records are accessible to patients.
- Patients contribute to the information presented in the electronic medical record showing that the patient voice is valued.
- *Needs are anticipated.* Ideas:
  - Query-driven information systems can tailor information based on age, region of the country, ethnicity, and religious affiliation, to name a few.
  - Proactive opportunities to maximize patients' ability to remain healthy as well as minimize the impact of disease states.
  - Online, individual usage patterns are used to recommend resources that can be used to minimize GRDs.
- *Waste is continuously decreased.* Ideas:
  - Patient education-portal connecting patients with webcasts/videos of their physician describing the general information related to common health and illness conditions, thus eliminating the need for the physician to repeatedly restate this information and instead focus time on developing personal relationships.
  - Electronic medical records with built-in checks to minimize unnecessary duplication of medical services.
- *Cooperation among clinicians is a priority.* Ideas:
  - Electronic medical records allowing medical service providers to easily share information related to the treatment of medical procedures.
  - Professional discussion forums and virtual meeting spaces.
  - Opportunities to support virtual medical teams where primary care physicians provide patient care across the lifespan and appropriate specialty providers are brought in for consultation and services as appropriate.

While successfully harnessing innovation and twenty-first century technologies to support healthcare system change is an enormous challenge, equally challenging will be aligning payment policies with quality improvement and preparing the health workforce to practice in this new context (IOM, 2011).

Conclusions

In closing, we would like to refer back to Antonovsky's proposed five stages to bring together all the information presented in this chapter. In this section, our recommendations related specifically to *Information and Communication Technology in Health Care* are intertwined with Antonovsky's general considerations related to how each stage offers an understanding of the source of salutogenic strengths. "At each stage of the process, structural factors—characteristics of the external world and of one's relationship to it—are decisive in determining whether the experience will indeed be salutogenic" (Antonovsky, 1994b, p. 7).

1. The self and the environment: linkage versus isolation. "A basic assumption of all who deal with well-being is that all of us live in a world of other persons. Linkages with these other people are the essential prerequisite for all salutogenic strengths" (Antonovsky, 1994, 7). When considering patient-centered care, one question that may be asked is how can we help individuals feel connected with instead of isolated from their healthcare and the practitioners who provide important medical services? Findings reported by Olson and Windish (2010) from Yale University School of Medicine suggested that only 18% of patients knew the name of the physician in charge of their hospital stay and only 57% left the hospital knowing their medical diagnosis. This illustration of less-than-optimal communication may leave patients with the feeling Antonovsky (1994, 7) described as "You do not really exist for us. You may be objects to be maltreated, exploited, or even cared for, but you do not count," a less than salutogenic outcome! Technology-facilitated interactions can play a key role in helping individuals feel linked to rather than isolated from their environment. A message on the hospital room's television containing the names of medical providers as they enter the room can help put patients at ease. Secure podcasts of medical diagnoses that patients can be given unlimited access to during their stay and take with them to have

following discharge can help improve a patient's interaction with valuable information related to their health needs.

2. Environmental input: information versus noise. "For the development and maintenance of a salutogenic strength, the nature of the messages must have two qualities. First, they must have some degree of clarity … . Second, it is not enough that the messages contain information, in contrast to noise. The message must contain content that allows a moderate degree of freedom and choice … " (Antonovsky, 1994, 9). Again, a focus on patient-centered care brings cultural and language barriers, education and health literacy levels, and previous experiences (to name a few!) into intervention discussions. Antonovsky (1994, 9) suggested that even if the action required is adverse and painful, "the salutogenic strength is enhanced if one recognizes the legitimacy of the demand and sees the alternative as making less sense." Technology-facilitated interactions allow patients to select information resources that fit with their unique understanding of the world around them. Tailoring based on current knowledge, reading levels, and available resources can also enhance feelings of coherence.

3. Internal processing: integration versus chaos. "Salutogenic strengths, then, are contingent on repeated experiences of linkage to and benevolent (or legitimately aversive) information from the suprasystems. Such information, however, must be processed … . Whatever the source of the information, it must be sorted out, translated, coded, and integrated" (Antonovsky, 1994, 8). Technology has the ability to help sort, translate, and code information so it can be successfully integrated into each individual's current construction of the world. Given the number of messages individuals are exposed to each day, this will allow for movement from chaos toward coherence and will have health-enhancing effects on individuals. Antonovsky (1994) commented that "The problem is not only what to do with noise and brutal information, but how to order and set priorities to the complexities of even

the benevolent information that bombards us. To the extent that we succeed in doing so, our strengths are enhanced. An experience of chaos (note, not failure) debilitates" (p. 10). While both technology and emerging media are often considered culprits contributing to feelings of bombardment with information, filters to minimize the information that reaches individuals and person-driven placement of that filtered information within the environment can contribute to feelings of coherence and enhanced well-being. Other innovative design features may also contribute positively to information integration.

4. Output: availability of resources. "All plans, to be carried out, require resources: motivational, emotional, cognitive, and instrumental-personal and social" (Antonovsky, 1994, p. 10). While technology does not have the ability to generate resource for individuals, it can help identify and access resources, including some that may be low or no-cost. Developing searchable web portals to help minimize time commitments and identify allies and using emerging media applications to stay connected with friends and allies can improve the resources available to individuals. In Antonovsky's (1994) words, " ... plans are only meaningful if one has the money, the time, the friends, and the freedom to carry them out" (p. 10).

5. Feedback: responsiveness versus rejection. "When one sends a message to the environment, two questions become critical: Does it listen? And does it respond in the anticipated, desired way?" (Antonovsky, 1994, p. 11). Well-designed, patient-centered technology has the potential to create an environment where individuals feel their needs and interests are being heard. According to Antonovsky (1994), "In order for an experience to be salutogenic, the environment must carefully regard the actor's existence and respond benevolently." (p. 11).

References

Antonovsky, A. (1987). *Unraveling the mystery of health.* San Francisco, CA: Josey-Bass.

Antonovsky, A. (1994). The salutogenic model as a theory to guide health promotion. Health Promotion International, 11–18.

Antonovsky, A. (1994). A Sociological Critique of the 'well-being' movement. *The Journal of Mind Body Health,* 10, 6–12.

Dabbs, A.D., Myers, B.A., McCurry, K.R., Dunbar-Jacob, J., Hawkins, R.P., Begey, A., & Dew, M.A. (2009). User-centered design and interactive health technologies for patients. *Computers, Informatics, Nursing,* 27(3), 175–183.

IOM, Institute of Medicine, Committee on Quality of Health Care in America (2001). *Crossing the quality chasm: A new health system for the 21st century.* Washington, D.C.: The National Academies Press.

Johnson, C.M., Johnson, T.R., and Zhang, J. (2005). A user-centered framework for redesigning healthcare interfaces. *Journal of Biomedical Informatics,* 38, 75–87.

Mayhew, D.J. and Mantei, M. M. (1994). A basic framework for cost justifying usability engineering. R.G. Bias and D.J. Mayhew (Eds.) Cost-justifying usability. (9-48) New York: Harcourt Brace.

Olson, D.P., & Windish, D.M. (2010). Communication discrepancies between physicians and hospitalized patients. *Archives of Internal Medicine,* 170(15), 1302–1307.

3

HEALTH INFORMATION EXCHANGE

DAVE YODER

Contents

What Is Health Information Exchange?

Health Information Exchange (HIE) in its simplest form is the transmission of health information from one entity to another. The data it generally transmitted in a common format that allows it to be accessed or sent to third parties that need access to the data. The advantage is that multiple healthcare providers—whether a hospital, lab, insurer, or government entity—can access the data in near-real-time. The intended end result of HIE is to provide improved outcomes for patients and realize efficiencies by reducing redundancies in the healthcare process.

History of HIEs

The concept of health information exchange is not new; in fact, there have been functioning HIEs since the mid-1990s. There are a few well-developed and mature HIEs around the United States that are providing services to healthcare providers, most notably in Indiana, Utah, and North Carolina (Rosenfeld et al., 2006). Adoption of HIEs has been a long, ongoing process due to the long adoption period for Electronic Health Records (EHRs) by healthcare providers.

Current State of HIEs

With the passing of the American Recovery and Reinvestment Act's State Health Information Exchange Cooperative Agreement Program (CAP), the U.S. Government has allocated hundreds of millions of dollars to the states to help fund HIE initiatives. The HITECH Act authorized the formation of the CAP while the American Recovery and Reinvestment Act (ARRA) provided funding that could be allocated to the states to finance the development of these programs. As a result, every state has started an HIE program so that they can receive federal funding for this undertaking. So far, $547,703,438 has been allocated to the various states and territories in the United States equaling fifty-six recipients (ONCa, 2010).

The current structure that exists in most states is a state-designated entity that oversees HIE activities within the state. Most states have multiple entities performing HIE, often referred to as Regional Health Information Organizations (RHIOs). The purpose of these RHIOs is to bring together local health organizations to facilitate information exchange between them. In this model, information would flow from the local RHIO to other RHIOs within the state or region and potentially into a national health information organization (see Figure 3.1).

Currently, government funding focuses on making sure that smaller rural facilities are able to implement electronic health records. The approach being taken is that government funding has gone to develop a program called the Health Information Technology Extension Program. This program authorizes the development and funding of Regional Extension Centers (RECs). There are currently

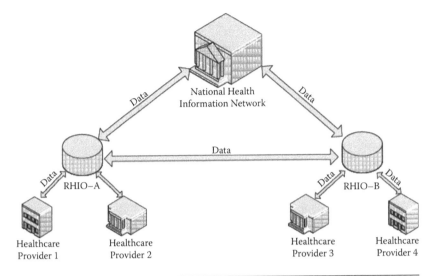

Figure 3.1 Diagram showing a very simple Health Information Exchange. Data flows to and from each entity in the diagram. The process begins with the healthcare providers (e.g., hospitals, primary care physicians, laboratories, or any other entity that gathers medical information). The data flows securely from the healthcare providers to the RHIOs (which are connected so that they are able to share data with one another). Finally, the data flows to the national network.

sixty-two such centers throughout the country that have received varied amounts of funding. The purpose of the RECs is to do the following (ONCb, n.d.):

- Provide training and support services to assist doctors and other providers in adopting EHRs
- Offer information and guidance to help with EHR implementation
- Give technical assistance as needed

The creation and funding of the RECs is an important first step in facilitating HIE between all healthcare entities. Currently, hospitals and large health systems are the primary adopters of EHR systems, while small providers and primary care clinicians have been much slower to adopt EHR systems due to cost and staffing constraints. HIE cannot exist without widespread adoption of EHR systems, so it is vital to the long-term success of HIE that every healthcare provider adopt an EHR system.

Current Usage

There are many practical applications for HIE that are currently being utilized. The federal government has delved into the HIE by starting a program with the Department of Veterans Affairs. The Department of Veterans Affairs announced the development of a pilot program that would allow both public and private healthcare providers access to veterans' health records through HIE. The project would be voluntary for veterans and they would have to authorize any HIE that occurs (Lee, 2010). This pilot program is slated to run through 2012 and could serve as a template for the development of a nationwide program with the entire Veterans Affairs healthcare system.

Another widespread use for HIE is through delivering lab results, radiology reports, and other clinical information. This allows for emergency departments, outpatient centers, and other entities to have near-real-time access to results through a web portal. This model of the RHIO, acting as an intermediary between health organizations, seems to be most prevalent and has provided a quick entry for HIE into real-world applications. In Michigan, an organization called Medicity is providing a service like this that is linking providers to move data from disparate EHRs (Anonymous, 2009). Medicity's approach has been to link healthcare providers and bypass third-party governance, and is referred to as the "organic HIE model" (Lassetter, 2010).

Software vendors that have developed EHR systems are also starting to realize the benefits of health information exchange. The EHR vendor Epic has a system that allows for this exchange of information; it is called Care Everywhere (Epic Systems Corporation, n.d.). Some vendors are enabling customers on the same platform to exchange information across their systems with the software vendor acting as the health information exchange. This is an interesting approach and certainly is beneficial in the short term, as most states are nowhere near being able to transfer data between healthcare providers. This also allows data to be transmitted across the country if healthcare providers authorize the exchange of data and participate in their EHR vendor's information-sharing program. The obvious shortcoming of this type of interchange is that one healthcare provider must be on the same vendor platform as the other healthcare provider. This use of vendor-based HIE could be a catalyst to implementing HIE nationwide as this will create real-world usage scenarios and highlight the benefits of information exchange.

Another trend that is beginning to emerge is consumer-driven demand for access to their health records. What has emerged from this is the development of a Personal Health Record (PHR), which is different from an EHR because it is managed by the patient and is a combination of information from multiple sources. This has spurred several companies—most notably Google, Microsoft, and WebMD—to offer their own tools for managing PHRs through the Internet (McGraw et al., 2009).

Barriers to Adoption of HIE

While health information exchange definitely holds potential, there are many issues that should be considered.

Business Model

Currently, most RHIOs are financed through a combination of federal and state grants and other income generated through selling of services. These services vary among the different RHIOs but generally involve a method of delivering information or clinical results electronically. This service provides several benefits in that it can be much faster to get test results and can be integrated into their existing EHR systems. The question that remains for the healthcare provider is whether it is more cost effective to adopt a clinical messaging and delivery system as opposed to conventional means (courier, fax, etc.). There are studies that indicate HIE can produce significant savings by reducing duplicate tests and paper-handling costs (Colpas, 2010). Second, if the HIE service is more expensive, is there a benefit that can be realized somewhere else in the healthcare process and thus offset the additional cost? These are questions that remain unanswered and may vary across regions.

The RHIO model that has been adopted may also impede the growth and adoption of HIE. This model could lead to a potential waste of tax-funded grant money by funding RHIOs that will not survive due to the lack of a sustainable business model. A 2007 survey of more than a hundred RHIOs around the United States revealed that only twelve of them were considered self-sustaining and not relying on

Table 3.1   Comparison of Operational/Non-operational RHIOs

	PARTICIPANTS	DIFFERENT TYPES OF DATA EXCHANGED	DATA FOCUS ON SPECIFIC POPULATION	PLANNING HIE ACTIVITIES
Operational RHIOs	4.8	3	28%	16 months
Nonoperational RHIOs	3.6	3.8	50%	36 months

grants to fund normal operations (Rudin et al., 2009). A recent survey showed that the RHIOs that develop a successful business model early and have the right volume and participant mix will be more likely to succeed than RHIOs that rely heavily on government funding (Adler-Milstein, Landefeld, & Jha, 2010). Another unknown is finding the correct balance for the minimum population required to support an RHIO. Currently there are no standards that exist to mandate that an RHIO serve a minimum percentage of a state's population.

From what little data has been gathered nationwide as HIE is in its infancy, Table 3.1 presents some early indicators of success and sustainability (Adler-Milstein, Landefeld, & Jha, 2010).

The results of this survey and the subsequent study reveal some interesting trends in operational HIEs and some cautionary tales for nonoperational HIEs:

- Participant mix:
  - It is important to have more participants and to continue to add participants over time. RHIOs that had more participants were more successful, possibly due to developing different revenue streams through varied participants.
- Types of data exchanged:
  - The fewer types of data exchanged, the higher probability of success. The more data types exchanged, the higher the cost as the information exchange process becomes more complex.
- Focus on specific population:
  - Medicaid was the most popular population that was focused on, and HIEs that took this approach were more likely to be nonoperational.
- Planning for HIE activities:
  - Operational HIEs planned for sixteen months, non-operational HIEs planned for thirty-six months. This could be due to a variety of reasons, such as complexity of

operations, more data types exchanged, and community healthcare involvement and buy-in.

Lack of Standards

One other potential barrier to adoption could be a lack of standards from both a state and nationwide level. Some states have projects underway or have planned to standardize data that are exchanged between RHIOs and stakeholders. This will be a critical piece to ensuring that data can be interchanged between states and at a national level. The Department of Health and Human Services has started a project to further define the standards for national health information exchange called the Direct Project. According to their website, The Direct Project "develops specifications for a secure, scalable, standards-based way to establish universal health addressing and transport for participants (including providers, laboratories, hospitals, pharmacies, and patients) to send encrypted health information directly to known, trusted recipients over the Internet" (The Direct Project, n.d.). The Direct Project will expand the standards and is not intended to replace the NHIN standards that are currently in place.

Statewide HIE design is another area that has few standards. The federal government is allowing states to decide the approach they will use in the design of their state's HIE. There are three approaches that are most common at this point in the evolution of HIEs (HIMSS, n.d.):

- Decentralized:
  - State coordinated, but services are market driven
- Mixed (hybrid):
  - State infrastructure may exist and RHIOs are allowed to choose connection with the state infrastructure or direct connection with participants
- Centralized:
  - State provides all infrastructure

The approach a state chooses may be driven by population, funding, or the presence of existing RHIOs performing HIE prior to federal funding. The federal government is taking a hands-off approach in this area, perhaps to allow states flexibility in their approach, as each state is unique in its particular stage of development in terms of HIE.

Security and Privacy

Security and privacy are two major concerns people have with HIE. Healthcare providers are very concerned with these issues and in a survey conducted in 2007, nearly 71 percent expressed concern about the privacy and security of HIE (Wright et al., 2010). The general areas of concern focus on the interpretation of federal and state health privacy laws, which influence how individual providers develop their own internal policies regarding privacy and security (Dimitropoulos and Rizk, 2009). This difference in interpretation and variations in state laws could create a major obstacle to implementing HIE. The Office of the National Coordinator for Health Information Technology (ONC) has started a program called the Health Information Security and Privacy Collaboration (HISPC) to address some of these concerns. The HISPC, through an environmental scan, has found several areas of concern, which include the following:

- Consent and permission:
  - There is general confusion among those involved in HIE as to whether HIPAA or state laws required consent to transfer data to a third party.
- Privacy and security:
  - Variations among HIE participants in security and privacy policies has impeded HIE adoption, particularly when one organization felt its security program was superior to another party that may be receiving the data.
- Authentication and authorization:
  - Variations among HIE participants in authentication and authorization standards has slowed HIE adoption and third-party access to health information.
- Linking data to one person:
  - There is currently no standard method for matching records to guarantee that the data you are viewing should be included in that patient's health record.

Consumers are also getting more involved in managing their own health records; this has driven several large information technology companies into the personal health record (PHR) market. PHR providers like this are exempt from HIPAA (Health Insurance Portability and Accountability Act) and only fall under applicable state health privacy laws (McGraw et al., 2009). Employers are also beginning to take an interest in PHRs and some have begun offering these to their employees. Large U.S. employers Walmart, AT&T, and BP America all offer their employees the option to participate in an employer-sponsored PHR program. Data collected from the PHR of employees are used to develop preventative health programs that will hopefully reduce healthcare costs to the organization (Wynia & Dunn, 2010).

State Spotlight: Indiana's Approach to Implementing Health Information Exchange

Background

Indiana has been a leader in the adoption of EHRs, due largely to the work of the Regrenstrief Institute. The Regenstrief Institute was a pioneer in the development and adoption of EHRs. They have been involved in EHR development since the 1970s and developed one of the first functioning systems, the Regenstrief Medical Record System (RMRS). The RMRS is said to have been operational since 1973 and contains 660 million distinct observations (Regenstrief, n.d.). Most early adopters of EHRs discovered it was great to have all this information but it had little value outside the organization. This was the case in Indiana as well, and in 1994 HIE began occurring in Indiana with the launch of the Indiana Network for Patient Care (INPC), which is comprised of eleven separate hospitals, county and state public health departments, and Indiana Medicaid (Regenstrief Institute, n.d.). This system allowed information to be shared across EHR platforms and healthcare providers.

Current State of HIE

Operating within the state of Indiana are five separate RHIOs that serve different healthcare providers throughout the state. Indiana Health Information Technology (IHIT) is the state-designated entity responsible for overseeing HIE in the state. IHIT has developed a strategic plan and allocated funds to ensure that certain objectives are met. IHIT guides RHIO's general direction through grant funding to ensure that essential services are provided and that Indiana is meeting any federal mandates required.

The model Indiana has adopted for implementing HIE is a *decentralized* model, which means that IHIT guides the RHIOs but the RHIOs maintain their own infrastructure. This model was best suited for Indiana due to the existence of established RHIOs prior to funding provided by the ARRA of 2009. Services provided by the RHIOs are primarily market driven and the services provide a revenue source.

Indiana received $10.3 million in funding through ARRA to further health information exchange. Below is a listing and description of projects the IHIT has selected to pursue with the $10.3 million in federal funding (IHIT, 2010):

- Connectivity Matching Grant Program ($2.65M):
  - The purpose of this program is to allocate funds to health-care providers in rural or underserved areas. The goal of this program is to allow access to HIE infrastructure by helping offset the cost of creating an interface with an RHIO. Funding ranges from $10,000 to $40,000 based on healthcare provider classifications.
- Data Mapping and Normalization ($750K):
  - The goal of this program to develop a common set of standards in accordance with national guidelines on data exchanged between RHIOs as well as data exchanged with stakeholders. This program would also put a change process in place for all future data additions and standards.
- Privacy and Security Policy Development ($200K):
  - This project will allow the IHIT to do a gap analysis between state and federal privacy and security regulations to ensure there are no barriers to intrastate and interstate HIE.
- HIO Connectivity ($5M):
  - Of the $10.3 million, approximately $2.2 million is planned to be spent on connecting the five different RHIOs in the state (IHIT, 2010). The IHIT also plans to allocate $2.8 million to fund interstate connectivity, which will be an important element for the ultimate goal of national connectivity.

- Web Communication Tool ($100K):
  - This would provide funding for communication tools to facilitate discussions and communication among RHIOs, stakeholders, and the state.
- Immunization Registry Integration ($1M):
  - This program would enable healthcare providers who provide immunizations to send their information to the Children and Hoosiers Immunization Registry Program (CHIRP). This program would focus on creating direct links with EHR to avoid double data entry and would allow for bi-directional data transfer. Currently, healthcare providers must keep this data in their EHR and maintain the record in CHIRP.

National Health Information Network (NHIN)

Having a statewide HIE that connects all healthcare providers together will be a huge first step in the development of HIE. The next logical step is to expand the system to a national network that would enable information exchange between states across the country. There are also many applications from a national healthcare level that are outlined below.

Applications of NHIN

One application of the NHIN that will be greatly improved is the ability to monitor public health trends across the country. This data could be gathered and reported in real-time, thus allowing trends to be identified earlier. The government has created a thirty-six-month program called the Beacon Communities Program that is intended to provide meaningful use for the information that is shared through HIE (ONCc, n.d.). Some potential applications for this program are to see trends with specific diseases such as diabetes or coronary disease.

Once the NHIN is functional, this will allow the Centers for Disease Control (CDC) to see trends in disease outbreak and react much more quickly through bio-surveillance. Bio-surveillance is the practice of analyzing health information to look for trends. There are currently some pilot projects across the country that are focusing on the area of bio-surveillance by utilizing HIE with laboratory data to immediately see trends for pathogens (Hoffman et al., 2003).

Electronic Health Records

One obvious advantage of an NHIN is that electronic health records could be available no matter where in the United States a person seeks treatment. This would eliminate the need to have medical records faxed or mailed to the patient's new provider. It would also allow for data to be captured from outlying visits to ERs and other immediate care facilities. Having access to this information in real-time will allow healthcare providers to have a better overall picture of the patient's health.

Conclusion

There are still many unknowns at this point in the evolution of HIE and they include the following, just to name a few:

- Can HIE and RHIOs survive without government funding?
- Will the lack of standards impede the widespread adoption of HIE?
- How will security and privacy issues be addressed on a state or national level?

While no one currently has the answers to these questions, it is clear that the government has taken a big leap toward modernizing health-care information technology. In the coming years there will enough data available to provide a roadmap on how to successfully implement a statewide HIE system as we currently see many different models across the country.

HIE will play an important part in the future healthcare system as the reimbursement model will be based on quality outcomes that will be reported through HIE.

Once the National Health Information Network is established, the way healthcare is delivered in the United States could potentially alter. Many of the reforms passed in the Affordable Care Act of 2010 will rely on the data gathered through HIE to ensure that better outcomes are occurring in healthcare. While there are still many areas that need to be addressed before national health information exchange can occur, the foundation is being built by the fifty-six different programs across the country that are developing HIE activities.

References

Adler-Milstein, J., Landefeld, J., & Jha, A.K. (2010). Characteristics associated with regional health information organization viability. *Journal of the American Medical Inform Association,* 17: 61–65. Volume 17 Issue 1.

Colpas, P. (2010, July). HIEs The future is now. *Health Management Technology* [serial online], 31(7): 8–12. Available from Health Business FullTEXT, Ipswich, MA. Accessed October 31, 2010.

Dimitropoulos, L. & Rizk, S. (2009). A state-based approach to privacy and security for interoperable health information exchange. *Health Affairs* [serial online], 28(2): 428–434. Available from: Academic Search Premier, Ipswich, MA. Accessed October 31, 2010.

Epic Systems Corporation. (n.d.). Epic Interoperability. http://www.epic.com/software-interoperability.php (accessed October 31, 2010).

HIMSS (Healthcare Information and Management Systems). (n.d.). Standards: State-level HIE Planning. http://www.himss.org/ASP/topics_News_item.asp?cid=74807&tid=33 (accessed 31 Oct. 2010).

Hoffman, M., Wilkinson, T., Bush, A., Myers, W., Griffin, R.G., Hoff, G.L., & Archer, R. (2003). Multijurisdictional Approach to Biosurveillance, Kansas City. (2003). *Emerging Infectious Diseases* [serial online], 9(10): 1281–1286. Available from Academic Search Premier, Ipswich, MA. Accessed October 31, 2010.

IHIT (Indiana Health Information Technology Inc.) (2010). Strategic and Operational Plan for Health Information Exchange in the State of Indiana. http://indianahealthit.com/images/stories/IndianaSHIECAP-OSPlan.pdf (accessed 31 Oct. 2010; revised December 20, 2010).

Lassetter, J. (2010). HIEs to transform. *Health Management Technology* [serial online], 31(1): 18. Available from Health Business FullTEXT, Ipswich, MA. Accessed October 31, 2010.

Lee, D. (2010). VA to use Indy exchange for e-records pilot. *Indianapolis Star,* August 25, Sect. A10.

McGraw, D., Dempsey, J., Harris, L., & Goldman, J. (2009). Privacy as an enabler, not an impediment: Building trust into health information exchange. *Health Affairs* [serial online], 28(2): 416–427. Available from Academic Search Premier, Ipswich, MA. Accessed October 31, 2010.

ONCa (The Office of the National Coordinator for Health Information Technology). (2010). State Health Information Exchange Cooperative Agreement Program 2010. http://healthit.hhs.gov/portal/server.pt/community/healthit_hhs_gov__state_health_information_exchange_program/1488 (accessed October 31, 2010).

ONCb (The Office of the National Coordinator for Health Information Technology) (n.d.). Health Information Technology Extension Program. http://healthit.hhs.gov/portal/server.pt/community/healthit_hhs_gov__ rec_program/1495 (accessed October 31, 2010).

ONCc (The Office of the National Coordinator for Health Information Technology) (n.d.). Beacon Community Program. http://healthit.hhs. gov/portal/server.pt/community/healthit_hhs_gov__beacon_commu- nity_program/1805 (accessed 31 Oct. 2010).

Anonymous. (2009). The Bottom-up Approach to HIEs. Bypassing third-party governance allows Spectrum Health to meet physician-practice needs across three hospital systems. *Health Management Technology [serial online]*, 30(12): 30–31. Available from Health Business FullTEXT, Ipswich, MA. Accessed October 31, 2010.

Regenstrief Institute Inc. (n.d.). Regenstrief Medical Record System. http:// www.regenstrief.org/medinformatics/rmrs (accessed 31 Oct. 2010).

Rosenfeld, S., Koss, S., Caruth, K., & Fuller, G. (2006). Evolution of State Health Information Exchange/ A Study of Vision, Strategy, and Progress. Prepared for The Agency for Healthcare Research and Quality (AHRQ), U.S. Department of Health and Human Services.

Rudin, R., Simon, S., Volk, L., Tripathi, M., & Bates, D. (2009). Understanding the decisions and values of stakeholders in health information exchanges: Experiences from Massachusetts. *American Journal of Public Health* [serial online], 99(5): 950–955. Available from Health Business FullTEXT, Ipswich, MA. Accessed October 31, 2010.

The Direct Project. (n.d.). http://nhindirect.org/ (accessed 31 Oct. 2010).

Wright, A., Soran, C., Jenter, C.A., Volk, L.A., Bates, D.W., and Simon, S.R. (2010). Physician attitudes toward health information exchange: results of a statewide survey. *Journal of the American Medical Informatics Association*, 17(1): 66–70.

Wynia, M., & Dunn, K. (2010). Dreams and nightmares: Practical and ethical issues for patients and physicians using personal health records. *Journal of Law, Medicine & Ethics* [serial online], 38(1): 64–73. Available from: Academic Search Premier, Ipswich, MA. Accessed October 31, 2010.

4

UNIVERSAL DATA STANDARDS

COLLEEN WILLIS

Contents

Why Is There a Need for Data Standards

The healthcare and public health fields are changing the way they manage and utilize an individual's health information. There have been rapid improvements in information technology to advance the effectiveness, excellence, and security of healthcare (MN-PHIN Steering Committee, 2006). Public health agencies are a portion of this changing health information strategy. Most public health data come from hospitals, laboratories, and the private sector. Public health also has data that have health policy, research, and clinical value. For health information to be managed effectively and transferred from one health institution to another, health institutions must accept data standards nationwide (MN-PHIN Steering Committee, 2006).

Data standards are an arranged-upon, mutual, and reliable way to record information. They allow data to be traded between diverse information systems. The data that are transferred have consistent meaning from system to system, program to program, and agency to agency. Data standards are extremely important in health information exchange (MN-PHIN Steering Committee, 2006). They make it possible for health information to be exchanged from one institution to another safely, and adequately. There is a set of diverse standards and each set of standards serves a different purpose. For example, there are standards for coding nursing functions for diagnostic codes, billing for medical services, sending health data between different information systems, and coding lab results (MN-PHIN Steering Committee, 2006). Standards allow computers to direct data from one computer to another in the same format. In short, data standards are universally agreed-upon ways to handle data that ensures interoperability (MN-PHIN Steering Committee, 2006).

Data standards are very important in public health because they enable secure and safe transfer of information across different computer systems. Right now there are 2100 different standards being used in the healthcare field. This is a huge number that must be reduced so they are easier to work with and easier to understand. There are many factors we need to take into consideration, including

- The need for a more effective and receptive public health system that utilizes its data as a resource to advance community health and public health.
- The need to interchange data across public health information systems to help generate comprehensive and integrated summaries of clients, families, and communities.
- The need to exchange data between hospitals, private sectors, jails, state agencies, and local health departments.
- There is the frustration of working with silo information systems that cannot interchange data, do not support enhancements in public health, are incompetent, and make complete public assessments problematic.
- The healthcare industry is moving very fast and is moving toward adopting a set of data standards that are universal. All public health data will eventually be exchanged, so we need to

guarantee that information systems can accept and exchange that data (MN-PHIN Steering Committee, 2006).

Healthcare reporting, data quality, and consistency are critical to ensuring patient safety and communication. To assess the quality and consistency of data requires data standards. The Institute of Medicine's report entitled "Patient Safety: Achieving a New Standard for Care" states that "At the most basic level, data standards are about the standardization of data elements: (1) defining what to collect, (2) deciding how to represent what is collected (by designating data types or terminologies), and (3) determining how to encode the data for transmission." If there are not any data standards, the future of interoperability is desolate (Fenton, PS-1, 2007: 1).

The purpose of data standards is to have a more uniform connotation of how health data are collected, exchanged, and examined between hospitals, physicians, other public health officials, and researchers across geographical areas. The standards are proposed to enable data analysis and utilization by guaranteeing the comparability, quality, and accuracy of healthcare data. When healthcare institutions use data standards, they intensify the computerization of healthcare data for constant patient care, quality measurement, and research (AHRQ, 1999). When we endorse uniform, consistent, and computerized healthcare data, there can be advancements in medical research and improvement in the effectiveness of the private institution's healthcare delivery system and excellence in improvement measurement. Data standards cover areas such as diagnosis and procedure codes; demographics, employment, economic, health status, and other characteristics associated with health. They also cover the use and cost of services provided by healthcare providers and clinical and administrative data for use in computer-based patient record systems and in decision support systems (Health Care Informatics Standards Activites of Selected Federal Agencies, 1999).

Interoperability: What Is It?

In healthcare, interoperability means the ability "to use the information that has been exchanged which means not only that healthcare systems must be able to communicate with one another, but also that they must employ shared terminology and definitions" (Gibbons et al., 2007). Interoperability is being able to interchange data from information system to information system, without having to decode it into a new arrangement and being able to remember the same connotation (MN-PHIN Steering Committee, 2006). Interoperability permits individuals or organizations to communicate in general terms about systems cooperating with each other. It can be inter-institutional, intra-institutional, and intra-system, which is the system's capability to use covert codes utilized into a clinical description (Gibbons et al., 2007). Interoperability has many different definitions and can be used in almost every field. Interoperability is very important in biomedical and clinical research because there is an incessant cycle of clinical quality development that starts with patient-gathered data at the point of care, is upheld, and augmented in clinical databases. This is referred to as "arcs of interoperability" and this permits information to flow effortlessly among researchers, point-of-care practitioners, and computer software developers (Gibbons et al., 2007). Interoperability describes how one or more systems are measured in relation to each other. It can range from nonexistent to complete and relating entire transparency between two systems (Gibbons et al., 2007). There are three types of interoperability: *technical, process,* and *semantic.* They are all very important but we focus here mostly on the semantics.

Technical Interoperability

Technical interoperability is usually used in conjunction with other types of interoperability. Technical interoperability defines the basic hardware-based form of interoperability. Healthcare individuals also refer technical interoperability as "functional interoperability." It is the capability of two or more systems to exchange information so that it can read by humans who receive the data information (Gibbons et al., 2007). The term "technical interoperability" is better defined because it refers to hardware, transmission, and related functions such as access and security management. The importance of technical interoperability lies in the transportation of data and not the meaning of the data. If computers did not use their own written language, technical interoperability would be comparable to the level of interoperability delivered by voice communications (Gibbons et al., 2007). Technical interoperability incorporates the transmission and reception of information that can be used by an individual but it cannot be further managed into semantic parallels by software. Mathematical operations are completed at the level of technical interoperability (Gibbons et al., 2007). Technical interoperability is a reliable, secure connectivity transmission that has specific shared standards for exchange of data and programs. It is a dynamic and shared service (Gibbons et al., 2007). Technical interoperability has a lot to do with connectivity across the network and across applications. There are three types:

1. *Simple exchange:* The sending application sends a message over the network to another application, which receives it in a complete and correct form (Gibbons et al., 2007).
2. *Simple exchange with a defined message:* The sending application structures the message in an expected form. The data elements appear in a defined way within the message but the meaning of the data is not specified (Gibbons et al., 2007).
3. *More complex exchange:* The mapping of the data in an agreed-upon form (Gibbons et al., 2007).

Technical interoperability deactivates the effects of distance. It makes sure that data streams consistently from system to system (Gibbons et al., 2007).

Process Interoperability

Process interoperability is the newest type of interoperability and is still being clearly defined. It is a necessity for effective system implementation into authentic work settings. It was identified as a type of interoperability in Europe, and the Institute of Medicine is writing a report that recognizes this social or workflow business as an important way to cultivate protection and excellence in healthcare systems (Gibbons et al., 2007). Process interoperability covenants mainly with approaches for the optimal integration of computer systems into actual work settings. They may include the following:

- Explicit user role specification
- Useful, friendly, and efficient human-machine interface

- Data presentation/flow supports work setting
- Engineered work design
- Proven effectiveness in actual use (Gibbons et al., 2007).

Process interoperability organizes work procedures. It enhances the communication of information in a timely manner to organize the work procedures of the care team. Important documentation, protection, and quality notices can improve human interventions to guarantee that the care team can access information to treat the patient in the most efficient and safe way possible (Gibbons et al., 2007).

Semantic Interoperability

Semantic interoperability is utilized to exploit the usefulness of shared information and to apply applications like smart decision backing, which is a higher level of interoperability. Semantic interoperability is defined as the capability of information shared by systems to be understood so nonnumeric data can be administered by the receiving system. It is a multilevel notion, with the degree of semantic interoperability reliant on the level of arrangement of data content terminology and the content of models and patterns utilized by the sending and receiving systems (Gibbons et al., 2007). HL7 (Health Level 7) has defined a quality that is essential for best semantic interoperability to occur. The rationale of the HL7 semantic interoperability messaging standard asserts that "health information systems will communicate information in a form that will be understood in exactly the same way by both sender and recipient" (Gibbons et al., 2007: 25). Semantic interoperability requires less "human" processing. This is good because it delivers liberation from redundant, error-prone human data entry or inquiry. It also generates opportunities for the interference of deceptive information, even mistaken policies, into patient care procedures, if not considerately and sensibly developed, tested, and employed (Gibbons et al., 2007). Full semantic transparency is very important in HIT (Health Information Technology) informatics. It is also the highest scientific and moral challenge. Pretend that semantic interoperability describes an image printed on a puzzle and the image's ability to deliver information to individuals. Now understand that each person views the puzzle differently. The individuals accumulating the puzzle do not care how it was contrived, wrapped, transported, or gathered. They are only concerned with viewing the map to understand how the subway may be used from "here" to "there." Semantic interoperability communicates only the meaning of the data information (Gibbons et al., 2007). It provides organized sequenced, unambiguous, and concise information that can instantaneously be put to use in patient care. It can contribute to improved care and outcomes by allowing the communication of meaning. Semantic interoperability is at the core of deciphering scientific finding into care distribution. It has to do with the *meaningful* exchange of information along with the perspective of the information derivative from ontology (Gibbons et al., 2007). Semantic interoperability goes outside, configuring the data and gets into collaborating the intent or understanding of the connotation of the data to the sender to the information user. There are four ways that semantic interoperability can be defined, to include:

1. "Blobs" of data: this is meaningful to the user at either end of the conveyed message but is not meaningful to the primary computer applications involved in transmissions.
2. Free text: can be read by the receiving application but does not have a distinct structure. Accepted language processing software can be used to recognize structure within the free text so that it can be further used within applications.
3. Classification systems: which include the International Classification of Diseases (ICD-9) and Common Procedural Terminology (CPT) or other countless nursing technologies, which have hierarchical representations for exact explanations of diagnoses, procedures, and activities.
4. Standardized clinical nomenclature within structured messages: these are called reference terminologies and use compositional languages that can be post-coordinated to create typical names, and also be mapped to confident ontologies (Gibbons et al., 2007).

Semantic interoperability is vital as data moves from place to place between those who deliver, pay for, and profit from healthcare. Problems can arise in semantic interoperability when terms have multiple meanings or when two or more terms denote the same notion but are not easily documented as synonyms (Fenton, 2007). Semantic interoperability is a shared message syntax, a shared data model with a domain and specific standards, dynamic data models, ontologies, shared standards, and vocabularies (Gibbons et al., 2007). It is a thorough, natural, and logical order of data gathering. Semantic transparency is utilized to support all functions of semantic interoperability (Gibbons et al., 2007). Having explained why there is a need for data standards and what interoperability is, we now discuss some types of data standards being used today in the United States.

What Is HITSP?

The task of the Healthcare Information Technology Standards Panel (HITSP) is to assist as a supportive partnership amid the public and private sectors for the persistence of attaining a widely recognized and useful set of standards precisely to permit and support widespread interoperability among healthcare software applications, as they will interact in a local, regional, and national health information network for the United States (HITSP, 2009a). HITSP is dedicated to an open and translucent style of development that includes membership and participation open to all interested parties; work products are available for open evaluation and comment before approval, and all meetings are open for membership participation (HITSP, 2009a). The HITSP was founded in October 2005 and partners with the U.S. Department of Health and Human Services. The panel has two objectives, which are:

- "To serve and establish a cooperative partnership between the public and private sectors to achieve a widely accepted and useful set of standards that will enable and support widespread interoperability among healthcare software applications in a Nationwide Health Information Network for the United States.
- To harmonize relevant standards in the healthcare industry to enable and advance interoperability of healthcare applications, and the interchange of healthcare data, to assure accurate use, access, privacy and security, both for supporting the delivery of care and public health" (HITSP, 2009a).

The HITSP is a membership-only organization; to become a member, you must be within four major categories. There is no fee to participate in the HITSP or on any of its committees. The only requirement is registration (HITSP, 2009a).

HITSP Harmonization Framework

The HITSP Harmonization Framework defines a set of artifacts, known as "constructs," that postulates how to assimilate and constrain designated standards to meet the corporate requirements of Use Case (a use case in software engineering and systems engineering is a description of a system's behavior as it responds to a request that originates from outside the system), and outlines a roadmap to use in developing standards and to harmonize overlapping standards when resolved (HITSP, 2009b). The HITSP has four concept types that help decrease the range of possibility:

1. *Interoperability specifications:* These specifications integrate all constructs used to meet the business needs of a use case. They also classify technical system necessities to meet use case and set background for concepts used.
2. *Transaction packages:* These packages logically group transactions and describe how the HITSP constructs are used to maintain a stand-alone information exchange within a distinct background between two or more systems.
3. *Transactions:* These are logical grouping of movements that use modules. Compound standards must realize the actions. Also includes essential content and context, which all prosper or flop as a group.
4. *Components:* Logical alignments of base standards that work together, such as a message and terminology. Also an atomic concept used to support a material exchange or to meet an infrastructure obligation (e.g., security, logging/audit) (HITSP, 2009b).

There are exact rules that occur for each construct type, describing what the construct type can be used for and how the construct types can be nested. Each construct can

- Contain construct types that are less inclusive in scope
- Constrain any construct or standard it contains
- Be constrained by any construct that contains it
- Is a candidate for reuse and repurposing, if a new set of requirements and context can be fulfilled by the construct without impacting existing uses of the construct
- Is uniquely identified and version controlled (HITSP, 2009b)

HITSP Structure

The HITSP organizational structure is united to meet the harmonization needs produced by a growing number and increasing scope of Use Cases and the need to uphold reliability across Interoperability Specifications and Constructs (HITSP, 2009a).

The perspective and domain technical committees (TCs) are accountable for

- "Identifying and analyzing gaps and duplications within the standards industry as they related to each specific Use Case.
- Providing a description of the gaps, including missing or incomplete standards.
- Providing a description of all duplications, overlaps, or competition among standards for the relevant use cases.
- Providing a listing of all standards that satisfy the requirements imposed by the relevant use cases as well as testing criteria that shall be used to test the standard.
- Submitting these recommendations to HITSP for review, approval, and resolution" (HITSP, 2009c).

The domain technical committees focus on specific areas of healthcare IT interoperability and the perspective technical committees focus on Use Cases defined by the stakeholder (HITSP, 2009a).

The coordinating committees focus on industry liaison, internal policy, and governance activities (HITSP, 2009a). The HITSP is a great way to try to find ways to use a universal set of data standards. The next type of standard discussed is the messaging standard; it is the most widely used in the United States.

Health Level 7

The Health Level 7 (HL7) was initiated in 1987, Health Level Seven International (HL7) is a not-for-profit, ANSI-accredited standards emerging association devoted to providing a complete framework and related standards for the exchange, integration, sharing, and retrieval of electronic health information that supports clinical practice and the organization, distribution, and assessment of health services. HL7's 2300+ members include approximately 500 corporate members who represent more than 90 percent of the information systems vendors serving healthcare (HL7, 2010). The HL7 vision is to create the best and most widely used standards in healthcare. HL7 delivers standards for interoperability that increase care distribution, enhance workflow, reduce uncertainty, and improve information transmission among all of the stakeholders, including healthcare providers, government agencies, the vendor community, fellow SDOs (Standards Development Organizations), and patients. SDOs, voluntary consensus-driven organizations, are comprised of members from diverse federal and state government agencies, academia, and the private sector. Working together, they bring multiple strengths to standards development. More importantly, they develop agreed-upon standards that ensure the transfer of understandable, coherent, timely, and actionable health information. In all the procedures, they display timeliness, technical thoroughness, and practical proficiency without compromising transparency, responsibility, practicality, or the readiness to put the needs of stakeholders first (HL7, 2010). Level Seven "refers to the seventh level of the International Organization for Standardization (ISO) seven-layer communications model for Open Systems Interconnection (OSI)—the application level. The application level interfaces straight to and attains shared application facilities for the application procedures. Although other procedures have largely outdated it, the OSI model remains appreciated as a place to begin the study of network architecture. The HL7 Roadmap article is a commercial plan for products and facilities and was intended specifically to meet the professional needs of affiliates and stakeholders. Derived from cooperative efforts with members, government and nongovernment agencies, and other standards development establishments, the Roadmap encompasses five high-level organizational strategies that are maintained by a thorough strategic plan with clearly defined objectives, milestones, and metrics for success (HL7, 2010).

HL7 Version 2.3.1

The purpose of HL7 version 2.3.1 is to enable communication in healthcare settings by providing standards that interchange data among healthcare applications. HL7 makes no assumptions about the use of data but it does assume that the application and the source have privacy settings in place. Version 2.3.1 is silent on logic and physical construction of the patient longitudinal health record. HL7 makes no hypothesis regarding the ownership of the data being transferred and also makes no expectations about the strategy and construction of the application system receiving the material. HL7 is limited to the specification of communication between application systems and the events triggering them (SRDC, 2005). A trigger event is an event in the real world of healthcare that creates the need for data to flow among systems. HL7 transfers three types of information: datatypes, messages, and segments. Datatypes transmit codes or encapsulated data (Figure 4.1). Datatype Coded Elements (CEs) transfer codes and the text related with the code. The identifier means which code and the text is the description. The name referes to which coding scheme is being used. Datatype Encapsulated Data (ED) transfers data that is encapsulated and includes source application, type of data, data subtype, encoding, and other data (SRDC, 2005). Messages are the atomic unit of data transferred between systems. Segments are repeating structures (SRDC, 2005).

There were numerous problems with Version 2.3.1. The first issue was that it had problems with misunderstanding the specifications. This resulted in different implicit information models. It also misread conformance claims and had no vocabulary to describe conformance concepts. The implicit information model was not implicit and needed a controlled vocabulary. The version also had no explicit support for object technologies and security functions. Finally, it was troublesome and ubiquitous (SROD, 2005). Although this version had problems and is not used very much today, it remains important because it paved the way for HL7 Version 3, which is discussed next.

VALUE	DESCRIPTION
SI	Scanned Image
NS	Non-scanned Image
SD	Scanned document
TX	Machine readable text document
FT	Formatted text
SGML	Structured Generalized Markup Language
Image	Image data
Audio	Audio data
Application	Other application data, typically uninterpreted binary data

Figure 4.1 Type of data encapsulated.

HL7 Version 3

HL7 Version 3 was created to improve the internal consistency of HL7. This version has models that are used. The definition of a model for this purpose is a collection of subject areas, scenarios, classes, attributes, use cases, actors, trigger events, and interactions that depict the information needed to specify HL7 Version 3 messages. They are further divided into four specific models: a use case model, an information model, an interaction model, and a message design model (SRDC, 2005).

- The use case model defines precise circumstances in which communication among healthcare units is required.
- The information model is a thorough and exact description for the material from which all data content of HL7 communications is drawn. The information model is further broken down into the Reference Information Model (RIM). This is the root of all information models and provides a static view of information. It is an HL7 varied communal reference model that assimilates all Technical Committee domain views. The RIM has foundation classes, which are acts, entities, and roles (SRDC, 2005).
- The interaction model postulates all trigger events and message flows and specifies the application roles. Each interaction model consists of the trigger event, message ID, sender role, and receiver role. The application role classifies material achieved correctly for one of the subject classes. The

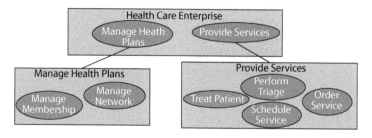

Figure 4.2   USE Case Model.

Interaction ID	PA231	PA232
Interaction Name	Send Registration to Trackers	Send Registration to Archivists
Trigger Event Name	Patient Registers for Encounter	Patient Registers for Encounter
Event Dependency	Account must be in the unregistered or pregistered state	Account must be in the unregistered or pregistered state
Message ID	A01	A02
Sender	Encounter Manager	Encounter Manager
Receiver	Encounter Tracker	Encounter Archivist
Receiver Responsibility		

Figure 4.3   Interaction Model.

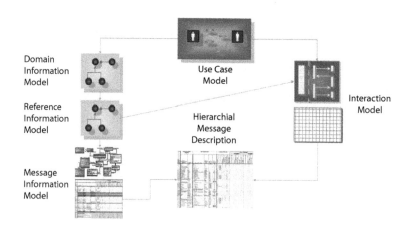

Figure 4.4   All models used in Version 3 of HL7.

responsibilities are creator manager, tracker, and archivist. Healthcare applications are supposed to be able to take on more than one application role.

HL7 Continued ...

The HL7 collaborates with other health data standards organizations, based not only in the United States of America, but all over the world. The HL7 model (Figure 4.4) is regulated and individuals must be a member to see any of the standards that they have created. Membership is accessible to everyone involved in the growth of a cost-effective approach to system connectivity. Participation and backing from HL7 members is vital to the continuing growth and development of the HL7 standard and the overall success of the organization (HL7, 2010). There is individual or organization membership. The membership cost is fair and worthwhile if interested in universal data standards. If anyone is interested in becoming a volunteer, there is no cost, and all volunteers are welcome. The challenge facing HL7 is that some of the versions have interoperability problems. HL7 is a shared model (HL7, 2010). Other data standards currently in use are discussed next.

Other Data Standards

The standard for Digital Imaging and Communications in Medicine (DICOM) was developed by the National Electrical Manufacturers Association (NEMA) in correlation with the American College of Radiology (ACR). DICOM covers most image setups for all of medicine and the stipulations for messaging and communication among imaging machines (SRDC, 2005). DICOM incorporates negotiation to permit peers to agree on the functions to be formed. It defines twenty-four data types and supports multiple character repertoires. DICOM has many features. It is a specific data model and has a UID mechanism; it has a number of new data elements; it defines classes of services for specific applications; and it has regulations that protect the patient's privacy and prevent data tampering. DICOM are especially concerned with confidential records being transferred over a data network. DICOM also want it to be mandated for access control. The security aspects are divided into three categories: policy, technical, and training issues (SRDC, 2005).

The Accredited Standards Committee (ASC) X12 develops uniform standards for interindustry electronic interchange of business transactions. ASC X12 advances, upholds, understands, distributes, and endorses the correct use of American National and UN/EDIFACT International Electronic Data Interchange (EDI) Standards. The ASC X12 members come together three times each year to create and sustain EDI standards. The main objective is to cultivate standards to enable electronic interchange concerning business communications such as order placement and processing, shipping and receiving information, invoicing, and payment and cash application data, and data to and from units tangled in finance, insurance, education, and state and federal governments. Committee members advance and endorse EDI standards that modernize business transactions. X12 standards enable these transactions by creating a shared, uniform business language for computers to interconnect across town or around the world. With more than 275 transaction sets, X12 standards can be used to automatically conduct nearly every facet of business-to-business operations (ASC, 2010). The ASC is a member-only organization and anyone in the healthcare business can join for a cost. The ASC is regulated for privacy (ASC, 2010).

The National Council for Prescription Drug Programs (NCPDP) is a not-for-profit organization that produces and endorses the transference of data related to medications, supplies, and services within the healthcare system through the growth of standards and industry direction. It was founded in 1993. The organization delivers an environment and backing where our various member can professionally and successfully grow and uphold these standards and leadership through a consensus-building procedure in association with other industry organizations (NCPDP, 2010). The NCPDP is a members-only organization. It is not very costly, but very worthwhile to join. It is regulated for privacy.

The Organization for the Advancement of Structured Information Standards (OASIS) is a not-for-profit organization that encourages the expansion, merging, and implementation of open standards for the global information society. It creates more web service standards than any other association. OASIS was founded in 1993 and has more than 5000 participants from 600 different organizations and individual members in 100 countries. OASIS is a members-only organization and its standards are regulated (OASIS, 2010).

The Continuity of Care Record (CCR) is an XML-based standard movement of "documents" between clinical applications. It helps organize and make transportable a set of basic information about a patient's healthcare that is accessible to clinicians and physicians. The Continuity of Care Document (CCD) is the effect of a cooperative effort between HL7 and the American Society for Testing Materials (ASTM) to synchronize the data format between the ASTM's Continuity of Care Record (CCR) and HL7's Clinical Document Architecture (CDA) stipulations (HL7 Standards, 2010). The CCD signifies a comprehensive execution of the CCR, combining the best of HL7 technologies with the richness of CCR's clinical data illustration, and does not disturb the existing data movements in payer, provider, or pharmacy organizations (SRDC, 2005). The CCD is regulated by HL7 and ASTM for privacy and policy issues.

The Systematized Nomenclature of Medicine-Clinical Terms (SNOMED) is considered the most complete, multilingual clinical healthcare terminology in the world. SNOMED aims to advance patient care through the expansion of systems to precisely record healthcare meetings. SNOMED CT is a "clinical healthcare terminology, a resource with comprehensive, scientifically-validated content, essential for electronic health records, a terminology that can cross-map to other international standards, and already used in more than fifty countries" (IHTSDO, 2010). SNOMED CT delivers the core general terminology for the Electronic Health Record (EHR) and covers more than 311,000 vigorous concepts with distinctive meanings and proper logic-based definitions prearranged into hierarchies. When applied to software applications, SNOMED CT can be used to characterize clinically pertinent information steadily, consistently, and systematically as an essential part of creating electronic health records. SNOMED CT was formed in 1999 in England and SNOMED was formed in 1965. It is a members-only organization that anyone in healthcare can join. The organization asks for a contribution for joining (IHTSDO, 2010).

Thus far we have discussed the data standards that will help information exchange from system to system. This is very important but the safety of drugs and medication is also very important. We now discuss the data standards that can effectively help the effective exchange of prescription drug information.

Bioinformatics

Bioinformatics is the design, expansion, and use of contemporary computer systems to competently and successfully manage the regulatory product information supply chain, along which medical product information travels among many relevant organizations. Bioinformatics management is used to assess a drug's safety and effectiveness. The current bioinformatics infrastructure is inefficient and needs to go through changes to make it better. It is outdated and irrelevant.

The Food and Drug Administration (FDA) has taken quantifiable stages to update its bioinformatics infrastructure, but the effort is costly, complex, and time consuming. It is still a necessary step to improve the critical path and enhance the benefit-risk assessments of drugs.

The FDA relies on efficient management of this information to assess a drug's safety and effectiveness. The current bioinformatics infrastructure that supports product information exchange is inefficient and is comparable to the antiquated infrastructure of the financial industry in years past. Bioinformatics modernization requires improvements in three important information management domains: access, standards, and interface. We must have better access to information, more standardized information, and a better interface with information (i.e., better tools to convert information into knowledge). Nonetheless, it is a necessary step to improve the Critical Path and enhance benefit-risk assessments of drugs (Oliva, 2007).

Bioinformatics is the design and development of computer-based technology to support the life sciences. The FDA is an important connection in this information supply chain, and guaranteeing the competent interchange of drug information among the FDA and its stakeholders is important to the FDA's mission to defend and endorse public health and to increase risk-benefit assessments of drugs. The FDA has made some progress in achieving a secure interoperable infrastructure to manage the exchange of regulatory product. They now have only one portal that information goes through to reach the agency electronically. All prescription drug labeling information is submitted electronically to the FDA. Although the FDA has taken these precautions, there still are inadequacies in the regulatory product information supply chain. The problem with bioinformatics is that most organizations use different technologies, different computer languages, and different terminologies. This makes communication of information inefficient and renders the information incomprehensible (Olivia, 2007). Even within the FDA itself, the technologies and terminologies are different and sometimes duplicated. There are also multiple submission formats, and most information received is still entered manually into computer systems that are different from one another. The inadequacies regarding bioinformatics can cause increased cost for human and technological resources, which makes the FDA's mission even more difficult to achieve (Oliva, 2007).

The FDA has been working on a solution to develop a modernized bioinformatics environment. This modern model would enhance the three key information management domains cited previously. These three domains can efficiently convert information into knowledge. Standards, access, and user-friendly interface tools work together to inspire the way we obtain, complete, and communicate material as part of regulatory decision making. Figure 4.6 details the three information management domains that must be enhanced and integrated. The three domains are represented as overlapping circles that work together to influence the way the information is received, managed, and communicated as part of regulatory decision making.

The FDA has created some standards for bioinformatics but not nearly enough to modernize the system. One standard they have created is that all information must be in English (Oliva, 2007). All standards and regulations address access issues. Some information must be sent directly to the FDA so they can access it first. Other information such as medical records must be kept at a specific off-site location and made available to the FDA at all times (Oliva, 2007). Mechanisms to interchange material electronically will also improve access. The FDA also measured access in terms of our skill to rapidly get to precise information contained in files and documents. It is not adequate to easily access a review of a new drug application because then anyone could access the information. We need rapid access to detailed information within a review, such as material about a rare adverse event. We must be able to "computerize institutional memory," to improve manage knowledge as well as information (Oliva, 2007). The interface helps information be readily available. If the interface is not appropriate, the usefulness of the information is diminished. The interface must be designed so that it can easily convert information into knowledge. The employees must also be trained to use these necessary tools. The three domains work interdependently to improve bioinformatics and decision making. It is the FDA's goal to attain a modern bioinformatics atmosphere that improves its decision-making proficiency and enables product information exchange. This means

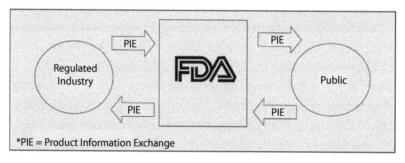

Figure 4.5 Bioinformatics FDA.

Figure 4.6 Information Management Domains.

that the information flowing through the regulatory product information supply chain is standardized, both information and knowledge are accessible electronically, and the tools for processing, analyzing, and reviewing information are both effective and user friendly (Oliva, 2007).

Conclusion

When we develop and use common standards, we create a common language for managing and exchanging health-related information, including research and study data. Universal data standards allow both individuals and electronic information management systems to communicate successfully and proficiently. Improving access means increasing the tools that make it easy to send, share, and receive information electronically. If the United States had a clear and concise set of standards that could be used to transfer information, healthcare would run more smoothly and there would be fewer problems. Healthcare technology will only grow in the future and the need for universal data standards will only increase.

References

AHRQ (Agency for Healthcare Research and Quality) (1999, September). Health Care Informatics Standards Activities of Selected Federal Agencies. Retrieved September 10, 2010, from Agency for Healthcare Research and Quality: www.ahrq/gov/data/infostd1.htm

ASC (Accredited Standards Committee) (2010). About ASC X12'. Retrieved September 10, 2010, from ASC X12: www.x12.org/x12org/about/index.cfm

Fenton, S. (2007, February). Data Standards, Data Quality, and Interoperability. Retrieved September 10, 2010, from AHIMA: www.library.ahima.org/xpedio/idcplg?IdcService

Pat Gibbons, G. D. (2007, February). Health Level Seven.

HITSP (Healthcare Information Technology Standards Panel) (2009a, January). About HITSP. Retrieved September 10, 2010, from HITSP: www.hitsp.org/about_hitsp.aspx

HITSP (Healthcare Information Technology Standards Panel) (2009b, January). HITSP Harmonization Framework. Retrieved September 10, 2010, from HITSP: www.hitsp.org/harmonization.aspx

HITSP (Healthcare Information Technology Standards Panel) (2009c, January). Technical Committees. Retrieved September 10, 2010, from HITSP: www.hitsp.org/technical_committees.aspx

HL7 (2010, January). About HL7. Retrieved September 10, 2010, from HL7: www.hl7.org/about/index.cfm?ref=nav

HL7 Standards (2010, March 10). CCD and CCR The Discussion Continues. Retrieved September 10, 2010, from HL7 Standards: www.hl7standards. com/blog/category/ccd

IHTSDO (International Health Terminology Standards Development Organisation) (2010). SNOMED CT. Retrieved September 22, 2010, from International Health Terminology Standards Development Organisation: www.ihtsdo.org

MN-PHIN Steering Committee (2006). Public Health Data Standards, Improving How Public Health Collects, Exchanges, and Uses Data. MN-PHIN, 1-6. Retrieved March 31, 2011, from www.health.state.mn.us/e-health/standards/pubhstandards08.pdf

NCPDP (National Council for Prescription Drug Programs) (2010). About NCPDP. Retrieved October 20, 2010, from National Council for Prescription Drug Programs: www.ncpdp.org/about.aspx

OASIS (Organization for the Advancement of Structured Information Standards) (2010). About OASIS. Retrieved September 22, 2010, from OASIS: www.oasis-open.org/who

Oliva, A. (2007, March 19). Bioinformatics Modernization and the Critical Path to Improved Benefit-Risk Assessment of Drugs. Retrieved September 22, 2010, from Federal Drug Administration: www.fda.gov/ ScienceResearch/SpecialTopics/CriticalPath Initiative/Articles

SRDC (Software Research and Development Center) (2005). Types of Data Standards. Retrieved September 10, 2010, from Software Research and Development Center: www.srdc.metu.tr/

5

HEALTHCARE INFORMATION EXCHANGE

KENT SUPANCIK

Contents

What Is a Healthcare Information Exchange and How Does It Fit into the Overall Healthcare Ecosystem?

Individual patient data (such as patient care summaries, vital statistics, clinical laboratory orders and results, radiology results, e-prescriptions and refill requests, eligibility and claims requests, immunization history, etc.) associated with healthcare delivery is generated in masses daily in a multitude of healthcare provider environments, pharmacies, payer organizations, and personal health tracking systems, among others. Each entity is looking at the patient from its own perspective

61

in the healthcare delivery value chain, each entity utilizing individual patient identifiers, patient record management systems, and billing and payment networks and systems, systems likely optimized for their originally defined environment. However, imagine if you took a look from the opposite direction, that of the patient receiving the services. Most likely, the view is fragmented, resulting in silos of information. Wouldn't it be ideal if a patient's entire medical history, regardless of origin or current location, could be available at the point-of-care, and be integrated with the most recent and relevant scientific medical knowledge to enable higher quality healthcare delivery? This electronic exchange of health records is where healthcare information exchange organizations and networks can play a vital role. By definition, health information exchange (HIE) refers to the sharing of clinical and administrative data across the boundaries of healthcare institutions, healthcare data repositories, academic and research organizations, personal health systems, and federal and state organizations. This is a rapidly evolving landscape with many innovative thoughts and ideas emerging daily. There are a multitude of areas to address, including standards, data ownership, privacy, security, data quality, unique patient identification, and many others. Public and private entities are taking leadership positions from both provider- and patient-centric perspectives at local, regional, and national levels to move these areas forward. As these efforts move forward, we can expect both tangible and intangible cost savings and benefits to be realized if parallel electronic and paper-based systems were replaced with a common electronic healthcare data exchange infrastructure linking clinical systems, Electronic Medical Records (EMRs), and the providers and organizations that leverage them (Miller, 2004). These efforts do not come without some level of investment, and much has been written regarding the challenges in incentivizing the various stakeholders to make the necessary investments in their healthcare information systems and infrastructure, without some level public and private support. Therefore, we won't explore those discussions here; instead, we'll take a look at some of the enabling efforts in defining and establishing interoperable healthcare information exchange in the United States.

What Key Initiatives Are Enabling the Development and Interoperability of Health Information Exchange?

There are several public and private initiatives driving the establishment of an interoperable, interconnected healthcare infrastructure. With privacy and security being a cornerstone of sustainable healthcare information exchange, the contents of medical records will continue to leverage aspects of the previously approved Health Insurance Portability and Accountability Act (HIPAA) of 1996 legislation to protect patients from unintended or inappropriate use of this information.

In addition, legislation established in February 2009, entitled the American Recovery and Reinvestment Act of 2009 (ARRA), created additional incentives. As a part of this legislation, $19.2 billion was set aside for Medicare and Medicaid Health IT incentives over a five-year period. This portion became known as the Health Information Technology for Economic and Clinical Health Act (HITECH) of 2009. Included was the official establishment of the Office of the National Coordinator for Health Information Technology (ONCHIT or ONC) within the U.S. Department of Health and Human Services, the establishment of the Health IT Policy and Standards Committees, and incentives through the Medicare Program for hospitals and physicians to accelerate the adoption and use of certified electronic health records (EHRs). In fact, looking ahead to 2019, the Congressional Budget Office (CBO) has estimated that prior to the HITECH Act, only 65% of physicians would have adopted EHRs, as opposed 90% under the incentives outlined in the HITECH Act (Athena Health, Inc., 2009). Furthermore, the CBO estimated that this accelerated level of adoption would deliver savings of over $60 billion between 2011 and 2019 (Athena Health, Inc., 2009). This is important because one of the requirements in order to receive incentives is to be able to demonstrate the electronic exchange of information in the form of an EHR that both improves the quality and coordination of care. Likewise, penalties will exist for failure to utilize EHRs.

The HITECH Act also established a federal entity called the Office of the National Coordinator for Health Information Technology (ONC). It is the responsibility of the ONC to coordinate national efforts to establish the electronic exchange of healthcare information leveraging the latest technology (U.S. Department of Health & Human Services, 2010e). The position of National Coordinator was created in 2004, by President George W. Bush, and then legislatively mandated in HITECH. The ONC is located within the Office of the Secretary for the U.S. Department of Health and Human Services (HHS). The mission of the ONC includes

- "Promoting the development of a nationwide Health IT infrastructure that allows for electronic use and exchange of information that:
  - Ensures secure and protected patient health information
  - Improves health care quality
  - Reduces healthcare costs
  - Informs medical decisions at the time/place of care
  - Includes meaningful public input in infrastructure development
  - Improves coordination of care and information among hospitals, labs, physicians, etc.
  - Improves public health activities and facilitates early identification/rapid response to public health emergencies
  - Facilitates health and clinical research
  - Promotes early detection, prevention, and management of chronic diseases
  - Promotes a more effective marketplace
  - Improves efforts to reduce health disparities
- Providing leadership in the development, recognition, and implementation of standards and the certification of Health IT products;
- Health IT policy coordination;
- Strategic planning for Health IT adoption and health information exchange; and
- Establishing governance for the Nationwide Health Information Network" (U.S. Department of Health & Human Services, 2010e).

Two key committees were created out of the ARRA and the HITECH Act to establish policy and standards. The first was the Health IT (HIT) Policy Committee. As the name suggests, this committee is responsible for healthcare information infrastructure exchange policy framework recommendations to the National Coordinator (U.S. Department of Health & Human Services, 2010b). The following workgroups, constructed of both stakeholder and subject matter experts, were formed by the HIT Policy Committee to provide further definition:

- Meaningful Use Workgroup
- Certification/Adoption Workgroup
- Information Exchange Workgroup
- Nationwide Health Information Network (NHIN) Workgroup
- Strategic Planning Workgroup
- Privacy & Policy Workgroup
- Enrollment Workgroup

The second was the Health IT (HIT) Standards Committee. This committee is responsible for making healthcare information infrastructure exchange and use standards, implementation specifications, and certification criteria recommendations to the National Coordinator (U.S. Department of Health & Human Services, 2010). Like the policy committee, several workgroups were formed to provide further definition, again comprised of key stakeholders and subject matter experts, including

- Clinical Operations Workgroup
- Clinical Quality Workgroup
- Privacy & Security Workgroup
- Implementation Workgroup

The definition of commonly agreed-upon standards will always remain a challenge in this environment given the number of diverse stakeholders and interests.

Several other nonprofit efforts are also providing significant leadership in enabling value to be realized from healthcare information technology deployment.

- *Healthcare Information and Management Systems (HIMSS).* HIMSS is a nonprofit organization representing over 30,000 individual members, the majority of which are healthcare providers or government or nonprofit organizations (HIMSS,

2010c). "HIMSS frames and leads healthcare practices and public policy through its content expertise, professional development, and research initiatives designed to promote information and management systems' contributions to improving the quality, safety, access, and cost-effectiveness of patient care" (HIMSS, 2010b).

• *Integrating the Healthcare Enterprise (IHE)*. IHE is sponsored by HIMSS as well as the Radiological Society of North America (RSNA) and the American College of Cardiology (ACC). The IHE reflects a mix between patient- and provider-centric perspectives. IHE is a multi-year global program that provides a standardized framework for accelerating healthcare information exchange among multiple providers at the local, regional, and national levels. Their primary focus is on demonstrating how existing standards can be implemented in actual healthcare delivery processes. Their defined Integration Profiles and Transactions facilitate reduced implementation costs, eliminate potential uncertainties, and enable relevant interoperability across systems and organizations in areas such as cardiology, radiology, and laboratory and Information technology infrastructure (IHE, 2010a).

What Infrastructure Is Developing to Enable the Exchange of Healthcare Information?

Several initiatives at multiple levels are beginning to put together the pieces of the puzzle—some driven from a healthcare provider or payer perspective and others from a patient perspective. In either case, it is expected that the greatest value will be achieved when both come together. Let's begin at the national level and then work our way down to the personal or patient level.

The national Health IT (HIT) agenda is presently focused on two primary areas: (1) to increase the adoption of Electronic Health Records (EHRs), and (2) to build a framework that facilitates the sharing of these records (U.S. Department of Health & Human Services, 2010a). In this section we focus on the framework that facilitates sharing, beginning with the Nationwide Health Information Network (NHIN) (Figure 5.1). The NHIN is not actually a network

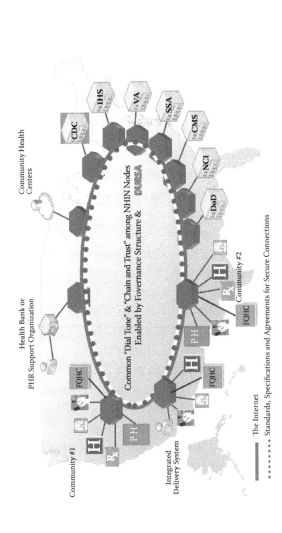

Figure 5.1 *Source:* From U.S. Department of Health & Human Services, 2010. http://healthit.hhs.gov/portal/server.pt/gateway/PTARGS_0_11113_911643_0_0_18/NHIN_Architecture_overview_draft_20100421.pdf

itself, but instead a set of core web-based service interfaces, standards, and legal agreements that establish a trust framework that allow healthcare data to be exchanged over the Internet.

Once operational, diverse entities such as providers, payers, patients, researchers, and administrators will be able to exchange and access data in a variety of repositories in communities across the United States. These services, when combined with regional and local efforts, facilitate the flow of healthcare information with the patient to the point-of-delivery, supporting the provider in clinical decision making (State HIE Toolkit, 2009). The NHIN began production in the early part of 2010 and remains an evolving entity though with a variety of initiatives aimed at both further defining and piloting the specifications and services as defined below.

What are the building blocks of the NHIN? The primary building blocks include two primary constructs, one being Nodes and the other Gateways.

NHIN Nodes are autonomous Health Information Exchanges (HIEs), Health Information Organizations (HIOs), or Regional Health Information Organizations (RHIOs) that join the NHIN. "In the context of the NHIN, a node is an HIO that participates in the exchange of health information with other nodes on the NHIN via a NHIN Gateway" (U.S. Department of Health & Human Services, 2010a). A Network and a Gateway component comprise a Node. A Network component is specific to each participant, representing both its systems and networks. The Network components then connect to an NHIN Gateway component and complete the NHIN On-Boarding Process to be officially connected (Puscas, 2009).

An NHIN Node can take a variety of forms, ranging from a single computer, to a server, to a network, to a hierarchy of networks running the core set of standard NHIN services and content and providing those services to the others (U.S. Department of Health & Human Services, 2010a). Obviously, when Nodes want to communicate with each other, specifications are required that define the standards and web services required for communication. Further discussion on the specifications appears later in this chapter.

"The types of HIOs initially exchanging information via the NHIN and those envisioned to do so in the future include: (a) Care Delivery Organizations (CDOs) that use Electronic Health Records

(EHRs), (b) Organizations that operate Personal Health Records (PHRs) and other consumer applications, (c) Organizations known as Health Information Exchanges (HIEs) that enable health related data exchange between state, regional or non-jurisdictional participant groups, (d) Other participant organizations that operate for specific purposes, including secondary users of data such as public health, research, and quality assessment" (U.S. Department of Health & Human Services, 2010a).

An implementation of the NHIN technical specifications that enables secure and interoperable healthcare information exchange is called an NHIN Gateway (U.S. Department of Health & Human Services, 2010a). Several options are available to an NHIO regarding their Gateway. First, they could implement the NHIN enterprise reference architecture on their own. Second, they could use one of two approaches that leverage another party, also having implemented the reference architecture. The first of those options is the Federal Health Architecture (FHA) CONNECT Gateway, and the second is a third-party (non-CONNECT) gateway. CONNECT was initially developed to support healthcare data exchange between federal agencies, but is now available as an open-source software solution to any organization that wants to establish an NHIN standard health information exchange or connect a healthcare organization into a regional network of exchanges (CONNECT, 2010). Implementation of an NHIN Gateway allows a Node to leverage NHIN specifications in communications with other Nodes but remain autonomous within its own environments (U.S. Department of Health & Human Services, 2010a).

In addition, two ONC Initiatives—the NHIN Exchange and NHIN Direct—are working to bring the NHIN to life. The NHIN Exchange, formerly called the NHIN Cooperative, is comprised of HIOs at the local, regional, and state levels as well as federal agencies, all working to help define the standards, services, and policies while demonstrating live exchange over the NHIN. Meanwhile, NHIN Direct is primarily a local-level effort, focused on how an entity such as a primary care provider can support Stage 1 of the meaningful use requirements. These ever-evolving efforts are important because the NHIN only comes to life in the end when organizations implement their specifications in support of healthcare business processes;

otherwise it only remains a set of specifications on paper (U.S. Department of Health & Human Services, 2010a).

Architectural Principles and Specifications of the NHIN

Given the complexity of facilitating healthcare information exchange at a national level, it is imperative to have a solid set of agreed-upon principles and reference architecture from which to build. The principles that the NHIN is being built upon are as follows (U.S. Department of Health & Human Services, 2010a):

- *Decentralization.* The NHIN is highly decentralized, putting the responsibility for patient information, including unique patient identification via master indexes and health record information, within the more localized NHIN Nodes.
- *Autonomy.* The NHIN Nodes are highly autonomous. This means that each NHIN Node has the right to decide whether information is released to another NHIN Node while abiding by appropriate state and federal laws and policies. This requires the requesting NHIN Node to provide enough information to the receiving NHIN Node so that it can make a decision as to whether to exchange the information requested.
- *Accountability.* Similarly, the NHIN Nodes are accountable for the information they provide, ensuring its accuracy, and providing a level of trust regarding its use to assist in the decision-making process by other NHIN Nodes as to whether the information should be accepted.
- *Standards and specifications based.* To enable and maintain interoperability, mutually agreed-upon standards and specifications must be adhered to by all NHIN Nodes.
- *Services oriented.* Underlying the discovery and information exchange services of the NHIN is a common foundation of messaging, privacy, and security services. The messaging services function as the common language between systems, leveraging a store-and-forward mechanism to achieve a higher level of reliability. Security and privacy services utilize

a combination of headers and tokens to enhance the authentication and authorization of users, granting or denying privileges to specific functions of a system.

Like any good IT system, there should be robust requirements to guide the design and overall architecture. In the case of the NHIN, the high-level guiding requirements include (1) the ability to discover and exchange healthcare information between diverse member organizations, systems, and technologies; (2) the ability to match patients to their data without a common patient identifier being used across member organizations; (3) the ability to allow patients to determine what information is exchanged, and who it is exchanged with; (4) the absolute ability to support secure and trusted data exchange, again a cornerstone for long-term success; and (5) support for the agreed-upon standards (U.S. Department of Health & Human Services, 2010a). The NHIN is built upon an Enterprise Reference Architecture that includes Governance, Health IT Business Cases, Capability Foundation, Operational Infrastructure, Technology Platform, and Policies, Standards, Validation (Figure 5.2). Each is briefly outlined below:

- *Governance.* This function defines the processes and organizations that provide oversight to the NHIN. Thus far, two organizations are in place serving in this oversight capacity. The first is the Technical Committee that provides guidance on the technical and security capabilities that will be supported. The Technical Committee leverages input regarding enhancements and new development from a broader public and private stakeholder group. They take these requests and put them through a prioritization process and then vote on which ones are actually carried forward to the production specifications (U.S. Department of Health & Human Services, 2010a). The second organization is the Coordinating Committee, which provides guidance on the operating policies and membership (Puscas, 2009). This committee also provides input into the specification development process (U.S. Department of Health & Human Services, 2010a)

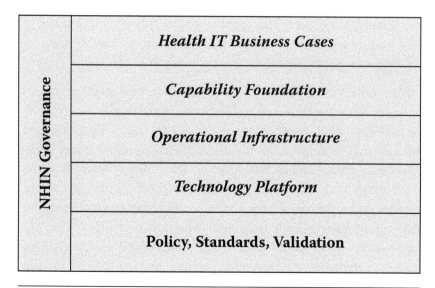

Figure 5.2   NHIN Governance. *Source:* From Puscas, K. (2009, July 10). National Health Information Network—Enterprise Architecture Overview Version: 1.0. Retrieved October 8, 2010, from HHS.gov: healthit.hhs.gov/.../PTARGS_0_11673_910398_0_0_18/NHINEnterpriseArchitectureOverview.doc.

- *Policies, Standards, and Validation.*
  - *Data Use and Reciprocal Agreement (DURSA).* The organizations currently committed to exchanging information via the NHIN have determined that they require a robust trust fabric, reflected in the Data Use and Reciprocal Support Agreement (DURSA). The DURSA is a comprehensive, multi-party trust legal agreement and is based upon a set of policy assumptions that bridge varying state and federal laws and regulations, as well as various policies. This legal contract, signed by all entities currently exchanging information via the NHIN, provides a framework of trust assurance to support multi-point health information exchange across the NHIN. The DURSA signators agree to be governed by its provisions, and require other parties who wish to exchange information with them to also sign the DURSA (U.S. Department of Health & Human Services, 2010a). As part of the NHIN's privacy, security, and messaging foundation, the NHIN Authorization Framework specification supports a multi-level approach to addressing security requirements in which NHIN

Nodes may exchange (or reference) transaction-specific agreements, if that requirement is established by the ONC. (U.S. Department of Health & Human Services, 2010a). Also, the monitoring functions of the NHIN will serve in a passive function when it comes to the collection or inspection of any personal healthcare information (PHI) (Puscas, 2009).

- *NHIN Testing and Validation Infrastructure.* Represents the set of tests, testing tools, test data, test environments, as well as interoperability and technical conformance that each prospective NHIO system must successfully complete to demonstrate their ability to securely exchange data (Puscas, 2009).

- *Operational Infrastructure.* This layer represents the operational runtime components necessary for data exchange by an NHIO, which can be located anywhere in the United States (Puscas, 2009). Key components include the services registry, security infrastructure, and operational monitoring. A brief overview of each follows:
  - *Services Registry*: As outlined earlier, each participating organization provides a set of standard services in order to facilitate information exchange. A Service Registry, based on the OASIS UDDI (Organization for the Advancement of Structured Information Standards—Universal Description, Discovery, and Integration) specification, allows other participating organizations to locate and utilize these services (Puscas, 2009).
  - *Security Infrastructure*: Three security principles need to be in place in order to establish a secure and trusted operational information exchange infrastructure: (1) assurance that only participating organizations can exchange information; (2) assurance of the integrity of all transactions across the NHIN; and (3) assurance that only participating organizations can both read and understand the information exchanged (Puscas, 2009). From a technical perspective, these principles are achieved through the use of a Public Key Infrastructure (PKI) that encrypts each message sent over the NHIN (Puscas, 2009).

- *Operational Monitoring*: With many participating organizations utilizing the network, disruptions need to be
  minimized and addressed quickly when they do occur.
  Therefore, it is important to understand the operational
  state of infrastructure and security components, as well as
  service registries in real-time (Puscas, 2009).

While all of these operational components can be hosted anywhere,
they appear to the participating organizations as a cloud. Participating
nodes just need to be able to access the cloud in order to participate
in the NHIN (Puscas, 2009). As you might expect, there is a cloud
for each of the operational components, one for the Services Registry,
another for Security, and finally one for Operational Monitoring
(Figure 5.3).

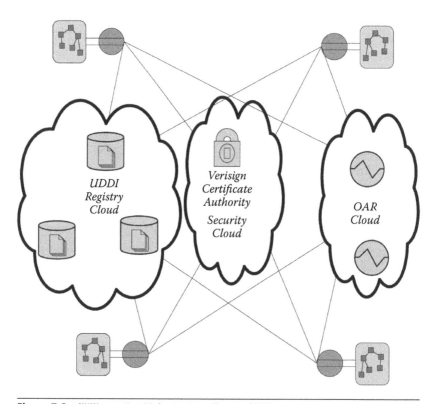

Figure 5.3 NHIN operational infrastructure. (Puscas, 2009)

This cloud approach reduces the level of physical infrastructure required and allows the network to scale and grow reliably over time. "The Registry Cloud is comprised of one or more UDDI servers. The registry information in these servers is replicated to each UDDI server so that access to any one provides the same information. The Monitoring Cloud is comprised of one or more systems for the collection of near real-time data about NHIO nodes. This information is shared among the different monitoring instances so that the NHIO nodes only need to access the cloud in order to obtain run-time information about any NHIO node. The final cloud is the Security Cloud. This cloud is implemented as a certificate authority operated by the Verisign Corporation. Verisign, under contract with HHS, will provide the tools necessary for managing the security trust fabric of the NHIN" (Puscas, 2009).

- *Technology Platform:* "The NHIN technology platform is based on the use of web services, as articulated within interoperability profiles established by the Web Services Interoperability Organization (WS-I). The WS-I provides interoperability guidance for core web service specifications created by standards organizations such as W3C and OASIS. These specifications cover the needs such as service description, registry, security, and reliability. Collectively, the WS-I Basic and Basic Security Profiles define a common platform for secure and reliable exchange of messages between participating organizations" (Puscas, 2009).
- *Capability Framework:* "The capability framework layer provides a set of core building blocks for supporting the architectural drivers. These building blocks are in the form of interface specifications that define a set of SOA based web services. These services provide such capabilities as patient look-up, document query and retrieve, and event based mechanisms for specific information. These services can be composed and choreographed into more complex healthcare information exchanges. The following is a list of the Core Services specifications that make up the Capability Framework layer

of the NHIN Enterprise Architecture" (Puscas, 2009). "Core Services specifications that define the following: (1) Message Platform Service Interface, (2) Authorization Framework Service Interface, (3) Subject Discovery Service Interface, (4) Query for documents Service Interface, (5) Document Retrieve Service Interface, (6) Health Information Event Messaging Service Interface" (Puscas, 2009). Many of these specifications are a further definition of the specifications published by the Integrating the Healthcare Enterprise (IHE) IT Infrastructure Profile and provide technology specific bindings based on the Technology Platform" (Puscas, 2009).

- *Health IT Business Cases:* "At the top of the NHIN Reference Enterprise Architecture are the business cases. These business cases represent the value added exchanges of health information for the purpose of meeting a business need. These business cases come from the healthcare and healthcare IT communities and reflect complex information exchange flows targeted to specific healthcare scenarios" (Puscas, 2009). Examples include electronic health records that contain lab results, biosurveillance, and medication management. "The ultimate goal of the NHIN Reference Enterprise Architecture is to support the Health IT Business Cases. ... "These Health IT Business Cases are implemented as interoperability orchestrations of the services provided by the Capability Framework, which are specified as bindings to the Technology Platform. The Technology Platform provides specifications for the implementation of the Operational Infrastructure. The Operational Infrastructure is defined and managed according to the policies, rules and governance practices defined in the Policy, Legal, and Governance Foundation" (Puscas, 2009).

Pulling all of these components together provides the foundation necessary for the reliable and trusted exchange of healthcare information at a national level. However, ultimately the success of a nationwide network must take root both at local and state levels (HIMSS, 2010d). This is where Health Information Exchanges, or Health Information Organizations, or Regional Health Information Organizations come into play.

Health Information Exchanges (HIE), Health Information Organizations
(HIOs), and Regional Health Information Organizations (RHIOs)

A Health Information Exchange (HIE) or Health Information
Organization (HIO) refers to the "electronic movement of health-
related information among organizations utilizing nationally recognized standards and policies" (NAHIT, 2008). It is the HIE that brings
together all the critical pieces of data at the point it is needed in the
healthcare service delivery process (HIMSS, 2009a). Meanwhile, the
definition of a Regional Health Information Organization (RHIO) is
broader. An RHIO is "an organization that oversees and governs the
exchange of health-related information among organizations according to nationally recognized standards. A health information organization that brings together health care stakeholders within a defined
geographic area and governs health information exchange among
them for the purpose of improving health and care in that community" (NAHIT, 2008). Although these definitions are now commonly
accepted, you could find the terms HIE, HIO, and RHIO used inter-
changeably, which can make it all the more confusing.

Up to this point we've focused primarily on the exchange of clinical data; however, some HIEs share other types of data. "For example, some HIEs are sharing exclusively specific types of nonclinical
data: (1) Eligibility determination (MassShare), (2) Transitions in
Care (Holomua Project), (3) Public Health and Biosurveillance
(CDC Projects), (4) Medication Histories (Sure Scripts, RxHub),
(5) Financial Transactions, and (6) Visit Histories (Holomua Project)"
(AHRQ—National Resource Center, 2010). As building blocks for
local and national healthcare information exchange efforts, HIEs
must make architectural, cultural, and technology decisions in order
to establish themselves as a viable entity.

What Fundamental Architectural Options and Cultural and Technology
Building Blocks Are Needed to Establish Health Information Exchanges?

Several common architectural options (centralized, federated, and
hybrid) for data sharing are available:

- "A centralized model has organizations sending patient demo-
  graphic and clinical information to a shared repository. This

centralized repository is queried to obtain a patient's clinical results and other information.

- A federated model allows the data source organization to maintain custodianship and control over the patient's medical record and indices. When requested, data is queried from the data source organization.
- A hybrid model is a mixture of the federated and centralized models" (HIMSS Health Information Exchange Best Practices Task Force, March 2009).

In addition to the architecture selected, HIEs must also provide a number of key components spanning technology, legal, and cultural boundaries:

- *Data sharing agreements.* These agreements define the standard policies, procedures, and terms under which data would be exchanged across organizational boundaries. This could also include agreement around data ownership, limits of liability, terms of use, and potentially compensation for use.
- *Network access.* This refers to the more physical connectivity to a telecommunications network that facilitates data sharing. This also includes access to the Internet.
- *Interface engines and translation services.* This refers to the messaging capabilities that provide for the interface and translation services between different systems. It can also encompass business rules engines that apply specific actions based on the data and processes being executed.
- *Record locator service.* This service provides the location of patient health information and where the care was provided, but not actual content of the health record.
- *Master patient Index (MPI).* This index provides either an algorithm or a common medical record number that allows a patient to be uniquely identified across multiple organizations (AHRQ—National Resource Center, 2010a).
- *Data repository or data warehouse.* An entity must either own a repository of health information to be exchanged or have access to a data repository owned by another entity. Electronic Health Records (EHR) would be one example of what could be contained in these repositories.

- *Standards and interoperability.* Standards are needed to achieve interoperability and ultimately success in the exchange of information across diverse HIE organizations and systems. Specifically standards need to exist for both message schemes and data encoding in order to support effective and efficient data exchange. Here are some common healthcare oriented messaging schemes and data encoding standards:
  - *Messaging schemes.* Thought of as the language or syntax used in the exchange to translate between different systems. Common messaging schemes include HL7, DICOM, ASC X12, and NIEM (emerging).
  - *Data coding.* Thought of as the common vocabulary, with common semantics (meaning), used to facilitate the level of understanding of what is being exchanged. Common data coding standards include ICD-9, CPT-4, LOINC-1, NDC, NCPDP, and SNOMED-CT.
- *Privacy and security.* As mentioned earlier, trust in both the privacy and security of the data is a cornerstone for healthcare information exchange. Failure to demonstrate that all possible precautions to safeguard this data have been taken, can have severe consequences. "Most organizations use all or a combination of the following privacy and security strategies:
  - HIPAA compliance
  - Access management (is a function of both user authentication and authorization. Authorization may be further constrained based on the sensitivity and use of data)
  - Role-based access (uses definition of roles to determine who is requesting the data and can also be used as a proxy for access control)
  - Entity/individual authentication/trust model (trust models and "chains of trust" are used where federated authentication is required)
  - Auditing/logs/review
  - Health Information Security and Privacy Collaboration (HISPC) (The HISPC project is tasked with the determination of appropriate privacy and security standards for HIE environments) (HIMSS Health Information Exchange Best Practices Task Force, March 2009)

- *Data quality.* Data quality is "the degree to which information and data can be a trusted source for any/or all required uses—the right set of correct information, at the right time, in the right place, for the right people to make decisions" (McGilvray, 2008). This definition implies a shared meaning as well.
- *Data transformation strategies.* Strategies focused primarily on normalization and encoding as well as data mapping and translation. "Normalization and encoding is the process of scrubbing the inbound data against a standard template which can 'normalize' data (make it conform to a specified format and data content). ... Data mapping/translation is a more simplistic process that maps data from one interface format to another or to an internal storage format with the ability to translate values as needed (e.g., Male = M = 1; Female = F = 2)" (HIMSS Health Information Exchange Best Practices Task Force, March 2009).

As you can see, many technical components and architectures exist in order to provide HIE capabilities at a local or state level to exchange healthcare information, including electronic heath records. Success at this level is imperative to improving the quality and cost-effectiveness of healthcare services over time. However, another rapidly growing area comes in the form of Personal Health Records (PHRs). As the name suggests, these are driven from an individual perspective as opposed to a provider perspective. It is here that you begin to see Personal Health Information Platforms and potentially Personal Health Information Networks emerge, linking personal data from multiple healthcare organizations and in some cases now medical devices. We'll briefly cover these platforms here.

Personal Health Information Networks (PHIN) and
Personal Health Information (PHI) Platforms

Much like managing your financial history and credit score has become a hot topic in the recent financial meltdown, so has the importance of managing your medical history. Individuals are taking a more active role in managing their over health and wellness. This is important when you look at the number of potential errors that exist in our medical records. "According to a report released by HEART Insight (*HEART Insight*, 3(4):7–9, November 2009. Patton, Carol), Medical Billing Advocates of America estimates that eight out of ten hospital bills are incorrect. Healthcare providers and insurers use complex coding systems to create a standardized system for health insurers to process claims and reimburse healthcare providers for their services. Since there are multiple coding systems, it is clear how hospitals and doctors' offices can easily make coding mistakes. Recording the wrong diagnostic or treatment code could lead to incorrect information in your medical records, or your health play be mistakenly charged for a test you never took" (Dossia, 2010c).

Whereas previous networks tended to initiate more from a provider perspective, the emerging landscape of Personal Health Information (PHI) Platforms (also can be called Personally Controlled Health Record (PCHR) Platform) and Personal Health Information Networks (PHINs) are initiated on behalf of, and controlled from a patient (individual) perspective. They offer a complimentary, voluntary, patient-driven approach to healthcare interoperability. They are built to manage and exchange Personal Health Records (PHRs).

"The PHIN and many applications supporting it create value both as stand-alone offerings and due to a strong network effect (the value of a network increases exponentially with the number of users (nodes) on the network. ... Thus, Google Health, HealthVault, Dossia and others are incentivized to grow collaboratively the total size of the network. ... The PHIN could be particularly disruptive to hospitals, health plans, physicians, and enterprise health information technology (HIT) vendors. ... There will be many beneficiaries of this disruption and many stakeholders will be keenly interested in promoting the amount and speed of disruption. For example, we anticipate that employers and government will be highly supportive of the PHIN" (Kuraitis and Kibbe, 2008).

As mentioned earlier, there are several influential vendors leading the way with regard to PHI Platforms. They include Microsoft HealthVault, Google Health, Dossia, and Indivo. As personal health record platforms, each puts the patient in control of their own data, on top of a private and secure platform. A platform because they can be extended beyond personal health records to include wellness metrics, disease management, education, as well as connectivity to medical and fitness devices. The Continua Alliance is one example of how companies like Cisco, IBM, Medtronic, and Intel, among others, are joining together to influence a broader ecosystem of interconnected personal health and fitness applications and services that could be leveraged by these platform vendors. These devices generate additional healthcare data that could be exchanged across the networks and infrastructure previously discussed. Another aspect of these platforms is that the patient can determine who has access to what data, and when. Each allows access from anywhere, at any time. Dossia and Indivo offer slightly different variations. Dossia is employer backed and can integrate tightly, leveraging single sign-on within a corporate environment. It can also be extended to deliver employee benefit programs. Indivo is an open-source solution, taking advantage of Advanced Programming Interfaces (APIs) to extend its platform with other applications. In addition, Indivo and Dossia have collaborated in delivering services. Each provides the ability for the patient to voluntarily enter data directly, import it from another electronic source, or in some cases they can engage a third-party service, often fee based, to assist in populating their information. All allow data to be integrated from disparate systems, and then centrally managed. All are free except Dossia, which has a monthly subscription fee (software-as-a-service).

As these platforms continue to evolve, and as individuals take greater ownership for managing their health and fitness, we will see the need to more tightly integrate this data with the HIE and NHIN networks.

Conclusion

The various types of healthcare information networks discussed in this chapter, when integrated, will assist in providing a more holistic and actionable picture to decision makers in the healthcare service delivery process. Data from hospitals, clinical labs, pharmacies, payers, medical devices, and many others can be brought together as never before. This is important in improving overall disease management, the quality of healthcare delivery, and in reducing the cost of healthcare delivery in the United States. This level of integration will not come without substantial effort at federal, state, local, public, and private levels. It will not come without increased levels of technology adoption to enable the infrastructure, as well as standardization, interoperability, trust in the form of privacy and security of the data exchanged, and harmonization that is agreed upon by all of these entities. The addition of medical device and wellness data will drive additional insights, as will the ability for others to use the combined data for the purposes of research, both to improve clinical and health economic outcomes. In the end, the promise of our entire medical history being available anytime, anywhere to support entire communities in healthcare delivery is definitely within our grasp.

References

(NAHIT), N. A. (2008, April 28). *Defining Key Health Information Technology Terms.* Retrieved October 20, 2010, from Healthit.hhs.gov: healthit.hhs.gov/portal/server.pt/gateway/PTARGS_0_10741_848133_0_0_18/10_2_hit_terms.pdf

Agency for Healthcare Research and Quality. (2007, February). *Health Information Technology: Overview—Program Brief.* Retrieved September 10, 2010, from http://www.ahrq.gov/research/hitover.htm

AHRQ—National Resource Center. (2010a, September). Health Information Exchange. Retrieved September 30, 2010, from Health Information Technology—Best Practices Transforming Quality, Safety, and Efficiency. Retrieved from http://healthit.portaldev.ahrq.gov/portal/

AHRQ National Resource Center—Health Information Technology. (2010b, September). *Architecture of Health IT.* Retrieved September 30, 2010, from http://healthit.portaldev.ahrq.gov/portal/server.pt?open=514&objID=5554&mode=2&hold

American Medical Association. (2009). American Recovery and Reinvestment Act of 2009. Retrieved October 4, 2010, from American Medical Association: http://www.ama-assn.org/ama/pub/advocacy/current-topics-advocacy/hr1-stimulus-summary

Athena Health, Inc. (2009). A Summary of the HITECH Act. Retrieved October 4, 2010, from athenahealth.com: http://www.athenahealth.com/HITECHAct

BioCrossroads. (2010, March 15). Indiana Collaborative Receives $10.3 Million in Federal Stimulus Funds to Improve Healthcare through Information Technology. Retrieved September 15, 2010, from http://www.ihie.com

CONNECT. About CONNECT. Retrieved September 07, 2010, from http://www.connectopensource.org/about/what-is-CONNECT

U.S. Department of Health & Human Services. The Connect Open Source Solution—A Gateway to the NHIN. Retrieved September 7, 2010, from http://healthit.hhs.gov/portal/server.pt/community/healthit_hhs.gov_connect/1323

Continua Health Alliance. (2010). FAQ's. Retrieved October 7, 2010, from Continuaalliance.org: http://www.continuaalliance.org/faqs.html

Dossia. (2010a). About the Personal Health Record. Retrieved October 7, 2010, from Dossia.org: http://www.dossia.org/for-individuals/about-the-phr

Dossia. (2010b). Dossia—Personal Health Platform. Retrieved October 7, 2010, from Dossia.org: http://www.dossia.org

Dossia. (2010c). Employee Q & A. Retrieved Ocotber 7, 2010, from Dossia.org: http://www.dossia.org/for-individuals/employee-q-and-a

Google. (2010). About Google Health. Retrieved October 21, 2010, from Google.com: http://www.google.com/intl/en-US/health/about/index.html

Health Information and Management Systems (HIMSS). (2010a). HIMSS Health Information Exchange (HIE). Retrieved October 5, 2010, from www.HIMSS.org: http://www.himss.org/ASP/topics_rhio.asp

HIMSS. (2010b). About HIMSS. Retrieved October 8, 2010, from HIMSS.org: http://www.himss.org/ASP/aboutHimssHome.asp

HIMSS Health Information Exchange Best Practices Task Force. (2009, March). Health Information Exchanges: Similarities and Differences. Retrieved October 8, 2010, from HIMSS.org: http://www.HIMSS.org

HIMSS. (2010c). HIMSS FAQs. Retrieved October 8, 2010, from HIMSS.org: http://www.himss.org/ASP/about_FAQ.asp

HIMSS. (2010d). HIMSS Health Information Exchange (HIE). Retrieved October 8, 2010, from HIMSS.org: http://www.himss.org/ASP/topics_rhio.asp

HIMSS. (2009a). 2009: Health Information Exchanges in the United States. Retrieved October 8, 2010, from HIMSS.org: http://www.himss.org

HIMSS. (2009b, July). Sub-Network Organization or SNO. Retrieved October 8, 2010, from HIE Topic Series—July 2009: http://www.himss.org

HITECHAnswers. (2010). EMR vs. EHR and HIE vs. HIO. Retrieved September 7, 2010, from http://www.hitechanswers.net/emr-vs-ehr-andhie-vs.hio/

IHE. (2010a). Retrieved October 9, 2010, from IHE.net: http://www.ihe.net

IHE. Changing the Way Healthcare CONNECTS. Retrieved October 8, 2010, from IHE.net: www.ihe.net

Indiana Health Information Exchange. (2010, September 8). Coumbus Regional Hospital Joins Nation's Largest Health Information Exchange. Retrieved Spetember 15, 2010, from Indiana Health Information Exchange: http://www.ihie.org

Indivo. (2010a). Indivo—Collaborators. Retrieved October 18, 2010, from Indivohealth.org: http://indivohealth.org/collaborators

Indivo. (2010b). Indivo—Home. Retrieved October 18, 2010, from Indivohealth.org: http://indivohealth.org

Indivo. (2010c). Indivo—Research. Retrieved October 18, 2010, from Indivohealth.org: http://indivohealth.org/research

Kansky, J. P. (2010, March 2). Health Information Exchange (HIE) Sustainability: Lessons Learned by the Indiana Health Information Exchange. Retrieved September 15, 2010, from Indiana Health Information Exchange: hhttp://www.ihie.org

Kuraitis, V. (2008, November 12). Picturing the PHIN as One Interoperable Network. Retrieved October 7, 2010, from e-care-management.com blog: http://www.e-caremanagement.com/picturing-the-phin-as-one-interoperable-network/

Kuraitis, V. and Kibbe, D.C. (2008, March 8). e-caremanagement.com blog. Retrieved October 6, 2010, from Birth Announcement: the Personal Health Information Network (PHIN): http://w-caremanagement.com/birth-announcement-the-personal-health-information-network/

Lee, D. (n.d.). Commentary—UPDATE. Retrieved September 15, 2010, from Indiana Health Information Exchange.

Leyva, C. A. (2009-2010). The HITECH Act and HIPAA. Retrieved September 7, 2010, from HIPAA Survival Guide: http://www.ihie.com and http://hipaasurvivalguide.com/hipaa-survival-guide-21.php

McGilvray, D. (2008). Executing Data Quality Projects—Ten Steps to Quality and Trusted Information. Burlington, MA: Morgan Kaufmann Publishers.

MGMA Connexion. (2004, August). Health Information Technology: The Government Moves towards a National Mandate. Retrieved September 18, 2010, from bNet Library: http://findarticles.com/p/articles/mi_qa4083/is_200408/ai_n9454324/

Microsoft. (2010a). Connecting Health Communities for Positive Health Out comes. Retrieved October 21, 2010, from Microsoft.com: http://www.microsoft.com/presspass/events/healthvault/docs/HealthVault2010FS.pdf

Microsoft. (2010b). Microsoft HealthVault Virtual Pressroom. Retrieved October 21, 2010, from http://www.microsoft.com/presspass/events/healthvault/default.mspx

Microsoft. (2009). Microsoft HealthValut Frequently Asked Questions. Retrieved October 21, 2010, from Microsoft.com: http://www.microsoft.com/presspass/events/healthvault/docs/HealthVault2010FAQ.pdf

Puscas, K. (2009, July 10). National Health Information Network—Enterprise Architecture Overview Version: 1.0. Retrieved October 8, 2010, from HHS.gov: healthit.hhs.gov/.../PTARGS_0_11673_910398_0_0_18/NHINEnterpriseArchitectureOverview.doc

Miller, R. H. and Sim, I. (2004). Physicians' Use of Electronic Medical Records: Barriers and Solutions . Retrieved October 21, 2010, from Healthaffairs.org: http://content.healthaffairs.org/cgi/content/full/23/2/116

State HIE Resources. (2009a, December 18). Nationwide Health Information Network (NHIN) Overview. Retrieved September 7, 2010, from State HIE Toolkit: http://statehieresources.org/the-toolkit/nationwide-health-information-network/nhin-overview/

State HIE Resources. (2009b, December 13). Planning Overview. Retrieved September 9, 2010, from State HIE Toolkit: http://statehieresources. org/the-toolkit/general-planning/planning-overview/

State HIE Toolkit. (2009, December 14). National Health Information Network. Retrieved September 7, 2010, from http://statehieresources. org/the-toolkit/nationwide-health-information-network/

U.S. Department of Health & Human Services. (2010a, April 21). Nationwide Health Information Network (NHIN)—Architecture Overview DRAFT v.0.9. Retrieved September 7, 2010, from http://healthit.hhs.gov/portal/ server.pt/gateway/PTARGS_0_11113_911643_0_0_18_architecture_ overview_draft_20100421.pdf

U.S. Department of Health & Human Services. (2010b, September 23). Federal Advisory Committees (FACAs). Retrieved September 27, 2010, from The Office of the National Coordinator for Health Information Technology: http://healthit.hhs.gov/portal/server.pt/community/ healthit_hhs_gov_federal_advisory_committees

U.S. Department of Health & Human Services. (2010c, September 3). Nationwide Health Information Network: Overview. Retrieved September 27, 2010, from The Office of the National Coordinator for Health Information Technology: http://healthit.hhs.gov/portal/server.pt/ community/healthit_hhs_gov_nationwide_health_information_network

U.S. Department of Health & Human Services. (2010d, February 12). ONC Initiatives. Retrieved September 27, 2010, from U.S. Department of Health & Human Services—The Office of the National Coordinator for Health Information Technology: http://www.healthit.hhs.gov/portal/ server.pt/community/healthit_hhs_gov_onc_initiatives/1497

U.S. Department of Health & Human Services. (2010e, August 13). The Office of the National Coordinator for Health Information Technology (ONC). Retrieved September 7, 2010, from http://healthit.hhs.gov/portal/server. pt?open=512&mode=2&cached=true&objID=1200

Wagner, M. (2009, December 1). InformationWeek.com. Retrieved October 21, 2010, from Microsoft, Google Face Off on Healthcare: http:// www.informationweek.com/news/healthcare/EMR/showArticle. jhtml?articleID=221901566.

6

HEALTH INFORMATION TECHNOLOGY IN THE UNITED STATES

Achieving Legal and Regulatory Results that Enhance Innovation and Adoption

STUART N. BROTMAN, J.D.,
GABRIEL G. BROTMAN,
AND JENNIFER E. PAUL

Contents

Introduction

In recent years, the U.S. healthcare community has seen dramatic developments in adopting information technology (IT) systems and practices. Among the largest national initiatives is the transition from paperless to digital health-related record-keeping. With significant federal, state, and private-sector investment in the market, Health IT (HIT) is emerging as a leading factor in ensuring the continued vitality of a first-class national healthcare infrastructure.

This chapter outlines the current HIT market, describes the regulatory environment encouraging HIT adoption, and presents future opportunities for the public and private sectors. It also highlights legal and regulatory issues—including critical privacy and security concerns—that health providers and IT vendors will face as HIT adoption proliferates.

Current Health IT Market (HIT) Overview

HIT encompasses a wide variety of technologies and administrative systems that help track, manage, and share patient information electronically, rather than through paper records. Doctors and hospitals are beginning to take advantage of electronic and mobile devices that aid in record-keeping, remote diagnosis, and monitoring; however, reports show that medical professionals have been slow to adopt the technologies to date. The major categories to consider include electronic health records and personal health records.

Electronic Health Records

According to the National Alliance for Health Information Technology, an Electronic Health Record (EHR) is an "aggregate electronic record on health-related information on an individual that conforms to nationally recognized interoperability standards and that can be created, managed, and consulted by authorized clinicians and staff across more than one health care organization" (NAHIT, 2008). As of October 2010, only 38.7 percent of medical offices in the United States had adopted EHRs, according to SK&A, a healthcare technology group.

New laws (such as the Health Information Technology for Economic and Clinical Health [HITECH] Act) may spur the adoption of EHR technology by providing incentive payments to healthcare providers who adopt and use EHRs, however. These payments, which are made after a provider begins the "meaningful use" of EHR technology (described more fully later in the chapter), are distributed by the Office of the National Coordinator (ONC) in the federal Department of Health and Human Services (HHS) and the Centers for Medicare

& Medicaid Services (CMS). They aim to advance significantly widespread Health IT adoption in the next five to fifteen years.

Personal Health Records

Under the final federal rules governing the meaningful use standard, all healthcare recipients are expected to provide patients with Personal Health Records (PHRs) by 2015. Like EHRs, PHRs contain health-related information about an individual. However, PHRs contain information drawn from multiple sources and are managed, shared, and controlled exclusively by the patient. PHRs allow patients easy access to their medical histories, prescriptions, and test results; however, lack of widespread broadband Internet access in rural and poor communities, consumer privacy and security concerns, and inadequate IT architecture have hindered the widespread adoption of the technology.

In a 2010 survey sponsored by the California HealthCare Foundation (2010), only 7 percent of respondents were using a PHR. Of these users, 64 percent found PHRs useful to make sure their health information is accurate, 57 percent enjoyed being able to look at test results, and about half of users found it useful to e-mail providers and renew prescriptions online. More than half of the PHR users said the records make them feel like they knew more about their health and the care that their doctor gives them. In the survey, nonusers cited privacy concerns and lack of an immediate need for PHRs as the biggest barriers to adoption.

A main concern among the Health IT community is the lack of interoperability in coding, vocabulary, standards, and architecture between PHR and EHR systems. In the past five years, many large hospital systems have partnered with blue-chip companies, such as Google and Microsoft, to provide patients with simple, interoperable EHR-PHR systems. For example, in April 2009, New York-Presbyterian Hospital and Microsoft created a service called myNYP.org that allows eligible patients to access their medical information from remote locations.

As Health IT adoption accelerates through 2015, the PHR market will create opportunities for smaller Health IT vendors to create strong, interoperable tools for patients' medical information.

One of the newest innovations in the personal health monitoring market is the proliferation of smart phone applications that allow users to track and monitor personal health information. The PHR data then can be stored for the user to analyze, or sent to physicians or caregivers for their analysis. The applications also can serve as tools to remind patients to take their medications and refill their prescriptions.

Surveys show that consumers are receptive to the adoption of these new applications, although their usage in the United States is not yet widespread. Nine percent of cell phone owners have software applications on their phones that help them track or manage their health, according to an October 2010 survey conducted by the Pew Internet & American Life Project (2010). In a separate survey, however, nearly one-third of respondents said they would use their cell or smart phones to track and monitor their personal health. Forty percent would be willing to pay for a remote monitoring device that sends health information directly to their doctor, according to PricewaterhouseCoopers (September 2010). PricewaterhouseCoopers estimated that the annual United States consumer market for remote/mobile monitoring devices and services is $7.7 billion to $43 billion, based on the range of consumers who said they would be willing to pay.

Federal Initiatives that Will Shape the Future of Health IT

HITECH Act

The Health Information Technology for Economic and Clinical Health Act (HITECH Act) was enacted as part of the American Recovery and Reinvestment Act of 2009. It created policy and standards committees, directed the Department of Health and Human Services Office of the National Coordinator (ONC) to establish new grant and loan funding programs, and instituted enhanced privacy laws. The HITECH Act also distributed approximately $27 billion to HIT federal programs, including an incentive payment program that encourages the implementation of EHR systems and discourages slow adoption. It allows eligible healthcare professionals and hospitals to qualify for Medicare and Medicaid incentive payments when they adopt certified

EHR technology and use it to achieve specified objectives. Eligible healthcare providers can participate in the program beginning in 2011.

The incentive payments are based largely on the "meaningful use" of EHRs, a term that was not defined until the Centers for Medicare & Medicaid Services (CMS) published its 276-page final ruling in July 2010 (CMS, 2010). This regulatory decision specified initial criteria for eligible professionals (EPs) and eligible hospitals to meet the Medicare and Medicaid incentive payment programs. Although both payment programs differ in administrative oversight, monetary benefits, and eligibility requirements, they share fifteen core objectives and measures that participating professionals and hospitals must meet by 2012. Additionally, both programs direct eligible professionals and eligible hospitals to choose five out of twelve menu objectives (e.g., implementing drug formulary checks, generating lists of patients by specific conditions).

The fifteen core objectives/measures in the regulations are

(1) (i) Objective. Use computerized provider order entry (CPOE) for medication orders directly entered by any licensed healthcare professional who can enter orders into the medical record per state, local, and professional guidelines.

(ii) Measure. Subject to paragraph (c) of this section, more than 30 percent of all unique patients with at least one medication in their medication list seen by the EP have at least one medication order entered using CPOE.

(2) (i) Objective. Implement drug-drug and drug-allergy interaction checks.

(ii) Measure. The EP has enabled this functionality for the entire HER reporting period.

(3) (i) Objective. Maintain an up-to-date problem list of current and active diagnoses.

(ii) Measure. More than 80 percent of all unique patients seen by the EP have at least one entry or an indication that no problems are known for the patient recorded as structured data.

(4) (i) Objective. Generate and transmit permissible prescriptions electronically (eRx).

(ii) Measure. Subject to paragraph (c) of this section, more than 40 percent of all permissible prescriptions written by the EP are transmitted electronically using certified EHR technology.

(5) (i) Objective. Maintain active medication list.

(ii) Measure. More than 80 percent of all unique patients seen by the EP have at least one entry (or an indication that the patient is not currently prescribed any medication) recorded as structured data.

(6) (i) Objective. Maintain active medication allergy list.

(ii) Measure. More than 80 percent of all unique patients seen by the EP have at least one entry (or an indication that the patient has no known medication allergies) recorded as structured data.

(7) (i) Objective. Record all of the following demographics:
(A) Preferred language.
(B) Gender.
(C) Race.
(D) Ethnicity.
(E) Date of birth.

(ii) Measure. More than 50 percent of all unique patients seen by the EP have demographics recorded as structured data.

(8) (i) Objective. Record and chart changes in the following vital signs:
(A) Height.
(B) Weight.
(C) Blood pressure.
(D) Calculate and display body mass index (BMI).
(E) Plot and display growth charts for children 2–20 years, including BMI.

(ii) Measure. Subject to paragraph (c) of this section, more than 50 percent of all unique patients age 2 and over seen by the EP, height, weight and blood pressure are recorded as structured data.

(9) (i) Objective. Record smoking status for patients 13 years old or older.

(ii) Measure. Subject to paragraph (c) of this section, more than 50 percent of all unique patients 13 years old or older seen by the EP have smoking status recorded as structured data.

(10) (i) Objective. Report ambulatory clinical quality measures to CMS or, in the case of Medicaid EPs, the States.

(ii) Measure. Successfully report to CMS (or, in the case of Medicaid EPs, the States) ambulatory clinical quality measures selected by CMS in the manner specified by CMS (or in the case of Medicaid EPs, the States).

(11) (i) Objective. Implement one clinical decision support rules relevant to specialty or high clinical priority along with the ability to track compliance with that rule.

(ii) Measure. Implement one clinical decision support rule.

(12) (i) Objective. Provide patients with an electronic copy of their health information (including diagnostics test results, problem list, medication lists, medication allergies) upon request.

(ii) Measure. Subject to paragraph (c) of this section, more than 50 percent of all patients who request an electronic copy of their health information are provided it within 3 business days.

(13) (i) Objective. Provide clinical summaries for patients for each office visit.

(ii) Measure. Subject to paragraph (c) of this section, clinical summaries provided to patients for more than 50 percent of all office visits within 3 business days.

(14) (i) Objective. Capability to exchange key clinical information (for example, problem list, medication list, allergies, and diagnostic test results), among providers of care and patient authorized entities electronically.

(ii) Measure. Performed at least one test of certified EHR technology's capacity to electronically exchange key clinical information.

(15) (i) Objective. Protect electronic health information created or maintained by the certified HER technology through the implementation of appropriate technical capabilities.

(ii) Measure. Conduct or review a security risk analysis in accordance with the requirements under 45 CFR

164.308(a)(1) and implement security updates as necessary and correct identified security deficiencies as part of its risk management process.

According to the CMS, eligible professionals can receive up to $44,000 over five years under the Medicare EHR Incentive Program, with an additional incentive for eligible professionals who provide services in a Health Professional Shortage Area (HSPA). The separate Medicaid EHR Incentive Program is offered voluntarily by individual states and territories and may begin as early as 2011, depending on the state. Eligible professionals can receive up to $63,750 over the six years that they choose to participate in the program.

The National Broadband Plan

Health IT's long-term success will depend largely on the implementation of The National Broadband Plan, released by the Federal Communications Commission (FCC) in March 2010 (FCC, 2010). The Plan devotes an entire chapter to health information technology. According to the Plan, HIT solutions "offer the potential to improve healthcare outcomes while simultaneously controlling costs and extending the reach of the limited pool of healthcare professionals" (FCC, 2010). The Plan offers recommendations concerning four areas in which the government should act to advance broadband and HIT: (1) better reimbursement, (2) modern regulation, (3) increased data capture and utilization, and (4) sufficient connectivity. The Plan's Health IT recommendations are as follows:

- "Create appropriate incentives for e-care utilization:
  i. Congress and the Secretary of Health and Human Services (HHS) should consider developing a strategy that documents the proven value of e-care technologies, proposes reimbursement reforms that incentivize their meaningful use and charts a path for their widespread adoption.
- Modernize regulation to enable health IT adoption:
  i. Congress, states and the Centers for Medicare & Medicaid Services (CMS) should consider reducing regulatory barriers that inhibit adoption of health IT solutions.

    ii. The FCC and the Food and Drug Administration (FDA) should clarify regulatory requirements and the approval process for converged communications and health care devices.

- Unlock the value of data:
  - i. The Office of the National Coordinator for Health Information Technology (ONC) should establish common standards and protocols for sharing administrative, research and clinical data, and provide incentives for their use.
  - ii. Congress should consider providing consumers access to—and control over—all their digital health care data in machine-readable formats in a timely manner and at a reasonable cost.

- Ensure sufficient connectivity for health care delivery locations
  - i. The FCC should replace the existing Internet Access Fund with a Health Care Broadband Access Fund.
  - ii. The FCC should establish a Health Care Broadband Infrastructure Fund to subsidize network deployment to health care delivery locations where existing networks are insufficient.
  - iii. The FCC should authorize participation in the Health Care Broadband Funds by long-term care facilities, off-site administrative offices, data centers, and other similar locations. Congress should consider providing support for for-profit institutions that serve particularly vulnerable populations.
  - iv. To protect against waste, fraud, and abuse in the Rural Health Care Program, the FCC should require participating institutions to meet outcomes-based performance measures to qualify for Universal Service Fund (USF) subsidies, such as HHS's meaningful use criteria.
  - v. Congress should consider authorizing an incremental sum (up to $29 million per year) for the Indian Health Service (IHS) for the purpose of upgrading its broadband service to meet connectivity requirements.
  - vi. The FCC should periodically publish a Health Care Broadband Status Report. (FCC, 2010)

The Health IT Road Ahead

Government policymakers, healthcare professionals, and technology companies all have recognized the importance of the Health IT market, and how potential technology could save money on healthcare costs while helping physicians to provide more efficient and effective care for their patients. While new laws are structured to provide federal money to incentivize the widespread adoption of Health IT, the up-front implementation costs are high, thus posing a formidable barrier to digital conversion.

Among the barriers to HIT adoption is the large financial investment by healthcare providers. According to a May 2008 report by the Congressional Budget Office (CBO, 2008), expenditures include (1) the initial fixed cost of the hardware, software, and technical assistance necessary to install the system; (2) licensing fees; (3) the expense of maintaining the system; and (4) the opportunity cost of the time that healthcare providers could have spent seeing patients but instead must devote to learning how to use the new system and how to adjust their work practices accordingly.

In the August 2010 edition of *McKinsey Quarterly*, consultants at the firm estimated that the cost to implement new healthcare IT at U.S. hospitals will average $80,000 to $100,000 per bed—about $120 billion nationwide—with only 15 to 20 percent of that cost being offset by federal incentive money. Because of these high start-up costs, many physicians and hospitals, especially those that do not qualify for federal incentive payments, may be hesitant to devote time and resources to implementing HIT systems.

At the same time, these providers should be aware that high up-front costs could have an even larger payout in the long run. The McKinsey consultants estimated that healthcare providers could save $40 billion annually by implementing effective HIT systems. Consequently, they recommended that providers take measured steps and strive to create an IT infrastructure that will minimize paperwork, reduce the number of unnecessary treatments, and lower the risk of drug and medical errors. To accomplish these goals and cut operating costs, the consultants wrote, providers must use a system to effectively house and store medical records, manage hospital resources more transparently, and define precise guidelines for medically authorized tests and procedures.

Hospitals and physicians' offices will need cutting-edge, simplified technology to aid them in reducing paperwork, unnecessary treatments, and medical errors. Technology companies have recognized that they will play a pivotal role in offering such solutions. In July 2010, IBM announced it would dedicate $100 million to health information technology research over a three-year span. IBM plans to collaborate with clinicians in medical institutions and hire physicians to work with its researchers to develop new technologies, scientific advancements, and business processes for healthcare and insurance providers.

In its press announcement, IBM (2010) said it would focus its research on three main areas:

- "Evidence generation, which uses scientific methods to utilize health data to help develop effective treatment methodologies, and then deliver it in a context-dependant and personalized way at the point of care;
- Improving service quality through simplifying the healthcare delivery process; and
- New incentives and models to shift the healthcare system to one that rewards based on patient outcomes rather than only treatment and volume of care." (IBM, 2010)

Other companies are focusing on how to create products that promote more effective, efficient home healthcare and monitoring. On August 2, 2010, for example, General Electric and Intel Corporation (GE and Intel, 2010) announced they had formed a joint venture to develop products, services, and technologies aimed at home healthcare.

The new company, owned equally by General Electric and Intel, will focus on three segments of home healthcare:

1. *Chronic disease management:* Products and services to help patients and their caregivers manage common conditions, including congestive heart failure, chronic obstructive pulmonary disease, hypertension, and diabetes.
2. *Independent living:* Wireless passive-behavioral monitoring products, to help keep the elderly living independently in their homes longer or more safely and comfortably in assisted living communities.
3. *Assistive technologies:* Products to enable people with learning disabilities or visual impairments." (GE and Intel, 2010)

These market investment initiatives could stall due to uncertain marketplace forces. Some HIT experts have expressed concern that consumer reluctance to adopt the technologies may act as a barrier to larger investment in the healthcare IT market. Without robust consumer demand, companies will not have sufficient profit incentives to create more efficient systems and applications. As David Cerino, general manager of the Consumer Health Solutions Group for Microsoft Corp., told MSNBC in January 2010 (Cerino, 2010), "consumers want digital healthcare to be transparent and secure, and allow patients to maintain personal control over their care. Until these concerns are addressed to their satisfaction, consumers won't fully buy into the idea of digital healthcare voluntarily," Cerino said.

Even if large numbers of consumers begin to seriously consider HIT options, government officials also have expressed worry that minority segments of the U.S. population will be shut out of the market. These policymakers have implored technology providers to take steps to ensure equal access. In an October 2010 letter, Dr. David Blumenthal (2010), the National Coordinator for Health Information Technology, asked that HIT vendors include in their sales and marketing efforts providers who serve minority communities. According to the letter, data from the National Ambulatory Medical Care Survey indicated that EHR adoption rates remained lower among providers serving uninsured black patients and Hispanic or Latino patients who are uninsured or relied upon Medicaid. The Obama administration, government agencies, and EHR vendors must make it a goal to "work together and focus substantial efforts on these priority populations," the letter said (Blumenthal, 2010).

Overall, healthcare providers, technology vendors, and government officials have established these policy considerations to support HIT innovation: (1) creating efficient, effective, and secure healthcare technology; (2) providing substantial cost-saving opportunities; and (3) enabling accessibility to a broad segment of the population.

What Barriers Must Be Overcome?

Although a nascent framework has been established to support the widespread adoption of HIT tools in hospitals and physicians' offices across the United States, significant barriers remain. Healthcare professionals, technology companies, and government officials must work together to ensure that such roadblocks can be addressed so they do not hinder timely adoption of HIT. Here are the key barriers that must be overcome.

Privacy Concerns

Privacy concerns and the risk of security breaches that disclose patients' personal information are the paramount barriers to the widespread acceptance and usage of Health IT systems and applications. In the case of EHRs, the privacy risk is clear. More electronic health records create the possibility of more personal medical information being breached and the opportunity for widespread medical identity theft. For the Department of Health and Human Services (HHS) and privacy watchdog groups, this threat already is a reality. From 2003 to 2009, the number of cases of privacy breached by healthcare providers rose considerably, according to the HHS Office of Civil Rights (2010). Moreover, reports estimate that millions of people are being affected by medical information breaches annually, a number that will grow exponentially as EHRs become more widespread.

Health professionals' mobile devices also could be a risk to patient privacy. If medical personnel save and transmit patient photos and written information on unsecured devices, patient privacy could easily be breached. Dr. Barry Chaiken, former chair of the Healthcare Information and Management Systems Society, thinks mobile devices are a "big problem" because of security concerns. "Now you have these unsecured networks sending personal health information over them," Chaiken told *HIStalk*, a healthcare blog (Chaiken, 2010). "That's a big problem. I think that problem needs to be addressed. As best as I know, there's no technology to specifically address it right now. I mean, I guess you can shut off everybody's smart phone, but still, they can take pictures and when they leave the hospital they can obviously send them." According to Chaiken, hospitals need to implement data privacy rules and educational programs. These must inform personnel about security issues and privacy issues that arise from using smart phones, iPads, and other devices, and emphasize why the rules should be followed.

PHRs also raise serious privacy concerns because they often may be facilitated by private websites that may not be covered by HIPAA privacy regulations. Consequently, patients' data potentially could be shared or sold to third parties. Patients must be instructed to carefully read the websites' privacy policies before they submit personal information to such sites. These written statements also must be written clearly so that patients understand how the privacy of their information may be compromised if submitted to a particular website.

Legal and Policy Obstacles

The healthcare technology market is unlikely to enact broad self-regulatory measures to ensure the security of patient data. Thus, federal government policymakers must be ready to step in to develop and implement privacy protections that affect HIT products and services — through Congressional legislation or Executive Branch initiatives. For example, HHS should identify clear standards that protect both the privacy rights of patients and hold accountable providers who implement weak security platforms in their EHRs. Congress also should broaden HIPAA so it applies to all PHRs, rather than only those offered by healthcare providers and health insurance plans.

Government policymakers also must not be too inflexible. Because HIT is developing so rapidly, product and service offerings are likely to change quickly. Slow-moving legislation that is crafted in reaction to current problems will not be sufficient. Rather, policymakers must work closely with industry experts to keep abreast of developing technology and marketplace trends to ensure that they are taken into account as legal and regulatory measures are considered.

All interested parties also must keep in mind that HIT issues are related to, but also somewhat distinct from, the healthcare reform laws that were enacted in March 2010. With continuing legal and political challenges to the Patient Protection and Affordable Care Act and the Health Care and Education Reconciliation Act of 2010, national healthcare reform likely will continue as a divisive political issue for the foreseeable future.

HIT, however, can best develop if it can be perceived as a separate issue from the fight over healthcare reform in the larger sense. It needs discrete, focused attention. Government policymakers should not let overall healthcare reform distract them from attending to the technological, economic, and privacy issues that arise out of HIT implementation.

Interested healthcare institutions, companies, and consumer groups can and should influence HIT policy development and adoption. Their views are needed to develop effective legal and regulatory measures that support an environment where widespread adoption is the norm.

Technology + Government-sponsored financial incentives for adoption + Consumer acceptance + Privacy policy and legislation/regulation may represent the optimal equation for promoting Health IT as it rolls out during the coming years.

References

Blumenthal, D. (2010). A letter to the vendor community: Health IT and disparities. Dated October 18, 2010. http://healthit.hhs.gov/portal/server.pt?open=512&mode+2&objID=3197 (accessed March 26, 2010).

California Health Care Foundaton (2010). Accessed August 24, 2011, from http://www.chf.org/publications/2010/04/consumers-and-health-information-technology-a-national-survey

CBO (Congressional Budget Office (2008). Accessed August 24, 2011 from http://www.cbo.gov/doc.cfm?indiex=8917

Cerino, David (2010). General manager of Consumer Health Solutions Group for Microsoft Corp., David Cerino. Interview on MSNBC, January, 2010.

CMS (Centers for Medicare & Medicaid Services) (2010). Accessed August 24, 2011, from http://www.cms.gov/PerformanceBudget/Downloads/CMSFY10CJ.pdf

FCC (Federal Communications Commission) (2010).

GE and Intel (General Electric and Intel Corporation) (August 2, 2010). GE, Intel to form new healthcare joint venture. http://download.intel.com/pressroom/pdf/Intel_GE_JV_Fact_Sheet.pdf (accessed March 26, 2010).

HHS Office of Civil Rights (2010) Accessed August 24, 2011 from http://www.hhs.gov/ocr/office/index.html

HIStalk (2010). Interview with B. Chaiken. Accessed August 24, 2011 from http://histalk2.com/2010/07/19/histalk-interviews-barry-chaiken/

IBM (2010). IBM bolsters scientific research to improve healthcare quality and costs globally. Hires M.D.s to work alongside scientists in new $100 million research initiative. Press release, July 15, 2010. IBM, Armonk, New York. See http://www-03.ibm.com/press/us/en/pressrelease/32125.wss (accessed March 26, 2010).

McKinsey Quarterly (2010). Accessed August 24, 2011 from http://www.mckinseyquarterly.com/Reforming_hospitals_with_IT_investment_2653

NAHIT (National Alliance for Health Information Technology) (2008). http://www.google.com/search?sourceid=navclient&aq=0&oq=National+Alliance+for+Health+Information+Technology+&ie=UTF-8&rlz=1T4ADRA_enUS421US422&q=national+alliance+for+health+information+technology+2008

Pew Internet & American Life Project (2010). Accessed August 24, 2011 from
    http://www.pewinternet.org/Reports/2010/Social-Media-and-Young-
    Adults.aspx
PricewaterhouseCoopers (September 2010). HRI consumer study.
SK&A (2010). Adoption of EHRs in Medical Offices Jumps 10 Percent. Press
    release, October 25, 2010. SK&A, Irvine, CA.

7

HEALTHCARE REGULATIONS, PRIVACY, SECURITY, AND INFORMATION AGE CONSIDERATIONS

SYDNEY MORRIS

Contents

Introduction

There are many important considerations in regard to standards in healthcare and privacy and security. Healthcare in America is changing with developments in technology and new legislation enacted by the Obama Administration. Organizations such as the Health Information Security and Privacy Collaboration (HISPC) and the Office of the National Coordinator for Health Information Technology (ONC) are striving to encourage health information exchange and provide rules, such as transfer of private data. With new technologies and the use of Web 2.0, or social media, providing new opportunities for healthcare providers, it is possible for patients to have unprecedented access to medical knowledge and generate rich discussions online with health professionals. These providers also have the opportunity to publish medical information and interact with their patients in a different way than before Web 2.0. Important standards to consider include the Health Insurance and Portability Accountability Act (HIPAA), Health Information Technology for Economic and Clinical Health (HITECH), the American Recovery and Reinvestment Act (ARRA), and the recently signed Patient Protection and Affordable Care Act (PPACA). These federal rules direct the way private data is released to the patient and also the way patients now seek medical care. In addition, there are state laws that govern the manner in which individuals obtain their information, and also address important issues such as medical identity theft and e-prescribing.

Privacy, Security, and the State

Overview of State Access Law

Almost every state has some legislative stipulation allowing an individual access to medical records. In some states these stipulations affect an entire range of healthcare providers, (Pritts, Kayne, & Jacobson, 2009), while in others, access laws affect only specific types of providers. For example, there are varied standards based upon the type of doctor (e.g., osteopathy, dentist, podiatrist, or chiropractor). The right to alter private health data is the standard least likely to be addressed in state law (Pritts, Kayne, & Jacobson, 2009).

Overall, this right to change individual health data is not likely addressed by state law. In addition, most state laws require doctors or hospitals to allow access to not only private data, but also to any data on record through another healthcare provider. Due to these laws, some providers do not supply a full record of patient data. With regard to a required format, there are also ambiguities. Some states require doctors or hospitals, upon inquiry, to provide "an explanation of any code or abbreviation used in the record or in a form that is understandable to the patient" (Pritts, Kayne, & Jacobson, 2009). Although some organizations, in practice, already direct patients' attention for professional terms to medical dictionaries and articles. In terms of response time for patient inquiries, state law varies greatly. Most states require doctors or hospitals to respond within thirty days for private medical data. In some cases, state law even allows sixty days' response time. With regard to fees charged for services, some states permit a "reasonable" charge. Most states (forty-one to be exact) require a fee timetable for data distributed to patients and copying charge limits. These fees also may include charges per-page. Under these state laws, the limit of copying fees for one page may reach $40; the limit for copying approximately 100 pages might surpass $140. With regard to record-holding rules, almost every state has requirements. In all states, ten years is the common requirement for holding time. With regard to accessing the private data of minors, parents or legal guardians generally command the right of their child's records. Complications arise when the minor may legally consent to his own medical aid (Pritts, Kayne, & Jacobson, 2009).

Consent

With regard to privacy and security, consent is also an important consideration. According to the Department of Health Policy, privacy or the capability to utilize authority over one's private data is the primary issue in Health Information Exchange (HIE). The consent standard changes with each state. Although there is no standard for consent, the central terms are no consent, opt-out, opt-out with exceptions, opt-in, and opt-in with restrictions. In no consent, patients have no choice, and their data is "automatically included." In terms of opt-out, the "default is for health information of patients to be included automatically," yet patients still have the option to fully decline. In terms of opt-out with exceptions, the "default is for health information of patients to be included, but the patient can opt out completely or allow only select data to be included." In terms of opt-in, the "default is that no patient health information is included; patients must actively express consent to be included, but if they do so, then their information must be all in or all out." The final term, opt-out with restrictions, typically allows "no patient health information [to be] made available ... but the patient may allow a subset of select data to be included" (Goldstien, Rein, & Hughes, 2009).

Federal-Based Organizations

Health Information Security and Privacy Collaboration (HISPC)

The HISPC or Health Information Security and Privacy Collaboration, an organization and a contract with the Department of Health and Human Services, strives to guide privacy and security issues derived from health information exchange within multiple states. Every member possesses the assistance of an area administrator and guides a group on related business matters. Currently in phase 3, starting in April 2008, the organization consists of forty-two states and territories. In addition, the organization is conducting seven multi-state coordinated privacy and security research undertakings to examine consent law. Specifically, the study will focus on "intra-state and interstate consent policies, developing tools to help harmonize state privacy laws, developing tools and strategies to educate and engage consumers, developing toolkits to educate providers, recommending basic security policy requirements, and developing inter-organizational agreements" (ONC 2010a).

Office of the National Coordinator for Health Information Technology (ONC)

The ONC, or Office of the National Coordinator for Health Information Technology, is an organization devoted to guiding the healthcare industry. They are at the front of the country's health IT endeavors, act as a guide to the whole health network in gaining health information technology and encouraging a nation-oriented health information exchange. They work within the Office of the Secretary for the U.S. Department of Health and Human Services. The ONC is the primary federal organization responsible for the management of national goals, the utilization of the most progressive health information technology, and the transmission of data over health information exchanges. Their mission in promoting a health information exchange consists of guaranteeing security, superior care, decrease in cost, data concerning when and where medical judgments occur, the opportunity for public participation, higher collaboration among healthcare professionals, decreasing the time reaction to national or private health emergencies, and the encouragement of research. In addition, the ONC strives to fill a national leadership role in guiding the healthcare industry: as the governing figure of a potential health information exchange. They strive to provide standards for the use of health IT, and general health IT rule implementation (ONC, 2010b).

Regulations

Health Insurance and Portability Accountability Act (HIPAA)

HIPAA, or the Health Insurance and Portability Accountability Act of 1996, an overarching law of The Privacy Rule, is a document permitting individuals to alter their health information for greater accuracy or entirety, (Pritts, Kayne, & Jacobson, 2009). HIPAA and the Privacy Rule grants rights to individuals regarding their private data and also establishes guidelines for who may access their information (HSS, 2010a). HIPAA, established on August 21, 1996, requires the Secretary of Health and Human Services (HHS) to "publicize standards for the electronic exchange, privacy and security of health information." Initially, HIPAA necessitated the Secretary of HHS to form privacy rules for the use of private data if Congress did not pass a related law within three years after the passage of HIPAA. It followed that Congress did not pass such legislation and HHS established a recommended rule to be circulated for public commentary. They published this rule for public perusal and received over 52,000 comments. The final rule, the Privacy Rule, was issued December 28, 2000. In March 2002, they drafted provisions to the Privacy Rule and circulated these changes to the public again for commentary. The response was over 11,000 comments. This is the most current version today of the Privacy Rule, which was released on August 14, 2002 (HSS, 2010b). According to the Department of HSS, organizations that must abide by these laws are referred to as "covered entities." These organizations include three main categories: health plans, most healthcare providers, and healthcare clearing houses. Health plans comprise health insurance companies, HMOs, and some government programs that provide healthcare. The category "healthcare providers" includes any medical organization that conducts business electronically. Healthcare clearinghouses are organizations that transfer nonstandard health data they obtain from other health organizations into standards (HSS, 2010a).

A goal of the Privacy Rule is to guarantee that private health data are appropriately utilized while facilitating the proper function of the healthcare industry. The establishment of this rule is, first and foremost, for a national set of standards with regard to the privacy and security of specific information. This Privacy Rule establishes national standards for individual rights (HSS, 2010b).

These standards are very specific, but general aspects include what an individual is entitled to with regard to accessing information, maximum time response restrictions, a specified amount a provider can charge, restraints rejection of an individual's access, establishing a way to review such rejections, and a way to edit private data. Private health data that is protected includes any material that healthcare providers put into an individual's health record (HSS, 2010a). More precisely defined, these data include all "individually identifiable health information." These data include exchanges with an individual's healthcare provider, data held by a health insurer, and billing information. More specifically, the protection of this private data does not exclude data in an individual's history, any provision of medical treatment to the patient, or any payment, regardless of time. In addition, it includes de-identified health information, which may be defined as data that neither classifies nor grants an understandable foundation to identify an individual. The two modes to de-identify information are an official result by a professional statistician and the elimination of certain identifiers of the individual. More specifically, an individual's rights include viewing or obtaining records, the ability to make corrections, giving consent, and acquiring a detailed document about these rights. With regard to uses and disclosures, the Privacy Rule servers to describe and restrict the protection of an individual's data. This private information may not be divulged unless the statutes of the Privacy Rule allow or the individual consents in writing (HSS, 2010b).

Required disclosure of private data is only present in two circumstances: when an individual inquires for access or the HSS is legally inspecting an individual. More specifically, with regard to uses and disclosures, the Privacy Rule only allows release to certain entities: "the individual, treatment, payment, Health care operations, uses … disclosures with opportunity to agree or object, incidental use … disclosure, public interest … benefit activities, and limited data set." According to HIPAA, an individual is defined as "a covered entity may disclose protected health information to the individual who is the subject of the information." As regards medical treatment, charges, or other healthcare acts, a related organization may release information for these acts when working with any healthcare provider. Treatment may be defined as the "provision, coordination, or management of health care and related services for an individual." Payment pertains to an arrangement to pay. Healthcare operations include "quality assessment … , competency assurance activities … , conducting or arranging for medical reviews, audits, or legal services … specified insurance functions … business planning, development, management, and administration" (HSS, 2010b). With regard to informal consent, or releasing and utilization of information with an individual's permission, it may be obtained by requesting it of the individual or instances when the individual possesses the ability to grant permission. Such cases of when an individual is not capable of consent include "when the individual is incapacitated, in an emergency situation, or not available" (HSS, 2010b). In the case of unintended utilization or release, the Privacy Rule does necessitate that each exception in this kind of disclosure of data be eradicated to ensure access to previously stated information. An individual utilizing or disclosing data may only do so if it is regarded as an "incident" or is otherwise authorized under another portion of the Privacy Rule. The data must also be disclosed at the smallest level necessary. In addition, there are twelve reasons to obtain disclosure under circumstances of national need:

1. *Mandated by law:* Any information required by law to be revealed should be disclosed.
2. *Endeavors of public health:* Data may be divulged under the conditions that a Public Health Organization is sanctioned to protect the general community from disease, injury, disability, reports of child abuse of neglect; in addition, information may be released if organizations are required to adhere to FDA regulations, patients who may have developed infectious diseases, or employers request information in consideration to the medical needs of their employees.
3. *Victims of abuse, neglect, or domestic violence:* Under specific circumstances, data may be disclosed in regard to the injured party.
4. *Health oversight activities:* Organizations that supervise the healthcare system may divulge data if authorized by law as a health oversight activity, such as auditing or inspections.
5. *Judicial and administrative proceedings:* If a demand for data is made by court order or administrative proceeding, then this information may be disclosed. In addition, this information may be released if requested by a subpoena or any other legal directive.
6. *Law enforcement purposes:* Private data may be released for law enforcement reasons when legally mandated, in order to ascertain a suspect, fugitive, witness, or missing person, to comply with the request of a official, to notify a law enforcement official of a death, or in case of a specified emergency.
7. *Decedents:* Data may be released to funeral directors in ascertaining a deceased person, establishing the reason of death, or complying with related laws.
8. *Cadaveric organ, eye, or tissue donation:* Information may be disclosed in order to assist in the donation of certain organs, tissues, or the eye.
9. *Research:* Defined as "any systematic investigation designed to develop or contribute to generalizable knowledge." Instances when research allows for necessary documentation, to comply with a specific research procedure, or only for the purpose research.
10. *Serious threat to health or safety:* Data may be divulged in the event that it might prevent a severe risk to health or safety.

11. *Essential government functions:* Permission is not required to perform crucial government tasks or roles such as ensuring the completion of a military operation, facilitating national security activities as legally allowed, assisting in the protection of the President, constructing medical advice for U.S. State Department employees, ensuring the health of inmates or employees in a correctional institution, and ascertaining the qualifications of individuals for certain government benefit programs.

12. *Workers' compensation:* In compliance with workers' compensation, data may be released.

In a limited data set, private data are secured under specific circumstances for certain individuals. In order for individuals, their relatives, household members, or employers to obtain disclosure, they must adhere to a data user agreement. In addition, the data must be utilized for the purposes of research, healthcare functions, or public health reasons (HSS, 2010b).

With regard to who can access this private data, the rule includes treatment, payment of doctors or healthcare providers, and any individual personally connected individual who is involved in the subject's medical care, to ensure good healthcare, in the security of the public (e.g., to report if a flu is in the area) and to aid by certain laws by reporting necessary information to the police (HSS, 2010b).

Some would argue that HIPAA protects the individual by restricting the way information is distributed and protected. Others agree that HIPAA is costly. Giacalone and Cacciatore (2003), in the *American Journal of Health*, argue that the benefit of HIPAA in ensuring the individual's privacy is expensive in comparison to its cost. The HHS calculates the cost for hospitals and healthcare professionals to comply with these rules to be $3.8 billion. The American Hospital Association estimates that same amount to be in a range from $22.5 billion to as much as $43 billion for hospitals (Giacalone & Cacciatore, 2003).

Health Information Technology for Economic and Clinical Health (HITECH)

In the ARRA, the section focusing on Health Information Exchange is also referred to as the HITECH act (Health Information Technology for Economic and Clinical Health). Generally, the goal of this act is to boost the healthcare economy and health information efforts. Of the $22 billion, $19.2 billion is for the purpose of Electronic Health Records (EHRs). In terms of the distribution of these funds, $18 billion is specified for Medicare and Medicaid compensation to hospitals or physicians who utilize an EHR system. A sum of $2 billion is allocated for the ONC (Office of the National Coordinator), charged with supporting EHRs. In addition, the ONC is responsible for altering the technology of the Department of Health and Human Services in favor of accommodating the needs electronic transmission of data. Another $1 billion is reserved for the refurbishment or construction of health facilities or to obtain health technology systems. An amount of $550 million is available for the acquisition of technology for health facilities specifically serving Native American individuals. Another amount of $400 million is dedicated to useful research in regard to the use, implementation, and societal effect of electronic information. An amount of $300 million is distributed to sustain health information exchange efforts both nationally and locally. A final sum of $40 million is reserved for the Social Security Administration in regard to EHRs to process disability claims (hitechanswers.net, 2010).

American Recovery and Reinvestment Act (ARRA)

The American Recovery and Reinvestment Act (ARRA) of 2009 consists of three main objectives: to (1) maintain or generate jobs, (2) encourage the health of the economy, and (3) cultivate new trust and respect for the ability of the government. To attain these objectives, the government will cut $288 billion in taxes to assist millions of citizens; raise federal monies to $244 billion for education and healthcare; obtain $275 billion for federal contracts, grants, or loans; and require all beneficiaries of recovery monies to account for all use of their funds in a quarterly report (Recovery Act, 2009).

Specifically in the healthcare industry, the ARRA will provide a total of $ 2.5 billion for the purpose of benefiting "Health Resources and Services." Of this amount, $500 million will be utilized for grants to health facilities; $1.5 billion is for the construction and maintenance of health centers, in addition to acquiring necessary health equipment and technology; $500 million is available for challenges or scarcities in the healthcare labor force; and $75 million addresses needs for scholarships, loan reimbursement, and grants for training courses. These funds will remain available until September 30, 2011. An amount of 0.5 percent of these funds will be provided for the administration of these monies. In addition, a separate amount of $1.3 billion, $1 billion, of which is portioned for the construction and repair of nonfederal research buildings, is provided for research. An amount of $300 billion may be utilized for the use of research technology. To the Office of the Director a separate amount of $8.2 billion is provided, for the necessary appropriation, to the National Institutes of Health (NIH) and the "Common Fund." These monies also are provided for the purpose of research. Restrictions to these funds include transfers to organizations such as the National Institutes of Health Buildings and Facilities, the Center for Scientific Review, the Center for Information Technology, the Clinical Center, or the Global Fund for HIV/AIDS, Tuberculosis, and Malaria. In addition, separate funds, ($500,000,000) are available to sustain other health facilities and institutes, specifically on the Bethesda, Maryland, campus. The ARRA will also provide funds for other areas of research to fulfill titles of the Public Health Service Act, the Social Security Act, and the Medicare, Prescription Drug, Improvement and Modernization Act of 2003. A portion of this amount, $700 million, is reserved for "comparative effectiveness research." These monies specifically should be utilized to:

> (1) conduct, support, or synthesize research ... and (2) encourage the development and use of clinical registries, clinical data networks, and other forms of electronic health data that can be used to generate or obtain outcomes data ... (Recovery Act, 2009)

Essentially, the goal of ARRA is to encourage effective, useful research and the implementation of health information exchanges (U.S. Senate and House of Representatives, 2009, p. 61–64).

PPACA

A new bill signed by President Obama on September 23, 2010, the Patient Protection and Affordable Care Act (PPACA) could alter healthcare laws in the future by placing tighter laws onto insurance companies; it offers greater Medicare options, tax credits for small businesses, and higher coverage for young adults. This step closer to standardized healthcare alters previous privacy and security issues for patients. The PPACA is an important consideration in how patients seek and receive health insurance. This law will establish "exchanges" or pools of insurance companies for consumers to have access to more competitive rates. In addition, patients will be allowed to choose the doctor they want to treat them through government mandate. Also, it is not necessary to obtain a referral to see an OB-GYN doctor or obtain consent to acquire emergency care outside of a patient's healthcare network. Yet these rules only affect group health plans (healthcare. gov, 2010). This law is a notable consideration for healthcare rules.

Considerations in the Information Age

Medical Identity Theft

Medical identity theft is relevant and significant, especially due to the emerging importance of Health Information Exchange. According to an ONC-sponsored report, two general issues of importance are privacy and security (Booz Allen Hamilton, 2009). Three important considerations in understanding this issue are prevention, detection, and remediation. As argued in the report, prevention is essentially defined as any activity that anticipates and deters identity theft. For health organizations, prevention is important because of its abil-ity to protect the private information of patients. Risks arise when healthcare providers update records or when there is an illicit breach of sensitive information. Detection is defined as any act that aids in the discovery and exposure of medical identity theft (Booz Allen Hamilton, 2009). Remediation is defined as the relief of injured parties of medical identity theft prior to the incident (Booz Allen Hamilton, 2009). In addition, "themes" or important considerations for comprehension include the centrality of the patient, information restrictions in subject, and the function of Health IT in Medical Identity Theft. The patient or "consumer" has the largest risk for dam-age. This individual is the most important party involved. Of course, other individuals may also be affected by such an event. The patient is the most significant consideration for action: prevention and remediation (Booz Allen Hamilton, 2009). Restrictions in information include how to categorize the issue. Many cases of medical identity theft are classified more broadly as healthcare fraud. However, there are cases that do not apply to such a broad category and demonstrate particular distinctions. Generally, the intention of this kind of theft is financial advancement; for example, a patient receives a bill from an erroneous organization for more costly labor than that provided. Yet theft can also apply to "the use of someone else's information to gain goods, services, and healthcare, which may result in different methods of addressing the problem (Booz Allen Hamilton, 2009). Health IT also has a significant function in addressing Medical Identity Theft. Health IT provides "comprehensive management of medical information and its secure exchange between Health care consumers and providers" (Booz Allen Hamilton, 2009). This entity provides the capability to examine and analyze information online. In this report, the ONC asserts that, if utilized properly, the Health Information Exchange potentially would "prevent, detect, and assist" with the deterrence of medical identity in a previously unavailable manner. As argued, prospective decisions, with respect to this topic, include "leadership, education, business processes and technology, and policies and laws" (Booz Allen Hamilton, 2009).

Leadership in Medical Identity Theft

According to an ONC-sponsored report, there is a "need for a strong national-level presence driving a standardized and coordinated approach to detection, prevention, education, and victim recovery" (Booz Allen Hamilton, 2009). The current guidelines for financial identity theft could also be utilized to draft guidelines or standards for medical identity theft. To achieve these guidelines, central procedures, rudimentary rules, and specialized approaches are argued by the report to be essential. The government also identifies the necessity for leadership in this area; for example, Executive Order 13402, allowing for the creation of the Presidential Identity Theft Task Force, consisting of fifteen federal departments and agencies. These entities finalized a specialized plan and written guidance. These recommendations are designed to address "data protection, data misuse, victim assistance, and deterrence" (Booz Allen Hamilton, 2009). As argued by the ONC-sponsored report, the government should take a more aggressive role in the healthcare industry. This role could be a "public-private task force, formation and membership of public and private entities, under government leadership to focus on medical identity theft that includes initiatives such as the HISPC." The government also could evaluate and investigate the procedure to approach financial identity theft and apply it to medical identity theft. In addition the government could create plans to recognize and categorize hazards. The report revealed that knowledge about medical identity theft is not well understood or disbursed. However, according to the Federal Trade Commission (FTC) from 2006 data, there are almost 250,000 injured individuals of this crime. There is a need for greater awareness of this subject. Another issue in medical identity theft is the kind of access individuals have to their private information. The manner in which individuals access this information may affect the privacy and security of that data (Booz Allen Hamilton, 2009).

E-Prescribing

E-prescribing is the act of advising patients on particular medicines online. Generally, laws are individually based upon by state administering the "prescribing, dispensing, of prescription drugs by licensed Health care professionals." There are federal laws that establish standards for the exchange of medicine (Pritts, Jacobson, & Connors, 2009). There also are laws that regulate generic drugs over brand name in order to support their sales and thus lower healthcare expenses. Almost every state has a law encouraging off-brand medicine. In addition, state law encourages these drugs through the limiting of Medicaid compensation when a generic drug is available. Almost twenty states have laws that address the substitution of generic medications with brand name and the encouragement of such purchases. In contrast, seventeen states have laws that require the provider to specify that the brand-name medication is more medically beneficial to the patient. Twenty states also mandate that a provider must provide handwritten documentation on the prescription in order to prevent generic replacement. Issues that complicate e-prescribing are prerequisites for prescription, documentation, exchange, and consent.

Further complications result from how to approach regulated substances, corresponding to 10 percent of total prescriptions. The majority of states do not allow e-prescribing of regulated substances (Pritts, Jacobson, & Connors, 2009).

Web 2.0

The Health Care Information and Management Systems Society (HIMSS) is a nonprofit organization devoted to imparting global leadership in the use of healthcare technology. The Northern Ohio Chapter of this organization published a Web 2.0 document concerning the potential role of Web 2.0 and also the use of social networking media in the healthcare industry. The benefits of Web 2.0 include reduction in cost, "the architecture of participation," "the web as a platform," and the ability to manage information directly (Sharp, 2006). In addition, many organizations are utilizing social networking sites to validate their businesses and engage in societal participation. Among the many resources or "tools" in this area are blogs, wikis, Google, Gmail, maps, Ajax, MySpace, Flickr, and YouTube (Sharp, 2006).

According to a recent report by the Health Care Performance Management Institute entitled "HPM in the Era of Twitter: Harnessing the Social Networking Phenomenon," social media are modifying the healthcare industry. The report specifies how organizations are able maximize the influence of healthcare technology in conjunction with social media to link sponsors, members, and the healthcare community. This online partnership is allowing for increased financing in wellness programs and the management of persistent diseases (HPM, 2010).

In a study entitled "Supporting Healthcare Knowledge Transfer through a Web 2.0 Portal" conducted by Steininger et al. (2009), they examine a patient's need for such a portal. This platform would be owned and supported by health professionals providing excellent information, possibly generating more reliability. Web 2.0 is defined as:

> Web 2.0 knowledge transfer portal does not only provide health information created by experts but also offer Web 2.0 functions like wikis, forums, chat rooms, or blogs. These functions shall allow patients and

interested people to share their knowledge concerning diseases or treatments as well as experiences ... (Steininger, 2009).

Essentially, Web 2.0 is a space for a host to edit information and users, or patients, to generate and gain knowledge. For example, users would be able to research a common cold on the Web and access information for treatment. Previously, a patient would speak to a physician about such a cold and the necessary treatment. Core principles to consider in this subject are "the web as a platform, harnessing collective intelligence, end of the software release cycle, lightweight programming models, software above the level of a single device, and rich user experiences." Prolific and successful examples of Web 2.0 platforms are www.wikipedia.org, RSS feeds such as www.webmd.com and www.medicinenet.com, blogs such as www.thehealthblog.com, and chat areas such as www.icq.com. Such a portal would be a space for patients and professionals to present questions and generate edited user content. The results indicate there is a significant possibility for hospitals to begin and maintain an effective Web 2.0 portal. These results are based on studies conducted within an Austrian central hospital: two questionnaires for patients and the professionals. In addition, the results demonstrate the patients' desire to participate more in their own healthcare. Many of these patients seek information from the Internet. Websites that provide such information include google.com and wikipedia.com. They assertively search the Internet for information about illnesses and potential cures. Searching for treatments online is actually one of the most prevalent actions on the Internet. Therefore, it is becoming a trend for organizations to provide this more efficient transmission of information and gain credibility with their audience (Steininger et al., 2009).

Web 2.0 is an excellent solution to the problem of how to effectively transfer knowledge to patients while also gaining their trust. Not only can such a platform be useful for patients to better understand their treatment, but also for doctors to share, save, and sort knowledge among themselves. Such transmissions of information could be helpful in diagnosing patients. With regard to the results of the study, prospective patients were questioned in a survey if they felt sufficiently educated on medical matters during their hospital visits. Only one fourth agreed to be completely educated. Another 35 percent

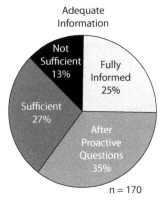

Figure 7.1   Data from the Steininger et al. (2009) study concerning how receptive patients and doctors may be to utilizing a web portal to transfer information. (*Source:* Courtesy of Morris, S., artist.)

agreed to also be completely educated but only after presenting specific queries; 13 percent did not feel fulfilled with the provided information during their hospital visits. When patients were questioned if they ever received medical treatment without understanding the reason, 35 percent stated they accepted treatment when they somewhat did not understand the purpose; 13 percent felt discontent with the medical professional's explanation, only 36 percent felt that all of their questions to medical professionals were fully answered, and 46 percent of patients were not fully happy with doctor discussions (Figure 7.1).

When patients were questioned about their favored source for further information after being diagnosed, the answers "attending doctor" and "Internet" accounted for 83 percent of the responses; 32 percent consulted books or journals. When asked if patients would utilize a Web 2.0 portal, 74 percent stated they would "definitely" benefit from such a platform offering health information; 24 percent stated they would "probably" benefit. Doctors who received the survey were questioned as to whether they felt patients were completely educated or even understood fundamental data after a discussion with a health professional: 51 percent stated that patients were not fully informed; 14 percent of doctors agreed that patients completely understood the information presented to them in conversations with professionals; 79 percent of doctors agreed that patients would utilize a Web 2.0 portal; 25 percent of doctors agreed they would distribute health information on such a portal, 28 percent agreed to only during paid time, and 29 percent agreed to sometimes; 42 percent felt that distributing such information would lessen their workload (Steininger et al., 2010). According to this study, patients and physicians are open to the idea of a Web 2.0 portal. In addition, some patients were not satisfied with the current level of communication they received from their current care providers.

Opportunities in Web 2.0 are available for health professionals to participate in and utilize to their maximum capability. This would allow greater transmission of knowledge among patients and doctors. In addition, there are state laws addressing issues such as e-prescribing, medical identity theft, and consent. Important standards to consider are HIPAA, HITECH, ARRA, and the newly signed PPACA. These federal rules direct the way that private data are released to the patient and also the way patients now seek medical care. The dynamic field of healthcare is evolving; new laws and opportunities are available for professionals to utilize.

References

Booz Allen Hamilton (2009). *Medical Identity Theft*. Washington, D.C.: Office of the National Coordinator for Health Information Technology.

Giacalone, R. P. & Cacciatore, G. G.(2003). HIPAA and its impact on pharmacy practice. *American Journal of Health-System Pharmacy, 60*, 430–442.

Goldstien, M., Rein, A. L., & Hughes, P. P. (2010). Consumer Consent Options for Electronic Health Information Exchange: Policy Considerations and Analysis. Washington, D.C.: Office of the National Coordinator for Health Information Technology.

healthcare.gov (2010). Understanding the affordable care act: About the law. Retrieved October 22, 2010, from http://www.healthcare.gov/law/about/index.html

hitechanswers.net (2010). About the HITECH Act. Retrieved October 22, 2010, from http://www.hitechanswers.net/about/about-the-hitech-act-of-2009/

HPM (2010). New report from HPM Institute: Employers can harness social networking technologies and processes to drive down costs and improve outcomes. From Healthcare Performance Management Institute. Retrieved October 23, 2010, from http://www.hpminstitute.org/node/207

HSS (U.S. Department of Health and Human Services) (2010a). For Consumers. From U.S. Department of Health and Human Services. Retrieved October 22, 2010, from http://www.hhs.gov/ocr/privacy/hipaa/understanding/consumers/index.html

HSS (U.S. Department of Health and Human Services) (2010b). Summary of the HIPAA Privacy Rule. From U.S. Department of Health and Human Services. Retrieved October 22, 2010, from http://www.hhs.gov/ocr/privacy/hipaa/understanding/summary/index.html

ONC (Office of the National Coordinator for health Information Technology) (2010a). Health Information Security and Privacy Collaboration (2010). From Office of the National Coordinator for Health Information Technology. Retrieved October 5, 2010, from http://healthit.hhs.gov/portal/server.pt?open=512&objID=1240&parentname=CommunityPage&parentid=2&mode=2

ONC (Office of the National Coordinator for health Information Technology) (2010b). About ONC. From Office of the National Coordinator for Health Information Technology. Retrieved October 5, 2010, from http://healthit.hhs.gov/portal/server.pt/community/healthit_hhs_gov__onc/1200

Pritts, J., Jacobson, R., & Connors, E. (2009). Report on State Prescribing Laws: Implications for e-Prescribing. RTI International, Chicago, IL.

Pritts, J., Kayne, K., & Jacobson, R. (2009). Report on State Medical Record Access Laws. Chicago, IL: RTI International.

Pritts, J., Lewis. S., Jacobson, R., Lucia, K., & Kayne, K. (2009). Report on State Law Requirements for Patient Permission to Disclose Health Information. RTI International, Chicago, IL.

Recovery Act (2009). Retrieved October 22, 2010, from http://www.recovery.gov/About/Pages/The_Act.aspx

Sharp, J. (2006). Web 2.0: Beyond Open Source in Health Care. NOHIMSS. Retrieved October 23, 2010, from www.nohimss.org/sharp.pdf

Steininger, K., Rueckel, D. R., Dannerer, E., and Roithmayr, F. (2009). Supporting Healthcare Knowledge Transfer through a Web 2.0 Portal. *Proceedings of AMCIS '09:* AISeL, San Francisco, CA.

U.S. Senate and House of Representatives (2009). *American Recovery and Reinvestment Act.* U.S. Government Printing Office, Washington, DC.

8

USABILITY

Patient–Physician Interactions and the Electronic Medical Record

CAROLYN K. SHUE, PH.D. AND LAURA L. S. O'HARA, PH.D.

Contents

In President George W. Bush's 2004 State of the Union address, he challenged the medical community to eliminate paper medical records by 2014. In support of this challenge, President Bush proposed allocating $100 million of the 2005 fiscal year budget and $125 million of the 2006 fiscal year budget to fund electronic medical record adoption efforts (Fletcher, 2005). President Obama's 2009 American Recovery and Reinvestment Act provided $20 billion in Health Information Technology (HIT) funding and physician adoption incentives in the form of Medicare and Medicaid reimbursements. The act also put into place financial penalties in the form of reduced Medicare reimbursements for physicians who have not adopted a certified electronic health record system by the end of 2014 (Ledue, 2009). The attention given to HIT also extends to the state level, as evidenced by the passing of 168 pieces of HIT legislation between 2005 and 2008 (HIT, 2009).

The political push for HIT stems from the desire to reduce health-related costs and increase health delivery efficiency. These goals, however, must be examined in light of HIT usability issues. The technology alone cannot guarantee the desired outcomes. Therefore, it is critical to examine the adoption of HIT in the U.S. health delivery system. Specifically, we will examine Electron Medical Records/ Electronic Health Records (EMRs/EHRs) within the hospital and clinical setting, the impact of EMRs/EHRs on patient-physician communication, and recommendations for EMR/EHR selection or development in light of current limitations and future expectations. By understanding EMR/EHR processes, we gain insight into what healthcare providers need this technology so that the outcomes of reduced cost, increased efficiency, and improved health outcomes can be realized.

Definition of Terms and Chapter Focus

According to the Department of Health and Human Services Office of the National Coordinator for Health Information Technology (HSS, 2008), there are three main HIT terms that refer to electronic information exchange at the patient level:

1. *Electronic Medical Records (EMRs):* "An electronic record of health-related information on an individual that can be created, gathered, managed, and consulted by authorized clinicians and staff within *one* [emphasis added] health care organization" (p. 6).

2. *Electronic Health Records (EHR):* "An electronic record of health-related information on an individual that *conforms to nationally recognized interoperability standards* [emphasis added] and that can be created, managed, and consulted by authorized clinicians and staff *across more than one* [emphasis added] health care organization" (p. 6).

3. *Personal Health Records (PHR):* "An electronic record of health-related information on an individual that conforms

to nationally recognized interoperability standards and that can be drawn from multiple sources while being managed, shared, and controlled by the individual" (p. 6).

There are also three main health IT terms that refer to electronic information exchange at the organization and community level:

1. *Health Information Exchange (HIE):* "The electronic movement of health-related information among organizations according to nationally recognized standards" (p. 6).
2. *Health Information Organization (HIO):* "An organization that oversees and governs the exchange of health-related information among organizations according to nationally recognized standards" (p. 6).
3. *Regional Health Information Organization (RHIO):* "A health information organization that brings together health care stakeholders within a defined geographic area and governs health information exchange among them for the purpose of improving health and care in that community" (p. 6).

While there are critical issues to examine at the level of the organization and community (e.g., accountable care organizations[1]), the focus of this chapter is on the patient and specifically on EMRs [and in some cases EHRs], for three primary reasons. First, EMRs/EHRs are the first step to larger organizational and community-level HIT adoption. Second, nationwide there has been more EMR/EHR adoption by clinics and hospitals with varying levels of success. Third, and most important, EMRs/EHRs can both positively and negatively impact patient-physician communication. One of the goals of this chapter is to examine specifically *how* EMRs/EHRs impact the clinical setting and patient-physician communication as a means of identifying directions for technological development that can promote clinical efficiency and increase positive health outcomes. To do this, it is important to keep the analysis at the level of the patient and on EMRs/EHRs. However, in our recommendations, we also identify areas for improvement in current EMR/EHR systems because of the ramifications for organizational and community-level coordination of health-related information, which ultimately affects patients.

The Current State of EMR/EHR Adoption

Currently, there are more than 300 EMR vendors, with an even larger number of EMR systems available to healthcare providers (Morgan, 2009). According to the National Center for Health Statistics' (NCHS) National Ambulatory Medical Care Survey, in 2008 41.5 percent of physicians report using a fully functioning to partial EMR/EHR system (not including systems solely for billing). Preliminary findings from the 2009 survey indicate that number has risen to 43.9 percent (Hsiao et al., 2009). Physicians in large group practices (fifty-one and more physicians), HMOs, and medical school faculty practices have been the earliest and most likely adopters of EMRs/EHRs while physicians in solo and small group practices have been less likely to incorporate EMRs/EHRs into their clinics (Grossman & Reed, 2006). Yet, physician adoption rates have increased for all types of practices from 2000 to 2007 (Grossman & Reed, 2006; HIT, 2008). Adoption rates by hospital types have varied as well, with less than 10 percent of nonfederal general acute care hospitals in the United States having comprehensive or basic EHRs. Larger hospitals (500+ beds), teaching hospitals, and urban hospitals, or hospitals that are members of a larger health-care system, are more likely to use EHRs (HIT, 2009).

Advocates for the adoption of EMR/EHR systems cite several compelling arguments. First, researchers' analysis of financial figures has demonstrated long-term cost savings and revenue generation. For example, Patil, Puri, and Gonzalez (2008) found that documentation costs decreased by $3.11 per encounter, average revenue increased by $117.88 per encounter, and the average revenue per provider increased by $184,627 during the four-year period after an EMR was adopted in an ambulatory surgical subspecialty clinic. In addition, the clinic increased the number of patient encounters by 13,075 over the course of the four-years post-EMR implementation. Second, EMRs/EHRs can improve the quality of patient care and decrease physicians' "cognitive load" (Shachak et al., 2008, p. 343) by providing decision-making aids, treatment guidelines charts, potential adverse drug interaction alerts, and easy access to information related to past visits and medical test results (Shachak et al., 2008; Tang et al., 2009). Third, electronic medical record systems can increase documentation accuracy and completeness. A *Wall Street Journal*/Harris Interactive Healthcare survey of patients found that, in general, approximately 30 percent of adults believe their physicians have a complete and accurate record of their medical history. For patients whose physicians use an EMR, approximately 50 percent believe their physicians have an accurate record (H&HN, 2008), a finding consistent with EMR satisfaction research (Freeman, Taylor, & Adelman, 2009). Galanter et al. (2010) demonstrated that an automated alert system based on medications ordered by physicians did, in turn, prompt physicians to increase their documentation of the diagnosis on the EMR problem list.

While there are many factors promoting EMR/EHR adoption, there are also several factors prohibiting it. Despite claims that financial costs of EMR/EHR implementation can be recovered (Patil, Puri, & Gonzalez, 2008), both physician practices and hospitals cite financial barriers as the primary reason why they have not yet adopted EMRs/EHRs (HIT, 2008, 2009). For example, one ambulatory surgical subspecialty clinic cited its EMR implementation cost at $10,329 per physician for a total cost of $293,406 (Patil, Puri, & Gonzalez, 2008). General industry estimates for EMR implementation per single provider office are approximately $33,500 in initial costs with subsequent yearly maintenance costs ranging from $3,000 to $10,000 (EMR Experts, Inc., 2009). In addition to high costs, physicians identify workflow disruption, loss of autonomy, and system barriers (i.e., lack of fit between the way the physician wanted to enter the data and the EMR/EHR format, processing delays, lack of access to records when the system is down) as reasons not to adopt EMRs/EHRs (Holden, 2010; Ross, 2009). In fact, some physicians argue that EMR/EHR use has created new types of medical errors in the form of typos, entering medical information into the wrong chart, and mistakenly selecting the wrong diagnosis or medication from a pull-down menu (Shachak et al., 2008). EMRs/EHRs can negatively impact patient care if physicians make treatment decisions based on errors documented in the EMR/EHR, ignore automated alerts because the system generates too many false-positive alerts, and spend more time documenting the medical visit than actually engaging in conversations with patients (Holden, 2010).[1]

The EMR/EHR and Patient-Physician Interactions

The communication that occurs between the physician and the patient is one of the "fundamental ingredients of medical care" (Roter and Hall, 2006, p. 4), and improving the quality of physicians' communication has become a top priority in the healthcare industry. For example, both the Surgeon General's *Healthy People 2010* and *2020* reports list as an objective increases in the number of persons who report that their healthcare providers have satisfactory communication skills (HSS, 2009). Related to this, there has been an increase in the empirical literature examining many specific aspects of physicians' communication behavior within the patient-physician dyad (e.g., Crane & Crane, 2010; Frankel et al., 2005; Mast, 2007; Rider & Keefer, 2006; Rider, Lown, & Hinrichs, 2004; Robinson, 2006; Roter & Hall, 2006).

One consistent theme in this body of literature is that maintaining excellent communication during healthcare encounters is often challenging for physicians, who need to manage a wide range of cognitive and physical tasks that do not necessarily follow a set sequence (i.e., gathering and recording information, examining patients, diagnosing illness, educating patients, and recommending treatments) while simultaneously attending to their interpersonal relationship with the patient (Frankel et al., 2005; Roter & Hall, 2006). Another consistent theme in the literature is that many physicians lack the training to enact appropriate communication skills during the medical interview (Crane & Crane, 2010; Ishikawa et al., 2006; Mast, 2007).

These challenges have become progressively more complex with the advent of the EMR, which demands more cognitive engagement from the physician as he or she performs "on the spot" such tasks as typing on the keyboard to enter patient information into templates, navigating searches, and ordering prescriptions (Frankel et al., 2005). Given that high-quality communication between the patient and physician is among the most significant factors in the healthcare visit (Crane & Crane, 2010; Kurtz & Silverman, 2005), with consequences for patient compliance (Schneider et al., 2004), patient satisfaction (Haywood et al., 2010), and ultimately, clinical outcomes (Rider & Keefer, 2006), there has necessarily been increased attention in the health communication literature focused on how the EMR affects the quality of patient-physician interactions.

Ideally, physicians should possess the communication skills needed to help patients express their medical concerns, explore the implications of these concerns, respond effectively and appropriately to their emotions, and validate their feelings (Cohen-Cole, 1991; Roter et al., 1995; Roter & Hall, 2006; Smith et al., 2000). All of these tasks involve critical verbal components (e.g., the ability to use simple, accessible language when communicating about complex medical topics; the ability to ask appropriate open-ended and probe questions at the appropriate time) and nonverbal components (e.g., the ability to orient one's body toward the patient and maintain appropriate eye contact to demonstrate appropriate levels of attention, the ability to change vocalic tone or facial expression to show concern or empathy).

The literature suggests that the EMR can improve the quality of medical information exchange between physicians and patients (Arar et al., 2005; Hsu et al., 2005; Kuo et al., 2007; Margalit et al., 2006) because it provides ready access to patient records, permits record sharing between physicians, and allows the physician and patient to view the EMR together, thereby opening up the potential for more collaborative communication about particular aspects of a patient's health. For example, Arar et al. (2005) demonstrated that the EMR helped physicians expand discussion about such topics as self-regulation and patients' adherence to medicines. Interestingly, however, despite patients' satisfaction with the physician's use of the EMR in this study, less than ten of the fifty videotaped interviews concluded with definitive agreement from both parties regarding the patient's prescribed medication routines.

Although the literature reveals general patient satisfaction with physicians' use of the EMR in terms of the quality of communication about *medical information*, patients often report less satisfaction with physician's EMR use in the realm of patient-centeredness. For example, in an observational study of Israeli primary care encounters, Margalit et al. (2006) reported that physicians routinely walked directly to the EMR after only a cursory greeting to the patient and spent nearly one-fourth of the visit time engaging in heavy keyboarding. Moreover, physicians in this study sustained eye-gaze with the

EMR up to 42 percent of the time during patient visits, often doing so while talking to patients or while patients were talking to them. Such behaviors have a clear inverse relationship to patients' perception of the physician's emotional responsiveness and patient-centeredness (Booth, Robinson, & Hohannejad, 2004; Kuo et al., 2007; Margalit et al., 2006; Ventres et al., 2006).

Research also suggests that patterns such as those described above may relate more to physicians' communication style than to his or her use of the EMR alone (Ventres et al., 2005). Given this, some of the physicians in these studies may have exhibited what Shackak and Reis (2009) classified as an "informational-ignoring style" (p. 645). Physicians with this style when using the EMR tend to focus on EMR-guided templates to gather and report detailed information, build less rapport with patients, share less information with patients via the EMR, turn away from patients while they type into the EMR, and gaze into the EMR screen even when they are engaged in conversation with patients. Although Shackak and Reis do not specify that such an "informational-ignoring style" contributes to diminished levels of patient-centeredness, hence diminished levels of patient satisfaction in patient-physician interactions in which EMRs are a part, earlier literature describing similar physician styles (e.g., Ong et al., 1995; Roter, Hall, & Katz, 1987; Stewart, 1984) suggests that there may be a relationship.

Conversely, scholars (e.g., Booth, Robinson, and Kohannejad, 2004; Shackak & Reis, 2009; Ventres et al., 2005, 2006) also discuss behavioral styles of physicians using the EMR that might be more effective in terms of balancing the need to attend to the task-focused elements of the EMR with the need to be patient centered. Specifically, Shackak and Reis (2009) describe a "controlling-managerial style" in which physicians tend to rotate their attention between the patient and the EMR into distinct periods within the medical visit by turning one's body or switching one's gaze to indicate that the "switch" from EMR focus to patient focus or vice versa has occurred. Additionally, a number of authors (e.g., Shackak & Reis, 2009; Ventres et al., 2005, 2006) describe an "interpersonal style" in which physicians tend to focus primarily on the patient, refraining from using the EMR at the start of a visit, spending less time entering data on the EMR throughout the duration of the visit, asking few, if any, EMR prompted questions, refraining from talking to the patient while using the EMR, but physically orienting themselves toward the patient when they are using the EMR. These physicians tend also to use the EMR as a tool to share information with the patient.

Not surprisingly, Frankel et al. (2005) found that physicians' use of the EMR tended to amplify both excellent and poor baseline communication skills when it was integrated into the exam room. In other words, physicians who performed communication skills well before the introduction of the EMR tended to be able to integrate it into their practice quite easily, while physicians who had poor baseline communication skills tended to be further inhibited in their communication with patients after the introduction of the EMR.

Thus far, we have focused primarily on the specific person-to-person communication factors of patient-physician communication as they relate to physicians' use of the EMR. However, there are other factors in this context that impact the quality of the communication that occurs between patients and physicians using the EMR. One of the most obvious of these is the spatial arrangement of the examination room and, in particular, the placement of the EMR in that room (Frankel et al., 2005; McGrath, Arar, & Pugh, 2007; Ventres et al., 2005). For example, Frankel et al. (2005) and McGrath, Arar, and Pugh (2007) describe a number of examination room configurations, including some in which the EMR was on a desktop, that forced the physician to sit with his or her back toward the patient. Ventres et al. (2005) documented physicians' satisfaction with EMRs that could be moved easily to facilitate more open communication with their patients (e.g., by enabling the physician to share information with the patient using the monitor, or by moving the computer so that the physician is face-to-face or side-by-side with the patient, rather than typing with their back turned toward the patient). However, despite the physicians' expressed satisfaction with the flexibility afforded by mobile EMRs, Ventres and colleagues observed "a relative lack of physician interest in fostering patients' involvement" (p. 128), surmising that this may be a result of "a predominance of biomedically focused practice styles" among physicians (p. 128). This observation was echoed by both Ann

King and Debra Roter (2010), leading experts in the field of health communication, at the *2010 Health Literacy Annual Research Conference.*

Another important factor in this context is what Frankel et al. (2005) term the physician's "computer navigation and mastery skills" (p. 680), which include the physician's ability to type quickly and accurately, search the patient record, and navigate the various templates and prompts in the EMR. Similar to their finding on physicians' communication skills, Frankel et al. (2005) found that physicians' use of the EMR tended to amplify existing baseline computer navigation and mastery skills (poor or excellent) when it was integrated into the exam room.

Recommendations for Implementing EMR/EHR/HIT Improvements

Research to date has demonstrated both the promise and problems associated with integrating HIT—in particular, the EMR—into clinical settings. Several recommendations emerge from the literature, from our work in the area of patient-physician communication,[2] and through our conversations with practicing physicians that must be addressed when selecting a new commercial EMR or considering improving future versions of EMR software. We organize these recommendations, and in some cases challenges, around the areas of (1) patient-physician interactions, (2) provider-patient usability, (3) care coordination, and (4) clinical and practice improvement research.

Patient-Physician Interactions

Increase communication training efforts to facilitate physicians' patient-centeredness when using the EMR/EHR: Margalit et al. (2006) argue that physicians' ability to remain patient centered when using the EMR/EHR can contribute to patients' improved understanding of their conditions, enhanced co-decision-making between patient and physician, patient empowerment, and ultimately, improved quality of care for the patient. While some physicians already possess the skills to better reach these goals, researchers (Margalit et al., 2006; Theadom et al., 2003) argue convincingly that many others do not, and that appropriate communication skills training can help these physicians develop such important patient-centered behaviors.

These skills include basic interpersonal communication (as described in the literature above) as well as methods for using the EMR/EHR as a teaching tool for the patient (e.g., integrating information from the EMR/EHR quickly and accurately; using simple, accessible language when discussing medical information with the patient; switching focus from the EMR/EHR to the patient). Specifically, this training can assist physicians in switching from a primarily "informational-ignoring" style (Shackak & Reis, 2009) in which a physician's focus on biomedical information exchange and data input into the EMR/EHR often leads to patients' perception that their physician is interpersonally distant, to a "controlling-managerial" style of communication (Shackak & Reis, 2009) in which the physician can alternate biomedical information tasks with more patient-centered communication.

Adopt and/or develop EMR/EHR software that encourages physicians to engage in patient-centered communication as well as bio-medical communication.

Interpersonal skill building. Clinics purchasing EMR/EHR software should consider a system that integrates theoretically sound principles of patient-centered communication (e.g., Cohen-Cole, 1991; Roter et al., 1995; Roter & Hall, 2006; Smith et al., 2000) into its design. For example, EMRs/EHRS could include communication prompts that remind physicians to ask patients questions that elicit the full spectrum of patient concerns and help patients explore the significance of their concerns at the appropriate time and in the appropriate language.

EMR/EHR as a teaching tool. Similarly, patients could benefit from EMRs/EHRs that facilitate more collaborative communication about particular aspects of the patient's health. For example, "quick switches" could help physicians toggle easily from a more complex version of the patient's record to a more "patient-friendly" and printable version that incorporates principles of low-health literacy patient education (Doak, Doak, & Root, 1996), such as graphs, simple language, or pictures. Included in these documents should be references to reliable resources for further information. In addition to these types of teaching tools, EMRs/EHRs should also incorporate patient-friendly and printable templates for common lists that are usually documented on the EMR/EHR by the physician but are only reviewed orally with the patient, thus potentially forgotten or overlooked by the patient once the appointment is over. Such documents could include lists of medications, the physician's recommendations after a particular visit, or a behavioral action plan. These documents could also include simple charts to track the patient's progress after the visit (e.g., for glucose monitoring, for charting diet and exercise). Prompts similar to those described above could also remind physicians to "toggle" to the patient-friendly versions of the physician record—particularly when reviewing lists of medications, recommendations, or behavioral action plans. As a host of researchers argue (Arar et al., 2005; Hsu et al., 2005; Kuo et al., 2007; Margalit et al., 2006), if used more effectively as a teaching tool, EMRs/EHRs could encourage more patient-physician collaboration, shared decision making, and negotiation between patients and physicians, thus potentially leading to higher patient empowerment and more positive medical outcomes.

Increase the flexibility of computer hardware in each examination room to facilitate more patient-centered communication. Research shows that the spatial arrangement of the examination room often has negative impacts on the physician's ability to simultaneously use the EMR/ EHR and engage in patient-centered communication (Frankel et al., 2005; Ventres et al., 2005). However, simple and relatively low-cost solutions for increasing patient-centered communication include making available extra batteries, charger stations, and computer-compatible power cords in each examination room, or at least in close proximity, so that physicians with laptop computers are not "bound" to the desk, which often forces them to work with their back to the patient. Additionally, when purchasing new EMR/EHR hardware systems, clinic IT personnel should consider laptops with such features as swivel screens so that appropriate information can be shared readily with patients. Although desktop screens present a larger mobility/flexibility challenge, efforts should be made to situate these screens so that physicians can share appropriate information from the EMR/EHR with both ambulatory and nonambulatory patients with a reasonable amount of effort.

Encourage/train physicians to take advantage of the flexibility of furniture in each examination room to facilitate more patient-centered communication. Previous research (McGrath, Arar, & Pugh, 2007) supports our own observations that for physicians using the EMR/EHR, the spatial arrangements in the examination room have an effect on the quality of patient-physician interactions. In our own observations, we have noticed that while some physicians "leave well-enough alone," others arrange the standard furniture available in the examination room to facilitate more patient-centered communication when using the EMR/EHR. Specifically, they sit on the short rolling stool (which is likely to send a strong nonverbal signal decreasing the perceived power distance between physician and patient). They use the examination table or their own lap as a perch for the EMR/EHR, most often facing the patient (who typically sits on a chair next to the examination table). When sharing information from the EMR/EHR with the patient, the physician will often move so that he or she is sitting at the patient's side so that both patient and physician can see the EMR/EHR screen, thus promoting the sort of collaborative, patient-empowering communication described above.

Provider and Patient Usability

EMR/EHR systems must be relatively easy to use. Health providers argue that EMRs/EHRs are neither intuitive nor are they easy to use. System constraints force physicians to alter their workflow to accommodate the system, and physicians have voiced usability frustrations highlighting how EMRs/EHRs are not designed by individuals who actually work with patients (Holden, 2010). Physicians argue that EMRs/EHRs do not "work like doctors think" (Holden, 2010, p. 76) and, consequently, physicians are likely to be inefficient when using the system (e.g., employing additional manual steps when an automated function is available [e.g., overusing free-text boxes when pull-down menus are available]) (O'Malley et al., 2010). Physicians argue that EMRs/EHRs should be designed with the individual clinician and department needs in mind (Holden, 2010). This recommendation on the part of physicians can be challenging in light of a call for increased standardization of data elements so that EMR data can be used beyond individual clinics (O'Malley et al., 2010). What is clear, however, is the need to ease usability burden in the next generation of EMR/EHR systems.

The automated and standardized functions must be correct and useful for clinical staff. O'Malley et al. (2010), based on interviews with physicians who have used a commercial EMR/EHR for two or more years and with EMR/EHR vendor medical directors, offer several recommendations for EMR/EHR functions, including the ability to link scheduling and EMR/EHR systems, a care plan summary screen that includes assessment information, more detail in the medication list fields, and enhanced capabilities within the EMR/EHR to link elements in the problem list to other EMR/EHR sections. In addition, providers need the automated alerts and features of EMRs/EHRs to be accurate and specific. False-positives generated as part of an alert system will lead to a lack of confidence in the system and the propensity to ignore alerts even when an alert is warranted. Standardized flowcharts or checklists that do not meet the needs of the clinical staff will be underutilized or misused.

Mechanisms for patient entry of information into the EMRs/EHRs. In the area of patient usability, a limitation of current EMR/EHR systems is the inability of patients to provide answers to basic medical history information electronically for use in an EMR/EHR. According to Moore, Gaehde, and Curtis (2008), there are (1) few interfaces available from vendors for importing electronic data into EMRs/EHRs, (2) current IT system infrastructure barriers, and (3) organizational IT policies that must be addressed.

Enable EMRs/EHRs to securely interface with patients' web-based health records. Patients like having access to laboratory results (Hess et al., 2007), and one study found that patients' pre-visit use of web-based health records that were linked to their EMRs/EHRs resulted in more accurate monitoring of their medications increased adjustments of diabetes-related medications (Grant et al., 2008). Although patients believe HIT systems in the form of patient portals can improve the communication they have with the clinic, they can become frustrated when messages are not answered and test results are not released (Hess et al., 2007). In addition, the information available to patients must be provided in a usable, accessible format. A test result without the information available to patients for accurate interpretation will confuse, scare, or intimidate patients instead of enhancing patient self-management and patient-centered care.

Care Coordination

Mechanisms within the EMR/EHR that help facilitate the change-over of patients from one set of clinical staff to another. During shift changes, critical information about the care of patients may not be communicated to the physician or nurse taking over the patient's care. Anderson et al. (2010) developed and tested an EMR/EHR handoff tool to improve shift change communication and standardize the types of information shared between shifts, including code status, medications, allergies, and the patient's location/room number. Anderson et al. found that the standardized EMR/EHR-based handoff software increased data accuracy, consistency in the type of information shared, and clinical staff's perceptions of patient safety, quality, and efficiency related to shift-change tasks.

Mechanisms to support the coordination of care from one clinic to another. According to O'Malley et al. (2010), current EMR systems lack the ability to support the coordination of care between clinicians and across clinics (e.g., between a primary care clinician and a specialist). This is, in part, due to the lack of standardization of key data elements for the exchange of information. Improvements are needed across coordination tasks, including tracking care plans, progress toward goals, referrals/consultations, and summaries from emergency departments/hospitals. O'Malley et al. (2010) provide many specific recommendations for how EMRs can support coordination across practices. Improvement suggestions include interoperability between settings (which requires moving from an EMR to an EHR), a balance between data standardization and ensuring that the data are clinically relevant/support patient care, and agreement on data entry elements. Coordination-of-care processes are going to become even more essential as many clinical settings move to the patient-centered medical home approach to patient care, and according to O'Malley et al. (2010), current EMR systems are "suboptimal" (p. 184) for meeting these needs. Coordination-of-care elements are also essential for achieving HIT goals at the organization and community levels.

Clinical and Practice Improvement Research

Explore ways in which EMRs/EHRs can impact clinical outcomes and/or improve practice procedures. Several studies have examined the relationship between EMRs/EHRs and disease management, with mixed results. For example, some research demonstrates little, if any, positive effect of EMR/EHR use on clinical outcomes. EMR/EHR-generated reminders did not increase colorectal cancer screening (Promoting Colorectal Cancer Screening, 2009), an EMR/EHR-based decision support tool for lipid management generally did not increase the quality of lipid management in the clinical setting (Gill et al., 2009), and an observational study of clinics that use EMRs/EHRs compared to those that did not found there was no difference in the quality of care provided to patients with diabetes (O'Connor et al., 2007). However, EMRs did improve documentation efforts associated with some interventions such as BMI documentation (Bordowitz, Morland, & Reich, 2007) and up-to-date lipid testing (Gill et al., 2009).

Yet, there is the potential for HITs designed to assist physicians in the management of a specific disease to have a positive effect on clinical outcomes. For example, in the area of diabetes management, Hunt et al. (2009) implemented an EMR/EHR system that included diabetes decision support tools, physician education, patient education, benchmarking tools, performance feedback, and other web-based population system features. They found significant clinical improvements in LDL and blood pressure goal attainments but did not see changes in average hemoglobin A1c scores. They also noted process improvements in the form of patients following through with scheduled laboratory testing, obtaining the medications necessary to achieve glycemic control, and receiving retinal and foot examinations. More work is needed, however, to determine how EMR/EHR applications can improve diabetes care outcomes (O'Connor et al., 2007).

Practitioners can learn from existing EMR/EHR data reviewed as a part of practice improvement projects[3] with the ultimate goal of increasing the level of care provided in their clinics. O'Connor and Asche (2007) used EMR/EHR-derived data to monitor diabetes care patterns across sixty-six primary care settings. They found great variation in the type of care provided. Analyses such as the one described by O'Connor and Asche can be done for other chronic diseases such as hypertension and heart disease. O'Connor and Asche argue that it is important to identify when patterns of care variation exist as the first step to understanding the origin of these variations and ultimately creating interventions to improve clinical practices.

Conclusion

Many of the challenges presented revolve around information and communication technology design translated into practice. Technology experts understand the abilities and limitations of IT but the context experts are the healthcare providers and patients who will be using the technology. Physicians and nurses need to work with technology specialists to develop EMR/EHR systems that facilitate the timely, accurate, and straightforward documentation of medical information (Green & Thomas, 2008). In addition, the patient perspective has been an underutilized resource in the design, implementation, and use of EMRs/EHRs (Mador et al., 2008). Having both providers and patients critique EMR/EHR prototypes can enhance implementation success in the clinical setting and has the potential to increase EMR/EHR usability and user satisfaction.

Realization of the EMR/EHR potential is not ensured once the system is developed, however. Appropriate training in how to utilize the technology and follow-up technical support are critical to the implementation of any EMR/EHR advancements. O'Malley et al. (2010) found that, in fact, many of the EMR system elements desired by physicians were currently possible in commercial EMRs but physicians were either unaware of the function or had never been trained on how to use all the EMR/EHR functions efficiently or effectively. Many physicians are willing to make the changes required by EMR/EHR systems when provided with a justification and explanation for why the system works the way it does. In fact, research has demonstrated that training and in-house technical support are more influential factors in EMR/EHR adoption than financial compensation (Ludwick, Manca, & Doucette, 2010). Building on current EMR/EHR successes, addressing the shortcomings, and incorporating suggestions for improvement in future versions will move EMRs/EHRs beyond data storage/retrieval/billing systems toward becoming a valuable tool for promoting effective patient-physician interactions, engaging in practice improvement or patient care research, and facilitating the coordination of care beyond the primary care setting.

Endnotes

1. For more information on accountable care organizations see a summary provided by Kaiser Health News: http://www.kaiserhealthnews.org/Stories/2011/January/13/ACO-accountable-care-organization-FAQ.aspx.
2. We observed patient-physician interactions when physicians used an EMR on a laptop computer. Laptop computers enable physicians to purposefully place the laptop in a position that can promote or inhibit interactions. For EMRs/EHRs to be effective in the clinical setting, however, there must be sufficient connectivity strength. If desktop computers are required to support the EMR/EHR, the desktop placement should enable physicians to interact with patients versus sitting at a desk or workstation with their backs to the patients.

References

Anderson, J., Shroff, D., Curtis, A., Eldridge, N., Cannon, K., Karnani R., et al. (2010). The Veterans Affairs shift change physician-to-physician hand-off project. *Joint Commission Journal on Quality and Patient Safety/Joint Commission Resources, 36*, 62–71.

Arar, N. H., Wen, L., McGrath, J., Steinbach, R., & Pugh, J. A. (2005). Communicating about medications during primary care outpatient visits: The role of electronic medical records. *Informatics in Primary Care, 13*, 13–21.

Booth, N., Robinson, P., & Kohannejad, J. (2004). Identification of high quality consultation practice in primary care: The effects of computer use on doctor-patient rapport. *Informatics in Primary Care, 12*, 75–83.

Bordowitz, R., Morland, K., & Reich, D. (2007). The use of an electronic medical record to improve documentation and treatment of obesity. *Family Medicine, 39*, 274–279.

Cohen-Cole, S. (1991). *The medical interview: The three function approach.* St. Louis, MO: Mosby.

Crane, J., & Crane, F. G. (2010). Optimal nonverbal communications strategies physicians should engage in to promote positive clinical outcomes. *Health Marketing Quarterly, 3*, 262–274.

Doak, C. C., Doak, L. G., & Root, J. H. (1996). *Teaching patients with low literacy skills (2nd ed.).* Philadelphia, PA: J. B. Lippincott Company.

EMR Experts, Inc. (2009). Sample EMR ROI Study. Retrieved October 23, 2010, from http://www.emrexperts.com/images/emr_roi.jpg

Fletcher, M. (2005). President promotes switching to electronic medical records. *Washington Post,* p. A07.

Frankel, R., Altschuler, A., George, S., Kinsman, J., Jimison, H., Robertson, N. R., et al. (2005). Effects of exam-room computing on clinician-patient communication: A longitudinal qualitative study. *Journal of General Internal Medicine*, 20, 677–682.

Freeman, M. C., Taylor, A. P., & Adelman, J. U. (2009). Electronic medical record system in a headache specialty practice: A patient satisfaction survey. *Headache*, 49, 212–215.

Galanter, W. L., Hier, D. B., Jao, C., & Sarne, D. (2010). Computerized physician order entry of medications and clinical decision support can improve problem list documentation compliance. *International Journal of Medical Informatics*, 79, 332–338.

Gill, J. M., Chen, Y. X., Glutting, J. J., Diamond, J. J., & Lieberman, M. I. (2009). Impact of decision support in electronic medical records on lipid management in primary care. *Population Health Management*, 12, 221–226.

Grant, R. W., Wald, J. S., Schnipper, J. L., Gandhi, T. K., Poon, E. G., Orav, E. J., Williams, D. H., Volk, L. A., & Middleton, B. (2008). Practice-linked online personal health records for type 2 diabetes mellitus: A randomized controlled trial. *Archives of Internal Medicine*, 168, 1776–1782.

Green, S., & Thomas, J. (2008). Interdisciplinary collaboration and the electronic medical record. *Pediatric Nursing*, 34, 225–240.

Grossman, J. M., & Reed, M. C. (2006). Clinical information technology gaps persist among physicians. *Issue Brief: Findings from HSC*, 106, 1–4.

H&HN, Patients want to e-communicate (2008, January). *Hospitals & Health Networks*, 82, 57.

Haywood, C., Lanzkron, S., Ratanawongsa N., Bediako, S. M., Lattimer, L., Powe, N. R., et al. (2010). The association of provider communication with trust among adults with sickle cell disease. *Journal of General Internal Medicine*, 25, 543–548.

Hess, R., Bryce, C. L., Paone, S., Fischer, G., McTigue, K. M. Olshansky, E., Zickmund, S., Fitzgerald, K., & Siminerio, L. (2007). Exploring challenges and potentials of personal health records in diabetes self-management implementation and initial assessment. *Telemedicine Journal & E-Health*, 13, 509–518.

HIT, Health Information Technology in the United States: On the Cusp of Change. (2009). Report from the Robert Wood Johnson Foundation, Massachusetts General Hospital, and The George Washington University. Retrieved October 23, 2010, from www.rwjf.org/files/research/hit2009execsummary.pdf

HIT, Health Information Technology in the United States: Where We Stand. (2008). Report from the Robert Wood Johnson Foundation, Massachusetts General Hospital, and The George Washington University. Retrieved October 23, 2010, from www.rwjf.org/files/research/062508.hit.exsummary.pdf

Holden, R. J. (2010). Physicians' beliefs about using EMR and CPOE: In pursuit of a contextualized understanding of health IT use behavior. *International Journal of Medical Informatics, 79*, 71–80.

Hsiao, C. J., Beatty, P. C., Hing, E. S., Woodwell, D. A., Rechtsteiner, E. A., & Sisk, J. E. (2009). Electronic Medical Record/Electronic Health Record Use by Office-Based Physicians: United States, 2008 and Preliminary 2009. Retrieved October 23, 2010, from the Centers for Disease Control and Prevention NCHS Health E-Stat: www.cdc.gov/nchs/data/hestat/emr_ehr/emr_ehr.htm

HSS (The Department of Health and Human Services Office of the National Coordinator for Health Information Technology) (2008). Defining Key Health Information Technology Terms. Washington, D.C.: Department of Health and Human Services Office of the National Coordinator for Health Information Technology.

HSS (U.S. Department of Health and Human Services) (2009). Proposed Healthy People 2020 Objectives—List for Public Comment. Washington, D.C.: The Office of Disease Prevention & Health Promotion, U.S. Department of Health and Human Services. Retrieved October 9, 2010, from http://www.healthypeople.gov/hp2020/objectives/TopicAreas.aspx

Hsu, J., Huang, J., Fung, B., Robertson, N., Jimison, H., & Frankel, R. (2005). Health information technology and physician-patient interactions: Impact of computers on communication during outpatient primary care visits. *Journal of the American Medical Informatics Association, 12*, 474–480.

Hunt, J. S., Siemienczuk, J., Gillanders, W., LeBlanc, B. H., Rozenfeld, Y., & Bonin, K. (2009). The impact of a physician-directed health information technology system on diabetes outcomes in primary care: A pre- and post-implementation study. *Informatics in Primacy Care, 17*, 165–174.

Ishikawa, H., Hashimoto, H., Kinoshita, M., Fujimori, S., Shitmizu, T., & Yano, E. (2006). Evaluating medical students' non-verbal communication during the objective structured clinical examination. *Medical Education, 40*, 1180–1187.

King, A., & Roter, D. (2010, October). Health Literacy: Measuring the Other Side of the Coin. Panel discussion presented at the annual *Health Literacy Research Conference*, Bethesda, MD.

Kuo, G. M., Mullen, P. D., McQueen, A., Swank, P. R., & Rogers, J. C. (2007). Cross-sectional comparison of electronic and paper medical records on medication counseling in primary care clinics: A Southern Primary-Care Urban Research Network (SPUR-Net) study. *Journal of the American Board of Family Medicine, 20*, 164–173.

Kurtz, S., & Silverman, J. D. (2005). *Teaching and Learning Communication Skills in Medicine.* Abingdon, Oxon: Radcliffe Medical Press.

Ledue, C. (2009, February). Physicians to receive incentives for EHR use. *Health Care Financial News.* Retrieved October 23, 2010, from http://www. healthcarefinancenews.com/news/physicians-receive-incentives-ehr-use

Ludwick, D., Manca, D., & Doucette, J. (2010). Primary care physicians' experiences with electronic medical records: Implementation experience in community, urban, hospital, and academic family medicine. *Canadian Family Physician, 56,* 40–47.

Mador, R. L., Shaw, N. T., Cheetham, S., & Reid, R. J. (2008). Whose record is it anyway? Putting patients' interests at the heart of the implementation and use of electronic medical records. *Healthcare Quarterly,* 11, 90–92.

Margalit, R. S., Roter, D., Dunevant, M. A., Larson, S., & Reis, S. (2006). Electronic medical record use and physician-patient communication: An observational study of Israeli primary care encounters. *Patient Education and Counseling,* 61, 134–141.

Mast, M. S. (2007). On the importance of nonverbal communication in the physician-patient interaction. *Patient Education and Counseling,* 67, 315–318.

McGrath, J. M., Arar, N. H., & Pugh, J. A. (2007). The influence of electronic medical record usage on nonverbal communication in the medical interview. *Health Informatics Journal,* 13, 105–118.

Moore, B. J., Gaehde, S., & Curtis, C. (2008). Architectural choices and challenges of integrating electronic patient questionnaires into the electronic medical record to support patient-centered care. *AMIA Annual Symposium Proceedings.* Retrieved October 23, 2010, from http://www.ncbi.nlm.nih.gov/pmc/articles/PMC2655980/

Morgan, B. (2009). Web portals enable electronic orders and results reporting. *Medical Laboratory Observer,* 41, 26–27.

O'Connor, P. J., & Asche, S. E. (2007). Using EMR data to assess variation in diabetes care quality of care across clinics and physicians. *Diabetes,* 56, A659.

O'Connor, P. J., Crain, A. L., Solberg, L. I., Asche, S. E., Rush, W., & Whitebird, R. R. (2007). EMR use is not associated with better diabetes care. *Diabetes,* 56, A313–A314.

O'Malley, A. S., Grossman, J. M., Cohen, G. R., Kemper, N. M., & Pham, H. (2010). Are electronic medical records helpful for care coordination? Experiences of physician practices. *Journal of General Internal Medicine,* 25, 177–185.

Ong, L. M., de Haes, J. C., Hoos, A. M., & Lammes, F. B. (1995) Doctor–patient communication: A review of the literature. *Social Science Medicine,* 40, 903–918.

Patil, M., Puri, L., & Gonzalez, C. M. (2008). Productivity and cost implications of implementing electronic medical records into an ambulatory surgical subspecialty clinic. *Urology,* 71, 173–177.

Promoting colorectal cancer screening which interventions work? (2009, July/Aug.). *CA: A Cancer Journal for Clinicians,* 59, 215–217.

Rider, E. A., & Keefer, C. H. (2006). Communication skills competencies: Definitions and a teaching toolbox. *Medical Education,* 40, 624–629.

Rider, E. A., Lown, B. A., & Hinrichs, M. M. (2004). Teaching communication skills. *Medical Education,* 38, 558–559.

Robinson, J. D. (2006). Nonverbal communication and physician-patient interaction: Review and new directions. In V. Manusov & M. L. Patterson (Eds.), *The Sage Handbook of Nonverbal Communication* (pp. 437–460). Thousand Oaks, CA: Sage.

Ross, S. (2009). Results of a survey of an online physician community regarding use of electronic medical records in office practices. *The Journal of Medical Practice Management, 24,* 254–256.

Roter, D. L., & Hall, J. A. (2006). Doctors Talking with Patients/Patients Talking with Doctors: Improving Communication in Medical Visits. Westport, CT: Praeger.

Roter, D. L., Hall, J. A., & Katz, N. R. (1987). Relations between physicians' behaviors and analogue patients' satisfaction, recall, and impressions. *Medical Care, 25,* 437–451.

Roter, D. L., Hall, J. A., Kern, D. E., Barker, L. R., Cole, K. A., & Roca, R. P. (1995). Improving physicians' interviewing skills and reducing patients' emotional distress: A randomized clinical trial. *Archives of Internal Medicine, 155,* 1877–1884.

Schneider, J., Kaplan, S. H., Greenfield, S., Li, W., & Wilson, I. B. (2004). Better physician-patient relationships are associated with higher reported adherence to antiretroviral therapy in patients with HIV infection. *Journal of General Internal Medicine, 19,* 1096–1103.

Shachak, A., Hadas-Dayagi, M., Ziv, A., & Reis, S. (2008). Primary care physicians' use of an electronic medical record system: A cognitive task analysis. *Journal of General Internal Medicine, 24,* 341–348.

Shachak, A., & Reis, S. (2009). The impact of electronic medical records on patient-doctor communication during consultation: A narrative literature review. *Journal of Evaluation in Clinical Practice, 15,* 641–649.

Smith, R. C., Marshall-Dorsey, A. A., Osborn, G. G., Shebroe, V., Lyles, J. S., Stoffelmayr, B. E., et al. (2000). Evidence-based guidelines for teaching patient-centered interviewing. *Patient Education and Counseling, 39,* 27–36.

Stewart, M. A. (1984) What is a successful doctor–patient interview? A study of interactions and outcomes. *Social Science Medicine, 19,* 167–175.

Tang, M., Tan, E., Tian, E., Loo, S., & Chua, S. (2009). Electronic e-isotretinoin prescription chart: Improving physicians' adherence to isotretinoin prescription guidelines. *Australasian Journal of Dermatology, 50,* 107–112.

Theadom, A., deLusignan, S., Wilson, E., & Chan, T. (2003). Using three-channel video to evaluate the impact of the use of the computer on the patient-centeredness of the general practice consultation. *Informatics in Primary Care, 11,* 149–156.

Ventres, W., Kooienga, S., Marlin, R., Vuckovic, N., & Stewart, V. (2005). Clinician style and examination room computers: A video ethnography. *Family Medicine, 37,* 276–281.

Ventres, W., Kooienga, S., Vuckovic, N., Marlin, R., Nygren, P., & Stewart, V. (2006). Physicians, patients and the electronic health record: An ethnographic analysis. *Annals of Family Medicine, 4,* 124–131.

9

REMEMBERING HUMAN FACTORS WHEN IMPLEMENTING TECHNOLOGY USE

A Case Study in Home Healthcare Usability

LORI A. BYERS, PH.D.

Contents

Introduction

Experts expect significant economic growth in healthcare services over the next decade. The healthcare industry is expected to add approximately 32 million new jobs between 2008 and 2018, more than any other industry in the United States (US BLS, 2010a). As close to 80 million Baby Boomers advance in age and as technological progress allows more people to remain at home during chronic and terminal illnesses, the demand for healthcare services at home is expected to increase exponentially. Specifically, the Bureau of Labor Statistics (Lacey & Wright, 2009) projects that the demand for home health aides will increase by 50% by 2018.

Even with the need for home health services increasing, financial sustainability of home health organizations has become increasingly difficult due to rising healthcare costs and reductions in Medicaid subsidies (Heck, 2010). Extremely high turnover rates complicate the picture. While the demand for home health aides is projected to increase by 50 percent over the next decade, turnover for this same group hovers around 71 percent (Institute of Medicine, 2008).

The fact that turnover for home health organizations tends to run high is not too surprising considering that the U. S. Bureau of Labor Statistics consistently categorizes most of the direct-care home health workforce, Certified Nursing Assistants (CNAs), among the lowest-paid occupations. According to one study of over 3000 CNAs, one-third of the CNAs received public assistance, and of those CNAs who were uninsured, 42 percent faulted low wages, reporting that they could not afford the insurance plan offered by their employers (Squillace et al., 2009). Direct-care home health workers also tend to be more likely to require food stamp assistance (Institute of Medicine, 2008). To add "injury to insult," more than half of the 3000 CNAs interviewed above reported sustaining at least one work-related injury in the year previous (Squillace et al., 2009). Considering the low wages, likelihood of injury, and overall stress of the job, the turnover rate remains perpetually high, and research consistently indicates that the best method of reducing CNA turnover involves increasing wages (Kash et al., 2006), a difficult achievement when most organizations are forced to do more with less.

Searching for means of financial survival, home health companies actively explore solutions for increased efficiency at every level or risk financial ruin.

Faced with the reality of high turnover, insufficient staffing, high operating costs, and low profitability in a struggling economy, many smaller and rural home health companies seek inexpensive solutions that promise significant returns.

Information technology vendors bombard healthcare organizations with messages presenting technology as a panacea to solve all the ills of home health organizations. Vendors dealing in information technology designed for healthcare contexts peddle their services in cleverly disguised press releases/advertisements appearing to be legitimate news articles in trade magazines, praising their wares for increased efficiency, accuracy, and ease of use.

If healthcare companies were not convinced of the popularity and perceived effectiveness of mobile devices as touted by the mobile device companies' advertising and PR departments, the monetary commitment made by the government via the American Recovery and Reinvestment

Act of 2009 (ARRA) to digitize electronic health records, more than $27 billion dollars, drove the point home (Schwartz, 2011). News outlets at every level exploded with news of the "massive investment" in information technology related to healthcare, or Health IT (HIT), allocated by the government with "no precedent" in terms of previous financial commitment (Steinbrook, 2009). The U.S. Department of Health and Human Services Secretary Kathleen Sebelius reinforced the praise for HIT in general by asserting that "this essential technology improves the quality of care we all receive and helps make care more efficient" (US HSS, 2010). Still, while HIT promises the potential to provide vast improvements in efficiency and effectiveness, as with all new technologies some products promise more than others.

For smaller healthcare companies, including many home health organizations in rural communities, IT vendors offer mobile phones as an "affordable," "flexible," and "familiar" alternative for home health companies wanting to improve efficiency, but that cannot afford or envision the long-term gains of purchasing the more expensive smart phones or tablets. The following is a case study of one such home health organization that recently adopted cell phones for tracking and reporting purposes.

Case Study

Exasperated with the latest news of another employee leaving, Mary felt as though her workload was always greater than the time available in each day. She already worked close to sixty hours each week, and the thought of the added work of advertising, interviewing, and training another nurse only added to her frustration. She understood why many of her colleagues in the home health industry commented about "finding warm bodies" to fill positions within their companies. It seemed as though she was always involved in searching for a new hire.

Already overwhelmed by long hours, office negativity, and worker burnout, Mary experienced increasing pressure from the regional director to cut costs and improve financial efficiency in the local office. As was the case with many businesses in the struggling economy, she was asked to do more with less. How could she do more with less when the company could not maintain a stable workforce?

A mobile phone sales representative visited Mary's office with what seemed to be the solution to many of Mary's efficiency issues. The representative promised increased communication between the caregiving team, improved point-of-care outcomes, a near-elimination of paperwork, and a means of tracking employee mileage via a GPS application.

The provider promised low-cost solutions to Mary's most pronounced problems. The office had very little money, and the salesperson bragged about the mobile company's market niche of offering affordable "low-end handsets." Mary recognized the phone as one of the most popular brands. She had owned what seemed to be a similar phone five years before, and had never experienced issues with it, so the phone appeared to be a solid choice. She had read literally hundreds of online articles in healthcare magazines touting the virtues of technology in healthcare, claiming to "eliminate … CNA's paper processes" (Hermann & Threats, 2010), and increase productivity and visit record compliance, while reducing costs" (Hermann & Jingle, 2008). Another article claimed that "By increasing efficiency, mobility applications are also driving up job satisfaction, which is critical for retaining nurses during a nursing shortage" (Enrado, 2009). One vendor claimed that their company's simple solution works and automates the field staff at the point-of-care with a very easy-to-use application working on a simple cell phone. It can be used by any home care or hospice agency, and it also proves how far we have come in the home health and hospice world. We can now start to use emerging technologies, or even simple ones like a cell phone, to improve patient care, gain better productivity, and implement a program that can save time and money for home care and hospice agencies (Hermann & Jingle, 2008).

These phones did seem affordable if they delivered as much as promised by the articles and by the sales representative.

Adopting the phones seemed like a simple, relatively low-cost solution to two of Mary's perceived immediate problems. First, employees would be able to input reports electronically immediately after seeing a client, cutting down on paperwork and speeding up the reporting process to the entire team of caregivers. One of the articles claimed the phones would "automate and eliminate costly manual paper processes" (Hermann & Jingle, 2008) at the point-of-care. The inordinate amount of record-keeping involved in home healthcare, particularly that required for Medicaid, proved overwhelming, so the possibility of reducing the mountain of paper in her office thrilled Mary.

Second, the office had experienced issues with a few workers in the past several years who made "ghost visits," claiming to visit clients when they were actually somewhere else. Mary also suspected that a few of her employees might over-report their mileage, even if simply rounding up numbers. The GPS tracking function would allow her to have constant access to the whereabouts of every one of her employees every minute of the day and to record that information.

After the new mobile phones were introduced, Mary was surprised by the uproar and outrage of the care team. The employees of the organization perceived that their integrity was being questioned. The care team felt insulted and not trusted by their employer. Over the following weeks, every single member of the care team expressed emotions ranging from frustration to rage, and Mary heard the phrase "big brother" whispered in many conversations. Over the course of time, Mary heard the following complaints concerning the new phones:

- One nurse expressed frustration with the compulsory brevity required by the device when documenting visits: "It doesn't really allow you to expound on things. We click on circles beside categories and questions. It needs to be more specific. It's difficult to type comments."
- The first complaints dealt with lack of privacy. One CNA complained, "I wish it didn't track every second of the day. It's an invasion of my privacy. If I want to use my own bathroom on my way out of town to see a client, I don't need everybody to know it. It tracks every second of your day. It tracks every address you drive by on the street. We should be able to put it on pause. They want to track us like animals."
- Another CNA mourned the lack of flexibility: "We have no flexibility in our schedule anymore. It used to be one of the perks of this job. I could pick up my kids between visiting clients. It's not like they give us good pay. What perks do we have now?"
- One CNA reported issues with connectivity: "We travel out to the country, and it takes a very long time for the phone to find a network. I'll push a button, and the phone will say,

"Searching … , searching … , searching … ." Sometimes it takes several minutes just to get started. I could have been on my way to the next patient, but instead I'm sitting in the driveway trying to get a connection to file my report. It takes flippin' forever to download a message. Meanwhile, my battery wears down on my phone. I'm lucky if my battery makes it to 2:15. I want to take the battery out and throw it away."

- The hope of radically cutting down paper usage fell short due to continued reliance on traditional file cabinets for information storage. According to one CNA, "We're cutting down forests. They make copies of copies of copies of copies. The printer spits out a page or two for every visit, every day."

- One of the care team's social workers expressed frustration with the mobile phone's obsolescence: "It would be great if we used a phone fabricated in the last decade. My company spent a ton of money on these damn phones. Buy me one that actually works, does what it is supposed to do, and is more a help than a hindrance. That's all I ask."

- Most care team members expressed frustration with the phone's lack of efficiency, caused by a variety of issues surrounding outdated technology. One care team member commented on being forced to "peck away on such a tiny keyboard. We need keyboards made in this millennium instead of the old-fashioned way of texting. Phones with decent keyboards are so cheap now." Another team member commented on the difficulty experienced viewing the small display.

- Many of the care team members commented on the disruptiveness of the phone, interrupting the flow of their day with slow computing times and lost connections. Several team members felt the mobile phone impeded their work and their relationships with clients. As one care team member asked, "What was I brought here to do? Take care of people or learn how to deal with the mess of reporting on this phone? The phone interferes with the task at hand."

Even Mary felt irritated by some of the glaring inefficiencies offered by the mobile phones. For example, she spent a significant amount of time each day correcting errors to the care team's mileage and care records. Each time a mistake was made in the field, whether by a person or by the device, Mary had to correct the mistake in the office. Sometimes it seemed as though every person on the care team required multiple corrections each day.

One care team member explained the frequency of corrections: "At the end of a visit, I must hit a button to finish the client's record, to submit it to the office. After I hit the button, the phone asks me six or seven questions that take forever to process, sometimes up to seven minutes. By then my mind has moved on to something else, and I forget to hit the button one last time to process all the information. I end up losing everything. It's very frustrating. Mary yells at everybody because she gets sick of doing these things. I understand her frustration, but it's not our fault we have these things."

Mary growled out loud the day she saw another article online that actually addressed the fact that people often forgot to register the beginning or the endings of visits, thus requiring corrections by the office administrator. The article simply brushed off the issue as "accepted as part of doing things a new way" (Hermann & Jingle, 2008). She never imagined that she and her company would experience so many issues with what first promised to be the answer to most of her problems.

Considering all the aggravation and complaining surrounding the phones, Mary wondered if the money she saved buying mobile phones instead of smart phones was worth it. Two employees had resigned since adopting the phones, and both cited the phone as part of their decision to leave. Technology was supposed to improve peoples' lives rather than make lives more complicated.

Discussion

Much of the information presented to healthcare organizations by IT vendors can be misleading. First, the organizational processes of each organization should be assessed to determine specific technological needs. Second, not all technology is created equal. Significant financial investments by home health organizations should be met by significant gains in productivity or efficiency, and mobile phones, although a relatively inexpensive investment compared to smart phones, cannot deliver data processing fast enough to result in significant advances in efficiency or productivity.

Analysis of the current case study points to several factors threatening retention of the home healthcare team. Studies of retention among direct-care health workers indicates that "lack of respect" constitutes the primary reason workers report leaving a job, while workers listed "flexibility" as one of the most important reasons reported for remaining on the job (Mittal, Rosen, & Leana, 2010). Similarly, the primary contributing factors to burnout point consistently to the underlying issues of workers' perceptions of respectful treatment, displays of appreciation, and feeling treated as though they are valuable to the organization (Bowers, Esmond, & Jacobson, 2003; Harahan et al., 2003). Several people on the healthcare team in the current case study cited the adoption of mobile phones as a symbol of disrespect and distrust of employees. Several reported mourning the demise of flexibility with the introduction of the tracking device installed on the phones. It is important for health organizations to remain mindful of the positive portrayal of the adoption of technology; otherwise the technology could contribute to higher burnout and turnover rates that disrupt the continuity of care for home healthcare clients, thus decreasing quality of care.

Although anecdotal evidence suggests that using technology increases efficiency, thus increasing retention and satisfaction, more research is needed to determine the best practices and best devices available for smaller organizations (Enrado, 2009), particularly concerning usability issues, paper efficiency ratings, time efficiency ratings, etc. When technology fails to deliver efficiency, and instead complicates one's workflow, satisfaction and retention will inevitably decrease.

HIT holds much potential for improving the processes of healthcare workers, as indicated by the hundreds of healthcare applications created for smart phones. In less than a year and a half after Apple introduced iPhones to the market, approximately 700 iPhone applications were created for healthcare-related services (Enrado, 2009), and the number of applications continues to increase. Of course, that does not help smaller and more rural health organizations who cannot afford to pay for the up-front costs of somewhat expensive smart phones.

Much of the healthcare industry remains fragmented, and many healthcare providers are small, making significant investments in technology extremely difficult. While the American Recovery and

Reinvestment Act provides incentives for larger hospitals and for physicians in private practice, the Act ignores the bulk of smaller health organizations contributing substantially to the mass of people in need of home healthcare. The possibility of a digital divide remains a reality even as advances in technology offer the opportunity for greater access than ever across the general population.

The potential for a digital divide exists for home health organizations, particularly those in economically disadvantaged communities who already struggle with financial sustainability. Although the Obama Administration would like all healthcare organizations to adopt electronic records by 2014 to improve access and quality of care, imbalances in access to technology continue to exist. Even with significant funds designated by the government to digitize healthcare records, many healthcare organizations cannot afford the initial investment required for successful implementation of systems for electronic health records. The digital divide in healthcare tends to follow the traditional boundaries of the digital divide in the United States, which generally tends to coincide with disparities in healthcare including smaller healthcare organizations or those located in more rural geographic areas (Glaser, 2007), healthcare organizations serving immigrants (Schwartz, 2011), and hospitals serving the poor (Jha et al., 2009).

At a the most basic level, connectivity must be increased for all to have access; for example, WiMax (Worldwide Interoperability for Microwave Access) capabilities could be implemented in isolated geographic areas to increase accessibility to wireless broadband. WiMax uses antennas instead of cables and wires, enables up to 75 Megabits per second broadband capability, and was created specifically for the handling of data, unlike traditional 2G and 3G networks created strictly for voice (Terry, 2009). As a result, WiMax provides faster connections and higher bandwidths with an inexpensive price tag, allowing accessibility in the most remote locations, including mountainous regions with more rugged terrain.

Emerging health information technologies hold much promise in terms of efficiency, mobility, and accessibility; but to achieve optimal results when implementing new technology, user-centered design and high usability prove essential. Implementation of HIT, from mobile devices to tablets, requires more than a casual decision, more than adopting technology for technology's sake. Creating highly usable technology involves "systems that are modeled after the characteristics and tasks of the users ... that are easy to learn, increase user productivity and satisfaction, increase user acceptance, decreases user errors, and decrease user training time" (Johnson, Johnson, & Zhang, 2005, p. 75). Adoption of new technologies contributes to quality of care and financial savings only if healthcare organizations consider all the issues involved in the usability and implementation of the technologies.

Maguire (2001) has outlined the benefits of designing and developing usable and intuitive systems:

- *Increased productivity.* A system designed following usability principles, and tailored to the user's preferred way of working, will allow them to operate effectively rather than lose time struggling with a complex set of functions and an unhelpful user interface. A usable system will allow the user to concentrate on the *task* rather than the *tool.*
- *Reduced errors.* A significant portion of "human error" can often be attributed to a poorly designed user interface. Avoiding inconsistencies, ambiguities, or other interface design faults will reduce user error.
- *Reduced training and support.* A well-designed and usable system can reinforce learning, thus reducing training time and the need for human support.
- *Improved acceptance.* Improved user acceptance is often an indirect outcome from the design of a usable system most users would rather use, and would be more likely to trust, a well-designed system which provides information that can be easily accessed and presented in a format that is easy to assimilate and use.
- *Enhanced reputation.* A well-designed system will promote a positive user and customer response, and enhance the developing company's reputation in the marketplace (Maguire, 2001, pp. 587–588).

Information technology has the potential to transform healthcare, but all technology must be reviewed for efficacy. If new systems cannot be learned with relative ease, then costs for the initially inexpensive device result in long-term costs involving time, redundancy of effort, and stress/burnout caused by frustration. When selecting technology, the daily activities and considerations must be taken into account; otherwise the daily workflow will be impeded.

If user-centered design and usability issues are not taken into consideration, the adoption of new technologies could prove threatening to employee morale and contribute to employee burnout. In occupations already ripe with stress, complicating one's workflow with ineffective technologies potentially increases the likelihood of stress and burnout.

If home healthcare organizations want to maximize returns on technological investments, it is important to conduct a task analysis and a user analysis to identify the specific needs of the population adopting the technology. Technology can be beneficial for improvement of healthcare and truly improve operational effectiveness only if user-centered approaches to technology are employed. Technology should enable home health workers to work smarter and more efficiently, and anything less should be rejected. Ultimately, "people costs" related to usability issues, including stress, burnout, and turnover, will be more expensive than technology costs in human-technology interactions.

References

Bowers, B., Esmond, S., & Jacobson, N. (2003). Turnover reinterpreted: CNAs talk about why they leave. *Journal of Gerontological Nursing*, 29(3), 36–43.

Enrado, P. (2009). Mobile devices, apps increase nurse job satisfaction, productivity. *Health Care IT News*. Retrieved from: http://www.healthcareitnews.com/news/mobile-devices-apps-increase-nurse-job-satisfaction-productivity

Glaser, J. (2007, October). The electronic health record: a digital divide? *Healthcare Financial Management (HFM)*, 61(10), 38–40.

Harahan, M., Kiefer, K., Johnson, A., Guiliano, J., Bowers, B., & Stone, R. (2003). Addressing Shortages in the Direct Care Workforce: The Recruitment and Retention Practices of California's Not-for-Profit Nursing Homes, Continuing Care Retirement Communities and Assisted Living Facilities. Washington, DC: IFAS.

Heck, J. (2010, May). Home health care agencies make tough business decisions amid Medicaid cuts. *Wichita Business Journal*. Retrieved from: http://www.bizjournals.com/wichita/stories/2010/05/17/story2.html

Hermann, S., & Jingle, V. (2008, July). The simple cell phone: Point of care solution for a hospice in Texas. *Caring*, 27(7), 36–38.

Hermann, S., & Threats, D. (2010). *CellTrak point-of-care provides Gaston hospice benefits to all areas of their hospice organization*. Retrieved from: http://www.prweb.com/releases/2010/09/prweb4561434.htm

Institute of Medicine (2008). *Retooling for an aging America: Building the health care workforce.* Retrieved from: http://www.iom.edu/Reports/2008/Retooling-for-anAging-America-Building-the-Health-Care-Workforce.aspx

Jha, A. K., DesRoches, C. M., Shields, A. E., Miralles, P. D., Jie, Z., Rosenbaum, S., & Campbell, E. G. (2009). Evidence of an emerging digital divide among hospitals that care for the poor. *Health Affairs, 28,* 1160–1170.

Johnson, C., Johnson, T., & Zhang, J. (2005). A user-centered framework for redesigning health care interfaces. *Journal of Biomedical Informatics, 38,* 75–87.

Kash, B. A., Castle, N. G. Naufal, G. S., & Hawes, C. (2006). Effect of staff turnover on staffing: A closer look at registered nurses, licensed vocational nurses, and certified nursing assistants. *The Gerontologist, 46,* 609–619.

Lacey, T. A., & Wright, B. (2009). Occupational employment projections to 2018. *Monthly Labor Review Online, 132*(11). Retrieved from: http://www.bls.gov/opub/mlr/2009/11/art5full.pdf

Maguire, M. (2001). Methods to support human-centered design. *International Journal of Human-Computer Studies, 55,* 587–634.

Mayhew, D. J., & Mantei, M. M. (1994). A basic framework for cost-justifying usability engineering. In R. G. Bias & D. J. Mayhew (Eds.). *Cost-justifying usability* (pp. 9–48). New York: Harcourt Brace.

Mittal, V., Rosen, J., & Leana, C. (2010). A dual-driver model of retention and turnover in the direct care workforce. *The Gerontologist, 49,* 623–634.

Schwartz, E. (2011, January 11). *Digital divide threatens health care.* Kaiser Health News. Retrieved from: http://www.kaiserhealthnews.org/Stories/2011/January/11/health-digital-divide-cpi.aspx

Squillace, M., Remsburg, R., Harris-Kojetin, L., Bercovitz, A., Rosenoff, E., & Han, B. (2009). The national nursing assistant survey: Improving the evidence base for policy initiatives to strengthen the certified nursing assistant workforce. *The Gerontologist, 49*(2), 185–197.

Steinbrook, R. (2009). Health Care and the American Recovery and Reinvestment Act. *New England Journal of Medicine, 360,* 1057–1060. Retrieved from: http://www.nejm.org/doi/full/10.1056/NEJMp0900665

Terry, M. (2009, March). WiMAX: Will fourth-generation broadband give telemedicine a boost? *Telemedicine and e-Health,* 132–136.

US BLS (United States Bureau of Labor Statistics) (2010a, February). Career guide to industries, 2010–11 edition: *Healthcare.* Retrieved from: http://www.bls.gov/oco/cg/cgs035.htm

US BLS (United States Bureau of Labor Statistics) (2010b, December). *Occupations with the largest job growth, 2008–2018.* Retrieved from: http://www.bls.gov/emp/ep_table 104.htm

US HSS (United States Department of Health and Human Services) (2010, June). *HHS awards $83.9 million in recovery act funds to expand use of health information technology.* Retrieved from: http://www.hhs.gov/news/press/2010pres/06/20100603a.html

10

SECURITY AND PRIVACY

Impacts of Evolving Technologies and Legislation

ROBERT FAIX, CHAD CAGNOLATTI, AND DAVID FLYNN

Contents

Introduction

Advancements in technology over the past decade have provided numerous tools for accessing and managing data. Historically, the healthcare industry has lagged behind other industries in the technology adoption curve. With recent legislation and technology advancements, most healthcare organizations are beginning to implement electronic tools to allow healthcare providers and patients access to confidential data. While providing access to confidential data is necessary, it presents healthcare information technology (IT) professionals with a challenge in securing this data from loss or misuse. Today more than ever, security and privacy challenges are a vital concern for healthcare organizations. A formal security management program that follows industry standards will provide a framework to ensure that confidential data are protected.

Evolution of Technology in Health Delivery

The healthcare industry has seen an evolution over the past decade where computer and data systems have become more commonplace. Health delivery organizations have embraced a number of transformative technologies for the purpose of improving clinical outcomes, enhancing the patient experience, and improving patient safety. These technologies provide for electronic storage of volumes of patient data that present security challenges for any organization. As new technologies such as online information portals, telemedicine for remote physician consults, or the ever-expanding capabilities of today's smart phones are adopted by health delivery organizations, the IT staff must always consider the security risks presented by adding new technologies to the environment.

The proliferation of network-enabled devices ranging from intravenous pumps to mobile communication devices and smart phones, along with the increasing amount of clinical patient data stored within clinic information systems, continue to challenge IT departments. Ensuring appropriate measures are taken to secure one of the organization's most valuable assets—its data—can feel like a never-ending game of cat-and-mouse. Adding to the complexity of securing networks and the devices using these networks is an expectation by the general public to have free and open access to the Internet. Today, access to the Internet from a wide variety of locations, including coffee shops, restaurants, bookstores, and hospitals, is expected by patrons. To address the demand for wireless access, hospitals typically implement two different wireless networks, one for guest access and one for clinical purposes. Guest networks are typically configured as "open" networks requiring little more than acknowledging a fair use message and provide access only to the Internet for personal browsing, checking e-mail, etc. Guest networks are typically isolated from all clinical systems through physical or logical configuration methods and may be limited to family waiting areas and patient rooms. Unlike guest wireless networks, clinical wireless networks are highly secured using leading-edge encryption technologies such as Wireless Equivalent Privacy (WEP), Wi-Fi Protected Access (WPA), Temporal Key Integrity Protocol (TKIP), Advanced Encryption Standard (AES), etc. to protect sensitive patient information transmitted between mobile devices and clinical systems and are likely to be centrally configured, monitored, and managed using any number of wireless network solutions.

Evolution of Caregiver Devices

Another developing paradigm that has underscored the requirement for increased data security management is the increased portability of data with an ever-expanding platform of mobile user interface devices. Laptops, tablets, smart phones, microstorage systems, and wireless and Bluetooth capabilities in smaller and more numerous electronics has expanded the sphere of vulnerability and therefore security concerns well beyond the centralized mainframe systems of the past. In older systems consisting of massive mainframes, servers, and hardware arrays, data were physically restricted to managed data center locations with "dumb terminals" displaying information to a user elsewhere in the facility. Today, personal information can be located on systems that are much more transportable and transmissible.

Among the first commercial successes for tablet-based computing in a clinical setting is the C5® tablet developed by Motion Computing. The C5 operates a modified version of the Microsoft Windows® operating system with touch-screen capability via stylus. Because this device used a standard operating system and provided for a reasonable screen size, recoding of client software by application vendors was largely unnecessary. With this device, caregivers were able to roam between patient rooms accessing clinical systems that were not otherwise designed for use on a mobile device.

More recently, the rapid adoption of Apple's iPhone® and iPad® for personal use has made significant inroads to the clinical setting. Recognizing this trend, leading healthcare information system providers such as Epic and Cerner have developed compatible applications to operate on these platforms, providing varying degrees of access. As proof of the continued evolution of technology, security, and safety, IT professionals need only recall that less than a decade ago hospital bans on cell phones were very common and enforced to varying degrees. These bans have since been largely abandoned. It is ironic that the very devices originally deemed as hazardous when used in the clinical environment are being integrated into the patient care experience.

Security Impacts of Legislation

As information has increasingly become digitized and the marketplace has become globalized through the proliferation of the Internet, privacy and identity misuse has unfortunately kept pace in growing as a common threat present in the digital age. Maintaining appropriate security and privacy levels for patient information in the healthcare industry has always been a high priority for management. That effort to ensure data security and privacy has received closer attention over the past years from privacy advocacy groups, consumer advocacy groups, software vendors, industry regulatory agencies, and the government. The Health Insurance Portability and Accountability Act (HIPAA) of 1996 represents one of the first major legislative moves toward standardizing security and privacy practices. HIPAA sought to improve protections given to patient data and first introduced the concept of Protected Health Information (PHI) of patients' data within electronic systems. This legislation outlines specific responsibilities of defined healthcare-related organizations, also referred to as Covered Entities, that routinely create, store, or use patient information as part of their normal business routine. At the time the legislation was passed, specific milestones for adoption of security-related safeguards were established along with corresponding penalties ranging from monetary fines to incarceration for the most egregious or repeated violations. HIPAA's initial objective of raising awareness for medical record privacy by Covered Entities and defining the rights of the patient to access their information has proven successful as an initial step toward a balance between protection and access to medical records. Throughout most of the late 1990s and early 2000s as Covered Entities were attempting to understand where they stood from a HIPAA compliance perspective, internal IT teams or third-party contractors were tasked with conducting HIPAA Security and Privacy Assessments (although the assessment objectives, requirements, and approach were created within each organization and varied widely in method), typically resulting in an assessment findings report, or scorecard and recommendations. Healthcare organizations used the results of these assessments to guide improvement in their security programs.

Among the criticisms of HIPAA is the fact that there has been very little oversight for compliance and assessment of penalties for willful noncompliance. Although a few high-profile healthcare organizations have paid significant fines due to willful neglect, the fact that HIPAA "has no teeth" has been generally accepted in the industry.

The American Recovery and Reinvestment Act (ARRA) signed into law by President Obama in 2009 contains the Health Information Technology for Economic and Clinical Health Act (HITECH Act), which among other things expands upon the original intentions of HIPAA for safeguarding patient information. Notable changes impacting the healthcare industry as a result of the HITECH Act included an expanded definition of Covered Entities. In 1996, several contemporary healthcare business arrangements such as Health Information Exchanges (HIEs) did not exist. As a result, there was ambiguity as to whether an HIE was required to comply with HIPAA and to what extent. The HITECH Act further defined required actions by Covered Entities when a breach of patient data has occurred. Under the HITECH Act, Covered Entities are required to notify the U.S. Department of Health and Human Services and local media when a breach involving 500 or more instances of Protected Health Information (PHI) has occurred. Public disclosure of all reported breaches involving 500 or more instances of PHI can be found on the U.S. Department of Health and Human Services website at www.hhs.gov.

Among the most significant technology advances in healthcare is the adoption of clinical information systems capable of generating comprehensive Electronic Medical Records (EMRs). Unlike traditional paper-based medical records, electronic medical records can be made available instantly to caregivers at remote locations, shared between affiliated hospitals, and easily compiled upon request by a patient. With the passage of the American Recovery and Reinvestment Act, health delivery organizations were given incentives for the adoption and "meaningful use" of electronic medical records as a means to increase adoption rates and improve clinical outcomes.

Security Awareness and Management

There is a saying among security professionals that the only secure network is that which has no devices attached. While true, this is obviously an exaggeration to illustrate a point that security vulnerabilities are ever-present. The most sophisticated and well-funded security programs of any corporation or government entity can only reduce the likelihood and impact of a security-related event, but cannot provide a 100-percent protection guarantee. With the addition of mobility, portability, and microsizing management, control and security grow increasingly difficult. Every day, minor security infractions such as accidental faxing of a patient record to an incorrect fax number occur in today's healthcare industry. While accidents do happen, it is human nature to have curiosity for certain information while fooling yourself into believing you will not get caught. When a celebrity or famous public figure visits a hospital, workers will be curious to find out information. To mitigate the risks created by human nature, organizations typically draft privacy and use policies. The success of these policies, as a deterrent for inappropriate access to information, has a wide range most often defined by the organization's culture and senior management's commitment to enforcing policy consistently.

To ensure the best possible protection of an organization's information assets, security professionals must remain current on evolving threats and mitigating technologies. As vulnerabilities are detected, members of the security team are responsible for developing an appropriate response and notifying the necessary leadership within the organization. Surveillance for improper use is usually managed in two approaches: random-use audits and focused exploration of a specific event. Detection of improper use generally occurs as a result of random log auditing, a report by department staff, or a complaint by a patient of suspected access, although there are technologies available to aid in this process.

The role of security as part of an organization's overall operations and technology function is (for better or worse) frequently managed as any other operations and technology expense. Organizations create annual budgets for continued maintenance and investment across all departments with examples of budgetary items likely to include workstation refresh, purchase of a new camera for the radiology department, or performing necessary software upgrades to existing clinical and business systems. Security, much like Disaster Recovery and Business Continuity Planning, is an area that can easily become viewed as a lower priority by management when faced with defining spending priorities for a limited budget—especially with a prolonged absence of a significant security event. The challenge of properly funding security-related programs and investing in technologies is only increased during tough economic times.

Unfortunately, it is only after an organization suffers a significant, possibly very public, security-related event that the role of security is given proper attention with necessary funding for the implementation of corrective measures. Common examples resulting in unwanted visibility may include the discovery of thousands of patient records thought to have been erased from a decommissioned piece of equipment; inappropriate viewing of a high-profile individual's medical record information, or a coordinated denial-of-service attack from an external entity.

Security Standards and Assessment Frameworks

The need to ensure that appropriate security and privacy controls are implemented continues to be at the forefront for leadership in Information Technology, Compliance, Internal Audit, and ultimately Executive Management. Over the years, several standards and frameworks have been developed to guide organizations in evaluating their current environment. Frequently referenced standards and frameworks typically include

- *National Institute of Standards and Technology (NIST),* an agency of the U.S. Department of Commerce. NIST has released a series of Special Publications, collectively referred to as the "800 Series," that provides guidance for proper configuration and enhancing security measures across a variety of technologies. With more than a hundred Special Publications and multiple revisions, the 800 Series has proven to be a very comprehensive body of work. Of all the documents contained in the 800 Series, one of the most frequently referenced publications is NIST 800-53 – Recommended Security Controls for Federal Information Systems and Organizations (most recently updated August 2009). NIST 800-53 provides a framework and defines specific controls for assessing all federal systems.
- *International Organization for Standardization (ISO)* is most commonly associated in business with the quality management ISO-9000 and ISO-9001 that standards organizations

have strived to achieve for many years. The ISO-27001 and ISO-27002 standards were published to specifically address security-related matters and complement each other as a "strategy" guide and "tactical steps," respectively. As noted in the ISO-27001 standard, the objective is to "provide a model for establishing, implementing, operating, monitoring, reviewing, maintaining, and improving an Information Security Management System."

- *Information Technology Infrastructure Library (ITIL)* is a comprehensive series of IT-focused operational guides. The current version of ITIL (Version 3, released May 2007) is organized around five volumes: Service Strategy, Service Design, Service Transition, Service Operation, and Continual Service Improvement. Within the Service Design volume is a section on Information Security Management and draws upon the guidance outlined in ISO-27002.

- *The Control Objectives for Information and Related Technology (COBIT)* originally released in 1996 and currently in version 4 is a framework to aid in understanding general security requirements of systems and establish appropriate evaluation criteria and controls to protect the organization. The COBIT framework is organized around 34 processes with 210 defined control objectives organized into four domains: Planning and Organization, Acquisition and Implementation, Delivery and Support, and Monitoring and Evaluation.

Although originally developed for different purposes, the content within many of the aforementioned standards and frameworks overlaps heavily. The overlap between these standards and other healthcare-relevant regulations are best depicted in Figure 10.1.

Selection and implementation of any of the standards noted above, along with regulatory guidance outlined in HIPAA, the HITECH Act, and other laws, can be a challenge to those charged with ensuring proper security configuration and management of IT assets. Further complicating the selection and assessment process is the general nature upon which the standards have been written. Organizations operating in the healthcare industry may find it difficult to define exactly what standard or assessment level within a standard is most

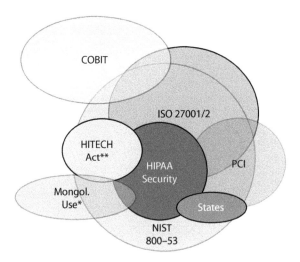

Figure 10.1 The overlap between standards and other healthcare-relevant regulations. (Source: From Healthcare Information Trust Alliance, Frisco, Texas.)

appropriate. Furthermore, these standards do not offer healthcare-specific mitigating controls when deficiencies are identified.

Recognizing the challenges for selecting an appropriate standard, the inconsistencies across various standards, and that auditing results are subject to interpretation of the assessor in some cases, the Health Information Trust Alliance (HITRUST) was formed. The following goals were defined by the HITRUST Alliance as the organization set out to create the Common Security Framework (CSF):

- A tool that normalizes existing standards and regulations to provide organizations of any size with prescriptive implementation requirements
- A single organization-wide security program for organizations to facilitate internal and external synthesizing [of] the requirements from ISO, PCI, COBIT, HIPAA, NIST, and others
- An industry consensus on the most effective way to address information security
- A means to manage and reduce the number, complexity, and degree of variation of security audits or reviews
- A methodology that organizations can use as a common baseline and mechanism for communicating validated security controls for third parties

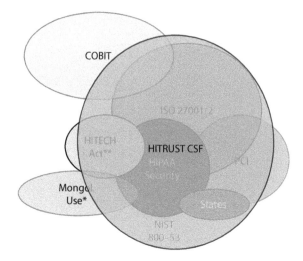

Figure 10.2 The reach of the CSF relative to the leading standards. (Source: From Healthcare Information Trust Alliance, Frisco, Texas.)

To accomplish these goals, the HITRUST Alliance partnered with leading organizations from all sectors of the healthcare industry, including health delivery organizations, health plans, pharmaceutical vendors, and device vendors, to build the CSF. Working closely with these partner organizations, the HITRUST team defined control specifications, implementation levels, and mitigating controls relevant to the healthcare industry. Figure 10.2 illustrates the reach of the CSF relative to the leading standards introduced earlier.

The CSF is organized around 13 Control Categories and contains 135 Control Specifications. Each Control Specification, where appropriate, incorporates three cumulative assessment levels of increasing restrictions. Lending further creditability to the content within the CSF, HITRUST documented one or more relevant source standards for each of the 135 Control Specifications. Organizations using the CSF as the basis for a security risk assessment can easily determine which standard or regulation influenced the CSF assessment criteria. As an organization prepares to conduct a Common Security Framework-based assessment, the appropriate assessment level for each Control Specification must be defined. Assessment levels are determined based on the unique characteristics of the organization being assessed. Factors influencing the assessment level include the number of users of a system, multi-state and international operations, whether the organization is subject to specific regulations such as the Federal Trade Commission's Red Flag rule, Payment Card Industry (PCI) compliance, the HITECH Act, and the Federal Information Security Management Act (FISMA). Responding to the organizational definition criteria will allow the assessor to create the assessment roadmap within the CSF.

Preparing for a Security Risk Analysis

Technology vendors are aware of the increased concern for ensuring the security of information assets and readily provide documentation outlining security measures. Most organizations will establish policies requiring a security review of new technologies introduced to an environment. A security review is typically conducted by a member of the information security department or an external vendor and will document device configuration and look for known security issues.

Conducting a security risk analysis, like any other project, can have a far-reaching or narrowly defined scope, depending upon several factors. Time, budget, resource availability, and motivating reason for conducting a security risk analysis should all be taken into consideration as an organization defines the project scope. Defining which standard will be used as the baseline for conducting the analysis is a critical question and should not be taken lightly as it will ultimately shape the observations and recommendations stemming from the engagement. Whether the project is conducted as an internal effort or contracted to a third-party consulting firm, it is essential for the project sponsor to have a clear understanding of exactly which systems will be assessed and what level of detail to cover in the final report.

Organizations conducting a security risk analysis for the first time should consider limiting the scope of systems to between three and five with a focus on critical applications. Keeping the initial scope small with a defined roadmap for subsequent assessment activities as part of the initial deliverables will increase the likelihood of completing the final report in a reasonable period of time and not overwhelming system administrators, network engineers, and application owners who are essential to the project.

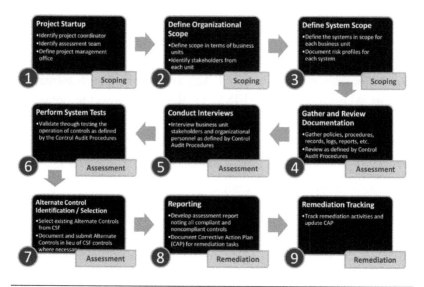

Figure 10.3 Outline of the nine key phases in the successful delivery of a security risk analysis. (Source: From Healthcare Information Trust Alliance, Frisco, Texas.)

The HITRUST Alliance has outlined the nine key phases shown in Figure 10.3 to the successful delivery of a security risk analysis. Each of these phases is outlined in further detail below:

- *Project Startup:* During this phase of the project, the basic project management structure is established. Elements addressed during this phase will include how an organization intends to conduct the project, that is, as an internal effort or contracting with a third party, identification of project sponsor and project manager, and initial goals of the engagement.

- *Define Organizational Scope*: In most cases, organizations are too large and too complex to be assessed in their entirety within a single project. Defining the organizational scope provides project sponsors with the ability to subdivide a large organization into smaller and more manageable units. Examples of organizational divisions may include individual facilities, departments within a large facility, or possibly users of a specific system.

- *Define System Scope:* Perhaps the easiest of scoping efforts is the definition for system scope. In most cases, a project sponsor will request an assessment of a particular system used within the organization. When defining the system scope, project sponsors should take into consideration the grouping of patient care systems, applications and devices; business systems and applications, infrastructure components, and supporting systems and applications. Additional considerations for defining the system scope may include the physical location where the system is hosted. Systems hosted by a third party may impact the level of detail or approach to information gathering. Assessors may be able to refer to documents such as a SAS-70 audit of a third-party data center and the Service Level Agreements defined and tracked between the organization and hosting provider.

- *Gather and Review Documentation:* Once the systems and organizational units have been defined, the assessor is able to begin developing a list of appropriate documentation to be reviewed. Examples of necessary documentation may include system configuration and recovery documents; network diagrams; contracts with third parties; new-hire training documentation; and organizational charts. Documents provided for the assessment will be reviewed for their thoroughness, last time they were updated, and (in the case of recovery documentation) the last time a system recovery was attempted along with the results.

- *Conduct Interviews:* As experienced with documentation review, the roles of individuals to be interviewed and the number of interviews necessary are directly related. However, regardless of the number of systems considered in scope for an assessment, the following roles are likely to remain part of the interview scope: Chief Information Officer, Chief Security Officer, Information Security managers, system administrators, and network engineers. Additional interviewees will likely include department managers for in-scope systems and the application administrators.

- *Perform System Tests:* For systems defined as in-scope, a series of tests will need to be performed. Standard tests generally include reviewing patch management practices, password management, account lockout capabilities and access control privileges for new hires, changes in system access levels as staff roles change, and confirmation of account deactivation as staff transition out of the organization.

- *Alternate Control Identification and Selection:* A variety of reasons may prevent an organization from configuring systems or implementing policies that align with the assessment framework's requirements. When it is not possible to meet a specific implementation specification, the assessor will work with the appropriate representatives to identify possible alternate controls that satisfy the intent of the control specification. These "work-arounds" are known as Alternate Controls.

- *Reporting:* At the conclusion of an assessment, the assessor will prepare a report identifying the key observations and outline recommendations where issues were identified. Recommendations from an assessment will typically be organizations and further detailed as part of a Corrective Action Plan (CAP). The CAP will serve as a roadmap for improvement and allow specific individuals or teams to be held accountable for the implementation of necessary changes to improve the overall security of a system.

- *Remediation Tracking:* With a properly developed CAP, management will have a clear understanding of the necessary actions to ensure that system compliance can be achieved. Depending on the nature of the recommended changes, remediation tracking may be incorporated into regular status reporting for urgent matters or reviewed on a quarterly, semi-annual, or annual basis for less urgent recommendations. In any case, it becomes the responsibility of all members of an organization with direct responsibility for an assessed system to ensure that the recommendations outlined in a CAP are adopted or modified accordingly.

Conclusion

Advances in technology aimed at improving the care-giving capabilities of the healthcare industry are continually announced by hardware and software vendors. While each vendor should have a rigorous process for ensuring compliance with federal and state regulations, it is incumbent upon the individual healthcare entities to develop specific policies and procedures to ensure compliance. Whether choosing one of the above-mentioned security standards or a more customized approach incorporating state and local guidance, the vast majority of the healthcare industry is in complete agreement that security and privacy must be treated as a top priority. Organizations proactively engaging and properly investing in an Information Security Management Program can significantly reduce exposure to unwanted events and respond quickly should such a security event occur.

11

NEW FACILITY PLANNING

A Healthcare Focus

TODD HOLLOWELL AND CARL FLEMING

Contents

Overview

The current healthcare environment in the United States is changing dramatically and competition is severe. These changes are driven by various dynamics, including healthcare reform under the Patient Protection and Affordable Care Act of 2010, the overall move to specialization, the goal of improving the quality of care while reducing or avoiding costs, and improving patient satisfaction as consumerism becomes an area of focus. The approach to addressing the required changes must be driven by process and workflow changes, with technology solutions being the enabler of change.

Combine the ever-changing forces in the healthcare market with the fact that many healthcare organizations are considering expanding or replacing facilities, and the appropriate new facility technology planning approach becomes extremely important. In the past, planning for and building a new hospital expansion or new replacement facility was a relatively straightforward process, based on years of experience, standard principles, and past practices. Some hospital executives and clinicians were moving toward a variety of new approaches around the patient-centered hospital, improved clinician workflow, specialized care, and other key initiatives, but the design and build of the core physical plant remained unchanged. Relying on the "old way" does not cut it any longer.

Today's new hospital facility, expansion or full replacement, is fundamentally different from that of a few years ago. Most, if not all, new hospital facilities are now being deemed a "smart hospital" or "hospital of the future," and the key assumption is that the building, and associated programs and processes, will leverage core technology capabilities that will assist in changing how care is delivered. Key questions now must be addressed by organizations earlier in the construction process and prior to beginning the technology planning process. For example, if more outpatient procedures are planned to be delivered and fewer dollars are available to a traditional hospital setting, what are the most effective procedures a new inpatient facility should look to provide? Additionally, how do hospitals with unused or underutilized facilities hold or increase their return on facility investments? Questions such as these have caused healthcare organizations to focus more strategically on technology planning for the new facility to meet their needs. The Information Services (IS) team and Chief Information Officer (CIO) are no longer being invited to the table after the building is nearly physically complete. Rather, the CIO and IS team are now contributing from the initial planning and visioning stages of a facility plan.

To assist organizations in thinking consistently about new facilities and associated planning efforts, The Joint Commission, in its *Guiding Principles for the Development of the Hospital of the Future* (http://www.jointcommission.org/assets/1/18/Hospital_Future.pdf)), identifies several key principles to guide technology adoption, including

- Establish the business case and sustainable funding sources to support the widespread adoption of health information technology.
- Redesign business and care processes in tandem with health information technology to ensure benefit accrual.
- Use digital technology to support patient-centered hospital care and extend that care beyond the hospital walls.
- Establish reliable authorities to provide technology assessment and investment guidance for hospitals.
- Adopt technologies that are labor-saving and integrative across the hospital.

One of the most critical actions completed during the construction of a new facility will be to determine the Technology Strategy. Similar to the other steps in planning for a new facility, the technology plan cannot be developed in a silo. In fact, it is required that the technology plan dovetails with the overall Master Facility Plan. Because the solutions identified within the technology plan can now account for up to 10 percent or more of the total construction budget, the technology plan demands early attention. Equally, the implementation of the technology solutions will have lasting effects on the organization's future operating and capital commitments and operating model. Ultimately, the ability to deliver the desired clinical outcome will be heavily impacted by the technology planning and implementation efforts.

Differentiating technology planning, and associated solutions, from medical equipment planning is also critical. While linked in a variety of ways, developing a Medical Equipment Plan and Technology Strategy are critically different. Medical equipment planning is the process of integrating the assessment, selection, and procurement of medical equipment into the overall construction project delivery process. With the increased sophistication of medical equipment and the reliance on these devices to improve efficiency and patient throughput, there is no doubt that it plays an important role in creating a "smart" hospital. However, this step often becomes an afterthought in the design and construction process because organizations (and teams) are so heavily focused on the "bricks and mortar." Assigning ownership of the Medical Equipment Plan to a dedicated resource or team, insourced or outsourced, must be completed early in the planning process.

Technology planning is the process of assessing current information systems, identifying technological needs, creating specifications and designs for major systems, and developing an accurate budget. Traditional new facility technology planning teams and consultants typically addressed system categories such as cabling, network and telephony infrastructure, security, television, code-compliant nurse call, wireless and mobility solutions, intercom, video and public address systems, and possibly other low-voltage systems. By contrast, most organizations are now also looking to address key applications or integration (convergence) needs related to clinical systems, including Electronic Medical Records, lab systems, radiology systems, and various other clinical applications. In addition to clinical systems, considerations for business systems such as patient registration and scheduling, patient accounting, supply chain, general ledger, human resources, and payroll are also being made.

The overall convergence of technologies is also causing organizations to define how technology solutions can improve communications for clinicians, patients, and families. Determining how and what to automatically integrate, while streamlining communications, is a goal of all new healthcare facility plans. Identifying which automated events or alerts can be routed to caregivers for faster response is being stressed—for example, integrating nurse call alerts or physiological monitoring alerts to wireless communication devices (IP phones) is becoming commonplace.

A key activity, early in the planning process, involves working with the organization to confirm and develop the technology *Guiding Principles* and *Planning Assumptions*. Ultimately, these principles and assumptions will be referenced as questions arise related to the specific types of solutions being considered, as well as which vendors should be considered. To begin planning, a cross-discipline team should be created. Included on this team should be the various stakeholders: the IS staff, the CIO, the Chief Medical Officer and/or the Chief Medical Information Officer, the Chief Nursing Officer and/or the Director of Nursing, the Chief Financial Officer, the Vice President of Facilities (or director and/or managers), and Biomedical Engineering (Clinical Engineering). Other key operational areas, including the ED, OR, Lab, Pharmacy, Radiology, Cardiology, and Medical Imaging, must be part of the planning and requirements-definition team also.

Key Concepts

With the various changes in how healthcare will be delivered and, maybe as importantly, reimbursed, the new facility planners must understand some key concepts behind these changes. Care delivery models are now focusing on several areas, including interdisciplinary and integrated care, population care, greater patient responsibility, while looking to shift locations of care as necessary. With team care models, providers and staff are now filling dynamic roles, including the greater use of physician extenders along with health coaches to advise patients on how to leverage the system to ensure coordination of care across the continuum. In addition, clinical and financial activities must now be integrated across the continuum among generalists and specialists.

In terms of population care, healthcare providers are becoming increasingly responsible for managing a defined population. The influx of Accountable Care Organizations (ACOs) is driving changes to how caregivers must interact. The goal of an ACO is to pay providers in a way that encourages them to work together, while not encouraging supplier-induced demand, and to create an organization that is rewarded for providing high-quality care. The design of a new facility, whether obvious or not, must consider how an organization sees itself fitting within the ACO model.

Regarding greater patient responsibility, a healthcare organization must look for opportunities to provide patients and families with more control over their healthcare, whether at home, during an inpatient stay, or as part of a clinic visit. The recent advent of patient consumerism is forcing healthcare organizations to view those who receive care not only as patients, but also as consumers with ever-increasing expectations. The patient-consumer leverages technology to research and educate himself and as a result wants control of his information and input into his own care. Organizations planning for a "Hospital of the Future" must ensure that the facility and its related technology solutions enable that control. Finally, shifting locations of care means more care will delivered in outpatient settings and new entities emerging, such as specialty hospitals, continuing care hospitals, and retail clinics, will cause more competition for the inpatient facility.

The new healthcare facility must be built to complement these new competitors and their offerings.

The final concept to recognize when planning for technology in a new healthcare facility is the idea that both the "Haves" and "Have Nots" exist in this market. The "Haves" are typically urban magnet or affluent suburban hospitals that have a strong payer mix made up of commercial insurance, self-pay, along with a more limited number of Medicare/ Medicaid patients. These organizations typically have top talent with an eye toward research, income, and innovation, and the facilities are most likely contemporary, inviting, and patient- and workflow-friendly. The "Haves" see technology as an enabler of quality and process improvement, even with the associated costs, and see mandated reforms, and the anticipated reimbursements, as "bonus" opportunities.

The "Have Nots" tend to be located in the inner city, in "fading" communities, or in rural settings, and they tend to have a more challenging payer mix, including a more significant Medicare/Medicaid patient population, unemployed and uninsured patients, and significant bad debt. Their blend of staff may be different, including altruistic or second-tier talent, while the facilities are more typically aging, confusing, and, often, not inviting to patients and workflow. Additionally, technology may be limited, second or third tier, and the organizations view mandated reforms and the associated costs to avoid reimbursement penalties as a "burden."

Therefore, a cookie-cutter or one-size-fits-all approach to technology planning for a new healthcare facility does not work. Right-sizing technology approaches and solutions for new healthcare facilities will vary greatly based on budget and financing availability, overall leadership's vision and objectives, the technology standards and guiding principles, the organization's location, and possibly most importantly, patient and staff demographics. To ensure a successful technology plan and implementation, a methodical approach to developing the plan and schedule must be followed.

The Approach

Many healthcare providers are either building replacement hospitals or building expansions to current facilities, and these construction efforts are usually driven by deficiencies within the current facilities.

New facility expansions present many more challenges than building a replacement facility as organizations must ensure that the older facilities and new expansions are truly integrated, across technology solutions and systems, clinical process and other workflows, and the patient flows and experience.

Determining which technology strategy to take, while also making educated guesses as to which vendors and solutions have staying power, becomes a critical consideration—all this in a time that allows very little room for error. A healthcare provider must make informed decisions, relative to its technology strategies and solutions, while making the right technology investments—under considerable pressure to contain costs. Ultimately, however, making sound investments in technology involves defining and setting the right priorities, identifying the appropriate technologies, undergoing a thorough solution selection process, and creating and executing a flawless implementation plan. In addition, this plan must align with the overall construction schedule and Master Facility Plan.

As we look to plan for the new healthcare facility, it is imperative that the team—leadership, architects, designers, construction team, etc.—understand and agree that technology infrastructure is as critical as "bricks and mortar." This technology infrastructure must support the needs of all stakeholders, including patients and visitors, hospital staff, and physicians and nurses, and the technology planning activities need to occur earlier in the construction project life cycle and then technology program management should continue throughout the construction process.

Begin by assessing the organizational readiness to adopt new technologies, including barriers, challenges, and opportunities. This readiness assessment will assist in producing a clearly defined and actionable "roadmap" that will lay the foundation for the new hospital's technology plan. The roadmap should support information sharing and information management capabilities within any current facilities, if not a replacement hospital, as well as the new facility. The ability to meet the future needs and requirements of the new facility should also be addressed. Finally, the roadmap must confirm the capital and operating cost models and appropriately allocate funding with respect to facility-related capital, other capital, and operating dollars.

If planning for an expansion rather than a full replacement hospital, keep in mind that it is much more costly to retrofit legacy facilities. Retrofitted patient rooms must be larger and technology enabled, such as new facility rooms to ensure standards of care across the enterprise. New rooms are typically private rooms with "family areas" for visiting, working, and sleeping. Additionally, older facilities (and old construction materials) are not conducive to new technologies, so an understanding of how legacy facilities impact various solutions and approaches must be considered. More specifically, how will the legacy facility accommodate biomedical and information technology convergence, a single (wired and wireless) medical-grade communication network, clinician mobility, flexible end-user device(s) for clinicians, and space needs for additional peripheral devices (workstations on wheels, bedside devices, etc.)?

A key activity, early in the process, involves working with the organization to confirm and develop the technology *Guiding Principles*. These principles are typically established and communicated by the organization's leadership team, ideally with input from various operational areas, but any technology decision should meet one or more of these principles. Second, the plan must include any *Key Planning Assumptions* made throughout the planning process. These assumptions must be identified and communicated to ensure that everyone— facilities staff, designers and architects, technology teams, leadership, other staff, patients and families—is thinking along the same lines. Ultimately, these principles and assumptions will be used as questions arise related to the specific types of solutions being considered, as well as which vendors should be considered. When developing the principles, the team should follow a methodical approach. The flowchart in Figure 11.1 highlights a proven new facility technology planning process. This process will take a large commitment of both time and effort.

Several common principles have begun emerging within the market and include the following:

- *All decisions for information system, telecommunications, and biomedical solutions must have a direct contribution to organizational strategies and objectives.* Technology solutions will be leveraged to drive process efficiencies throughout the organization and

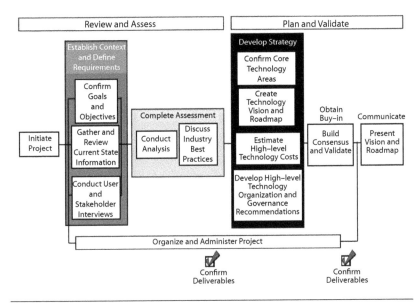

Figure 11.1 Flowchart of new facility technology planning process.

to assist with effective decision making (clinical quality, productivity, and economics) while enabling cost savings.

- *An enterprise-focused (not department- or individual-focused)
  vision will drive technology solution decisions.* A "single/common
  vendor" systems approach will be adopted and implemented
  whenever possible. Information sharing and system integration will "trump" full functionality (i.e., integration versus
  disintegration). Processes will be based on best practices and
  will be coordinated and standardized to ensure continuous
  quality, patient safety, and a consistent patient experience.
- *Centralized technology will play a lead role in enhancing the
  patient experience.* Patient portals, the patient education and
  entertainment system, and other solutions will be provided
  or enhanced to augment the patient care process. In this way
  patient and family members will have access to clinically relevant information.
- *Clinical information will be gathered at the point-of-care, and the
  data will be shared throughout the enterprise to support clinical
  needs, enhance patient care, and increase patient safety.* Electronic
  charting will facilitate clinical decision making, and an integrated clinical information system will be available throughout

the continuum of care, including results, order entries, imaging, pharmacy, nursing documentation, and clinical care analysis. Technology will enable improved documentation processes and replace manual keyboard entry and data capture, and medical equipment results will be recorded automatically to the electronic medical record whenever possible.

- *Stable technologies and solutions will be utilized.* Strategies will aim to provide the most cost-effective yet innovative solutions, and it is expected that all solutions must have a clinical or business value. Where there is an opportunity to move toward a future vision, the hospital will not wait for the perfect solution but may implement in stages to achieve efficiencies as soon as possible.

- *Governance and accountability will be structured to promote, recommend, drive, and make enterprisewide decisions.* All decisions must obtain buy-in, gain agreement, and have accountability. In addition, they must identify policies and processes for adapting new systems.

- *Clinicians will have immediate access to information in real-time and from anywhere.* Universal connectivity will be appropriately provided to all available internal and external information resources enabling a more efficient and effective paperless and film-less environment. Availability of data to inform real-time decision making will be enabled, and a common set of utilities will be provided to all authorized information technology users. Support for easy, rapid access to information systems utilizing technologies, such as single sign-on, biometric identification, and proximity badges will be considered. Automatic event notification will be enabled by a convergence of wireless communication devices, the enterprise network infrastructure, and critical systems (e.g., nurse call, physiological monitoring).

Once the *Guiding Design Principles* are established, the *Key Planning Assumptions* will be confirmed as stakeholders are more engaged, and these assumptions will typically cover such things as workflow standards (multidisciplinary and patient-centered approach), functional needs (new facility services will meet or exceed capabilities provided in legacy locations), and future requirements (flexibility required for easy incorporation of future changes in technology will be met). Every organization will also look to retain and leverage many, if not most, of their existing systems and vendor relationships. A new facility, however, may challenge both the hospital and the vendor to consider how to adapt those solutions to meet new needs ... without disrupting their current use in the older facilities. Finally, the plan must assume that the recommendations will maximize value; an organization cannot implement solutions for technology sake, and it must add value, improve patient care and safety, increase other efficiencies, or decrease costs.

Typical Topics and Solutions

Based on the *Guiding Principles* and *Key Planning Assumptions*, the cross-discipline team should begin to identify and evaluate each key solution proposed for the new facility. For instance, an Electronic Medical Record (EMR) or expansion of the current EMR may eliminate the need for a paper-based record. It should facilitate more real-time communication and support for administrative tasks and integrate information from various care settings and departmental systems. All care data, including text, images (PACS, etc.), photographs, video, etc. may be included. Ultimately, the EMR should provide sufficient access to documentation tools and workstations and allow for the electronic availability of patient results and reports to all appropriate providers along the care continuum.

In much the same way, Computerized Physician Order Entry (CPOE) should provide real-time, online ordering capabilities, facilitate efficient closed-loop medication management, enable clinical decision support, streamline care planning, and support comprehensive results reporting. Overall, the new building and the appropriate placement and use of technology can improve patient safety, quality of care, staff performance and satisfaction, while enabling the organization to better meet compliance requirements.

Improved staff communication is paramount in a new facility. Many times in new hospitals, nursing leadership is considering new means of distributing staff to provide better care. In a decentralized nursing approach, for example, wireless and hands-free voice communication devices integrated with key systems (e.g., nurse call, physiological monitors) will also provide an additional level of flexibility and safety.

Central to a hospital and outpatient clinic registration and scheduling process will be the capability to leverage self-service kiosks to allow patient check-in, way-finding, and payment of charges (e.g., co-payments).

Finally, improving the patient and family experience is vital. For example, including a patient education and entertainment system in many places, particularly in all in-patient rooms, can greatly improve the patient's ability to participate in his or her own care. These systems not only provide the basics—TV, movies, Internet connectivity—but also enable more enhanced capabilities—online surveys (patient satisfaction, pain management, etc.), real-time patient education integrated with the EMR, online food ordering, and many others. In addition to the patient experience, the family experience can be enhanced by various means. One particular technology has recently gained more traction: large-screen displays used for patient tracking and status information. These solutions have been in place for caregivers, particularly in the OR and ED areas, but more and more, these displays are being considered to provide "virtual waiting rooms" to allow family members to leave the patient's side while still staying informed.

Each service-related goal drives a specific set of technology directions. These goals drive and define both the processes and the technological and equipment directions to support those processes. Several infrastructure and application technologies play a significant role in supporting direct care delivery quality and efficiency. Each drives a specific set of technology requirements. The effect that each proposed technology has on both operations and infrastructure should be developed as a part of this plan. The objectives of the identified solutions are to ensure that collaboration efforts support the missions of the hospital, reduce operational barriers and enhance collaboration across the organization, increase customer service capabilities and support quality, leverage existing service delivery capabilities, and optimize past investments by utilizing and enhancing existing infrastructure and solutions.

After completing the initial planning, you will be able to develop your tactical plan. Elements of the tactical plan should include equipment and technology solutions, implementation guidelines, resource requirements, and projected costs.

Tactical Projects and Roadmap

The most thorough step within any technology planning effort should be the definition of the *Tactical Projects and Roadmap*. With this activity, the planner should ensure that the organization has identified the realistic projects that should be initiated to meet its goals. During this activity, more details should be specified for each initiative, including specific scope of work, the project approach (e.g., build, buy, outsource, etc.), specific deliverables and outcomes, the resources required (time, people, and dollars), and specific time frames, risks, and potential returns.

For each tactical initiative, the planner should attempt to quantify some Return on Investment (ROI) to assist executives in justifying the effort. The key is estimating "hard" metrics that can be predicted and monitored over time (e.g., the ability to meet HITECH requirements for reimbursement, improved patient satisfaction ratings, decreased costs associated with technology support, improved system response time, etc.). Even if these hard returns are difficult to estimate, each tactical initiative should offer various "soft" returns, such as increased staff productivity, improved patient service, improved efficiencies and processes, better branding, etc., and these returns should be identified as part of building the business case for the initiative.

Once the tactical efforts are identified and clearly defined, it is time to put the pieces of the puzzle together. More specifically, by identifying the *Roadmap* (i.e., tactical sequencing), the plan identifies key interdependencies and issues that may exist between the tactical projects. In addition to recognizing these interdependencies, now is the time to map more specific time frames to each initiative to ensure that they align with the overall construction schedule.

Budget Estimates

The final and, in many cases, most important outcome of the planning process is the creation of *Budget Estimates*. These estimates should provide the going-in specifics for the CFO or other individuals who will be focusing on the actual costs associated with the efforts. These estimates should include both capital cost estimates for each tactical initiative (identifying costs for hardware, software, and services), as well as identifying ongoing operational estimates for costs such as maintenance contracts, software updates, and labor.

The Transition Coordinator

Upon completion of the plan, it is critical to staff a Transition Coordinator. This resource—or team of resources, depending on size of project and numbers of technology projects—manages the overall technology plan. This resource will usually report to the leader of the IS team, but occasionally will report to the Facilities team, depending on each organization's governance model and "responsibility matrix." The Transition Coordinator provides and manages resources to oversee various projects, activities, tasks, including the network detailed design and implementation, device requirements and placement, blackout and other hardware-related testing, application readiness assistance and management, application assessment and configuration, "pilot" projects coordination, and application testing (test plans and execution). In addition, the Transition Coordinator should also participate with readiness activities.

Putting It All Together

You have been introduced to a number of themes, ranging from planning approach to roadmaps and budget. How do these themes flow? When do these activities occur? And what relationship do they have with the actual construction schedule of the new facility? The following paragraphs take a more in-depth look at each construction phase and the correlating technology activities that occur within.

For the sake of this discussion, let us break down the construction life cycle into six phases: Planning, Programming, Design, Construction, Transition, and Post Move. The technology plan and implementation must fit within these phases, and we also identify, and align, six technology planning and implementation phases: Visioning, Tactical Planning, Detailed Design, Implementation and Pilot, Testing and Go-live, and Operations/Support (Table 11.1 and Table 11.2).

Table 11.1 Project Lifecycle Crosswalk

CONSTRUCTION PHASES	TECHNOLOGY PLAN AND IMPLEMENTATION PHASES
Strategic Planning	Visioning
Facility Programming	Tactical Planning
Design (Schematic and Design Development)	Detailed Design
Construction	Implementation and Pilot
Transition	Testing and Go-Live
Post Move	Operations/Support

Table 11.2 New Facility Technology Project Phases and Activities

CONSTRUCTION PHASES	TECHNOLOGY PLAN AND IMPLEMENTATION PHASES
Strategic Planning	**Visioning** • Participate in planning Activities • Assess technology needs/integration • Research future technology options • Define technology guiding principles • Develop initial budget
Facility Programming	**Tactical Planning** • Review and understand program plans • Identify technology to support building programs • Gather technical and functional requirements • Develop technology assumptions • Identify technology space needs • Define technology program including biomedical convergence opportunities • Identify key pilot initiatives and location(s) • Update budget

Design
→ **Schematic**
→ **Design**
   Development
	Detailed Design
	Schematic Design
	• Provide technology specifications
	 • Physical space
	 • Network/Cabling/Infrastructure/etc.
	  • Input to building systems with technology implications
	• Review/refine IS Organization structure (if required)
	• Review equipment specifications for connectivity and/or integration requirements
	• Review and revise budget
	Design Development
	• Develop infrastructure design specifications, including selection of technology architects via RFP processes if necessary
	• Note any changes/"value engineering" activities
	• Confirm new technology to be piloted

Continued

Table 11.2 (continued)   New Facility Technology Project Phases and Activities

CONSTRUCTION PHASES	TECHNOLOGY PLAN AND IMPLEMENTATION PHASES
	Design Development
	• Update guiding principles if necessary
	• Create detailed network specifications and other infrastructure designs
	• Engage with equipment procurement team
	• Define network install requirements for biomed and any equipment requiring network connections, including 3rd party contracts
	• Confirm future state applications
	• Review and revise budget
Construction	**Implementation and Pilot**
	Infrastructure
	• Monitor construction activities for all technology areas
	• Note any changes or "value engineering" activities
	• Develop cabling and network infrastructure work plans
	• Build/Install network/infrastructure, including wireless
	• Complete cross connects
	• Test full network/infrastructure, including wireless solutions
	• Participate in building commissioning/testing
	Applications
	• Select/confirm and pilot applications/vendors
	• Implement pilot applications/technology solutions
	• Revise and update plans, specs, requirements based on pilot results
	• Workflow reviews for tech systems, apps and device placement
	• Confirm application usage assumptions
	• Determine/document application change requirements
	• Determine/document integration changes requirements
	Devices
	• Workflow reviews for technology systems and device placement
	• Determine detail device requirements/locations
	• Determine documentation approach for devices (database guidelines)
	• Start device procurement/select vendor(s)
	• Secure device staging space in new facility or warehouse
	Budget/Staffing
	• Allocate IS staff for remainder of project/update organization structure if necessary
	• Confirm new FTE requirements for ongoing operations of new facility

Table 11.2 (continued)   New Facility Technology Project Phases and Activities

CONSTRUCTION PHASES	TECHNOLOGY PLAN AND IMPLEMENTATION PHASES

Transition

Testing and Go-Live

Commissioning

- Define Commissioning approach
- Determine commission timing
- Define recourses required for commissioning
- Integrate commissioning activities w/bldg load
- Build commissioning work plan – all phases
- Develop application test plans (test in production environment)
- Execute tech commissioning – all phases
- Resolve any reported items

Readiness

- Participate in all readiness groups (bldg, ops, load, move, etc.)
- Provide training info to build training materials
- Define scanning strategy to archive/retain documents currently on paper
- Building Load
- Determine building load approach

Load Building

- Review device locations with users prior to connecting
- Adjust as needed
- Connect all devices
- Record all asset tags

Patient Move

- Participate in all move preparation
- Participate in any mock moves
- Build move day support schedule
- Complete device "sweep"
- Configure IS support room
- Configure Command Center and any other support areas
- Support "Move Day" activities
- Resolve and reported items
- Develop post opening support structure

Post Move

Operations/Support

- Document open items
- Set plan in place to resolve issues
- Invoke ongoing support structure
- Follow up any post opening items
- Complete post project review w/lessons learned
- Finalize budget processing

Strategic Planning—Visioning

Each phase of the construction life cycle has a set of inherent technology planning components. For example, the technology planning team should participate in Strategic Planning exercises and leverage insight gained during this phase for technology visioning: assessing technology and integration needs, and researching future technology options. Upon completion of the Strategic Planning and Visioning phase, the technology planning efforts should have a defined set of *technology guiding principles* and an initial rough order of magnitude technology budget.

Facility Programming—Tactical Planning

Facility Programming further defines the conceptual boundaries of the building by defining the services that may be performed within. As a result, the Tactical Planning efforts for technology can begin. Only after reviewing and understating the program plans can the Technology Planning team begin to gather the technical and functional requirements necessary to develop initial technology assumptions. For example, biomedical convergence or BMDI (Bedside Medical Device Interfacing—integration of bedside and point-of-care devices with the EMR and Nurse Call solutions) is a growing area of interest for nursing in general and certainly in new facilities. Beginning to identify pilot opportunities for these solutions as well as other identified technologies should occur in this phase. As with each subsequent phase, the additional understating of technology needs and wants provides an opportunity to revise the technology budget.

Schematic Design/Design Development—Detailed Design

The Design phase of new facility planning is where the first conception of the look-and-feel of the building takes place. While the programming phase provides the conceptual boundaries, Schematic Design provides the first glimpse of the physical boundaries and layout for the facility. Evaluating the patient floors, for example, allows the Technology Planning team to refine technology assumptions based on potential workflows in the perceived physical spaces. To further illustrate this point, a design that incorporates an alcove between two patient rooms provides the opportunity to allow caregivers to document in the EMR outside the patient room. Conversely, a flat work area in the patient room allows for the caregiver to document at or near the bedside. Other scenarios for patient documentation might include the use of tablets or computers-on-wheels (laptops affixed to a mobile cart). At the very least, the Schematic Design phase provides the opportunity to give input with regard to technology implications for building systems and device connectivity and integration requirements.

Further defining the physical space of the facility occurs in the Design Development phase of construction planning. At this stage, technology planning is occurring at a rapid pace and detailed infrastructure requirements and specifications for identified technologies are being developed. Note that future applications, technologies not available on opening day, should be considered in the infrastructure requirements and specifications process. The goal is a "Hospital of the Future" ... not just of today. Technology Guiding Principles may be revised if necessary and pilot technologies may be confirmed. Another round of budget iterations may occur as well.

Construction—Implementation and Pilot

The Construction phase of a new facility is long; many years can pass before the building is ready for patients. This is not a time to put initial technology planning documents on the shelf. Unfortunately, many strategic and tactical plans are tucked away and forgotten. These documents are living documents, dynamic and continually edited and updated. Ideally, the Transition Coordinator(s) would begin to manage the planning documents and use the roadmap and responsibilities matrix to guide him (them) through the completion of the project.

The Technology Planning team should continuously monitor construction activities for all technology areas and note any changes or "value engineering" activities and the outcome they have on existing technology assumptions. Consider three areas of technology focus during the construction phase. There are implementation and pilot components for *Infrastructure, Applications, End-User Devices and Budget/Staffing.* While the building is being constructed, the Technology Planning team should be developing the cable and network infrastructure workplans and eventually building and installing the network infrastructure (wired and wireless). Testing the full network and participating in building commissioning and testing will come toward the end of the Construction phase. Technology applications will be prioritized and vendors selected during this phase. Pilot initiatives for certain technologies will be implemented, and plans, specifications, integration requirements, and workflows may be revised based on the results of these pilot initiatives. Documentation requirements and devices will be evaluated and device placement assumptions updated based on workflow modifications. Device vendors will be chosen and facility device procurement will commence. A secure staging space for these new devices will be identified. In some cases, the feasibility of onsite staging is low and thus an offsite warehouse-type space must be secured. The above infrastructure, applications, and devices activities cannot be accomplished without the proper staffing in place and budget defined. The technology implementation and pilot phase must include the allocation of Information Services (IS) staff for the remainder of the project, which includes the confirmation of new staffing resource requirements for ongoing operations of the new facility. Staffing revisions may also require an update to the organization structure.

Transition—Testing and Go-Live

Once the building is complete and ready for occupancy, the transition from construction to occupation can occur. The Technology Planning and Transition team is responsible for a few essential components necessary to successfully ready the building for caregivers, support staff, and patients. Technology commissioning is a quality-oriented process for achieving, verifying, and documenting that the performance of technology systems meets specifications. The commissioning process tests systems to ensure that everything works as designed. The Transition team must build the commissioning process workplan, confirm the approach, determine timing, define recourses required for commissioning, and integrate activities with the building load activities. In addition, application test plans for the production environment must be developed. Finally, the team must execute on all phases of these commissioning activities and resolve any reported issues.

A new facility, new technology, and a handful of unknowns await both hospital employees and patients and their families. How ready is the organization to occupy the new space? Everyone reacts differently to change and, as a result, special attention must be given to the evaluation of Transition Readiness. Technology Planning and Transition plays a key role in ensuring that end users are comfortable with the new technology tools at their disposal. The Technology Planning and Transition team should participate in all readiness groups and provide information for the development of training materials.

Installing the devices in the new facility or "Loading the Building" is a huge undertaking. An important step for the Planning team is to develop a solid *Building Load Approach* that allows for review of device locations prior to load and make location adjustments as necessary.

The final step in the Transition phase is the Patient Move. Relocating potentially hundreds of patients is an arduous and delicate task. The Planning and Transition team will need to configure a Command Center to support "Move Day" activities and develop a post opening support structure. Participating in "mock moves" will allow the team to evaluate the ability to constantly monitor patients on transport monitors and provide valuable insight into how to leverage other technology to support patient transport. Moving quickly is not necessarily the goal, however; proper preparation, "mock moves," and a solid transport plan will allow for an expedient move.

Post Move—Operations/Support

Post Move, there are still a few tasks to complete. Open issues must be documented and a plan to resolve said issues must be developed. The ongoing support structure must be invoked and post-opening project review and lessons learned must be completed. Finally, the many budget iterations that occurred during the course of the project will result in a budget finalization process.

Critical Success Factors

To ensure success, several factors must be considered. As expected, communication and "buy-in" are critical across all operational areas, but the ability to work with internal and external parties is vital. Key success factors include planning in the pre-design phase, obtaining assistance from outside subject matter experts, and allocating sufficient time to inventory existing technology and equipment. Management, physician, and stakeholder support are critical and all must have realistic expectations based on facts, needs, and budget limits. Full transparency and constant information sharing should be incorporated throughout the life cycle. Teams should attempt to pilot new solutions in a legacy/existing environment if possible to confirm workflow impacts, user training needs, etc. And finally, *Transition Planning* should be integrated early into design, facility planning, and readiness efforts to ensure that conceptual plans (and assumptions) are fully realized and schedules are coordinated.

Conclusion

With all of the advances we have seen in technology over the past several years, it is easy to get distracted and confused. By planning early, engaging a multidisciplinary team, following a methodical process, and setting a realistic budget, the technology plan for a new healthcare facility should fulfill all of the teams' and patients' expectations.

12

DEVELOPING INNOVATIVE HEALTH INFORMATION FOR YOUTH

Communication Theory for Practical Emerging Media Applications

LOU ANN STROUP, CHELSEY SIGLER, AND JAY E. GILLETTE, PH.D.

Contents

Introduction: The Challenge of Effective and Innovative Health Communication for Youth

The Human Factors Institute for User-Centered Design, Development, and Deployment (HFI-UCD3, or "HFI" for short) is a research group at Ball State University's Center for Information and Communication Sciences Information and Communication Sciences. The HFI focuses its research on the interaction between humans and information and communication technologies.

We are increasingly interested in the new approaches to research and development that have emerged under the rubric of "open innovation." This is a term pioneered in the seminal work of Henry Chesbrough in his *Open Innovation: The New Imperative for Creating and Profiting from Technology* (Chesbrough, 2003).

Chesbrough says his work represents "a new vision of the innovation process. This vision eagerly seeks external knowledge and ideas, even as it nurtures internal ones. It utilizes valuable ideas from whatever source in advancing a company's own business, and it places the company's own ideas in other companies' businesses" (Chesbrough, 2003, p. xxxi).

The work inspired the development of the European Open Innovation Strategy and Policy Group (OISPG). They summarize five key elements in the new innovation process:

1. Networking
2. Collaboration involving partners, competitors, universities, and users
3. Corporate Entrepreneurship, especially corporate venturing, start-ups, and spin-offs

4. Proactive Intellectual Property Management: to buy and sell intellectual property and so create markets for technology
5. Research and Development (R&D): for competitive advantage in the marketplace (OISPG website, 2010)

In a personal communication, OISPG's Bror Samelin declared,

> "We would like strongly to communicate a more modern view on open innovation. We need to go far beyond, towards crowdsourcing, co-creativity and collaborative open innovation ecosystems."

In the spirit of open innovation, through the Fall 2009, the Human Factors Institute began a new project as part of its ongoing relationship with the Indiana Department of Health (INDoH). The INDoH is a leading participant in the "Indiana Coalition to Improve Adolescent Health" (ICIAH). Established in 2006, the ICIAH is comprised of individuals and organizations working statewide to improve the health of Indiana's adolescents and youth, defined as those between ages of ten and twenty-fours years. The coalition operates toward four major goals:

1. Increase awareness of health issues impacting adolescents.
2. Provide support and accurate health resource information to adolescents and those who serve and care for adolescents.
3. Encourage collaboration among agencies and organizations whose services and decisions affect adolescents' health.
4. Evaluate the distribution and use of the state adolescent health plan.

The research institute has been working in collaboration with ICIAH coordinators to re-design the promotional materials for youth throughout Indiana. Through its ongoing research efforts, the institute will assist the coalition with the first two goals.

The following groups have been working as a subcommittee of the ICIAH on this project:

- Indiana State Department of Health
- IUPUI School of Medicine
- Clarion Hospital
- Ball State University

Growing up a digital world, adolescents do not take in information as others have in the past. When the ICIAH came to the Human Factors Institute for assistance in creating a campaign of public service announcements, the team asked to initially create and distribute a media usage survey. With so many alternative media outlets available to adolescents, researchers want to ensure the ICIAH is reaching their audience effectively and with the greatest impact.

Through institute-wide collaboration, the team developed a twenty-six-question survey through the online survey site: www.surveymonkey.com. The survey provides general insight on a variety of topics, specifically media consumption, ownership of technological devices, and interest in health-related topics. The following sections contain a summary of research issues and preliminary findings to date.

Health-Related Topics

Ten health issues were identified by the ICIAH as affecting the well-being of Indiana youth and adolescents:

1. *Healthcare capacity:* How to talk to your doctor about health problems or concerns.
2. *Health insurance:* Benefits of health insurance.
3. *Binge drinking:* Drinking alcohol excessively in a short time period; the dangers of binge drinking.
4. *Cigarette smoking:* Consequences of smoking cigarettes or learning how to quit smoking.
5. *Dating violence:* Relationships that are physically, emotionally, or sexually abusive; how to prevent dating violence.
6. *Mental health services:* How to get counseling for issues such as stress, depression, and anxiety.
7. *Motor vehicle fatalities:* Driving issues such as seatbelt use, preventing accidents, and preventing distracted driving (texting, cell phone use).
8. *Obesity:* How to eat better and get more exercise.
9. *Sexually transmitted infections:* How to prevent sexually transmitted infections and where to go for treatment.
10. *Suicide:* Warning signs of suicide and depression.

Following client approval, a Human Factors Institute survey was sent out to several school systems throughout the state of Indiana through digital and paper copies. To date, over 125 surveys have been analyzed, with additional surveys awaiting data entry. The information received through the survey will better assist the Human Factors Institute in reaching out to adolescents in fresh and effective ways.

Using the results of the entered surveys, the research team is building a strategic and multifaceted campaign to promote the ICIAH and health information. They use various innovative media outlets, including Internet social media, text messages, broadcast e-mails, among other channels, as well as traditional outlets such as radio and television.

Researchers from the Human Factors Institute are also revamping the branding of the awareness campaign to focus on the three audiences the materials will be targeted to: youth, parents, and healthcare professionals. The branding efforts will be tested using focus groups of local students with varying formats, information, and statistics.

The current generation of teens growing up is texting an astonishing average of 2272 texts per month. This generation's use of information technologies is part of the reason that communication networks and media are changing and changing rapidly, just to keep up. These youth have grown up with the Internet and texting, and expect information to be available on demand and at fast speeds no matter what is being sent across the network, whether voice, text, data, or video.

Internet for Health Promotion across the United States

Health departments across the United States have been using media as an important tool to promote health campaigns, create awareness, and market health products. Traditional methods included promotions through print media such as newspapers and books.

Today, with the advancement in technology, the Internet is the medium and is beginning to be used aggressively to disseminate health messages. Social media have gained a lot of importance through Web 2.0 approaches. Health departments are making new efforts to use these social media to their advantage to promote healthcare.

Empowerment is often said to be a "key principle" of health promotion (Tones, 1996; Rootman et al., 2001). According to the survey conducted by the opinion Research Corporation in January 2008,

59 percent of adults use the Internet as their take-off point for health information. Therefore, the Internet is arguably an empowering resource for communication. The various elements of the Internet used for healthcare promotion include:

- Interactive websites
- Facebook
- Twitter
- MySpace
- YouTube and podcasting
- Wikipedia

As noted at the 2009 American Public Health Association's (APHA) 137th Annual Meeting, the above elements of the Internet are becoming widely used for healthcare promotion by American public health organizations.

With this background, the HFI arrived at the following research findings based on its preliminary research.

Preliminary Research Findings for Recommended Information Media Approaches

For the ICIAH, we recommend that the following alternative and innovative media in order to get health-related information to the age ranges of ten to twenty-four years.

Youth Communication

- YouTube
- Public Service Announcements (PSAs)
- High quality PSAs hosted on ICIAH channel
- Same PSAs as commercials used on MSM
- Facebook
- Indiana Coalition to Improve Adolescence Health web pages
- Host events
- Make all fact sheets available
- Link-related articles
- Link to YouTube and Twitter pages

- Notify of new PSAs
- Twitter
- Live stream of all ICIAH entities' happenings
- Live blog/tweet
- RSS feed
- Articles
- PSA releases
- Blogs
- Articles written on related topics (linked by Facebook and Twitter)
- Build hype for events

Doctor/Youth Patient Communication

The use of new technologies would help interest adolescents in learning about healthy lifestyles, including:

- Touch-screen technologies
- Web 2.0 communications
- Doctors have longer attention spans so they can concentrate more on in-depth fact sheets and advice on how to communicate with patient
- Doctors have the ability to translate terms for effective communication with a patient

Parent-Child Communication

- Parents need to know all the facts to effectively communicate with their child about healthy lifestyles.
- More specific and informative fact sheets are necessary for parents.
- Knowing what could happen to their child would potentially encourage them to speak to them more often.
- Fact sheets do not need to be as visually appealing.
- Downloadable smart phone applications providing fact sheet information.
- Public Service Announcements on encouraging parents to communicate with their children

Preliminary Research Findings for Health Information Content
Approaches: Reaching Youth Effectively by Submarkets

Public outreach efforts change in cooperation with technology. Obviously, with information technology becoming more and more accessible and familiar for today's youth, these areas become easy focal points for outreach. However, it is also important to understand when and where these individuals want to get information, and then to focus on how to do this.

From our preliminary data from research surveys, we find that respondents in these age categories obtain most of their health information through the Internet, news, school, and in doctors' offices significantly more than any other sources. To further extend this information, basic Internet use, e-mailing, and social networking were the most common web uses, proving these areas to be effective in reaching youth within this age range. To add value, television was very commonly used by those surveyed; however, it was not a desired means of obtaining health information.

This overall age category can also be broken into even smaller groups, or submarkets, because of the intellectual, physical, and emotional maturity differences between these ages.

Youth Ages 10 to 14 Years

With sample data from a recent research survey, it was a common finding in youth between the ages of 10 and fourteen to have little interest in learning health information. However, it was also common that these students had expressed learning most health information in schools and doctors' offices, and also a significant amount in religious organizations.

Information technology, although a growing trend among current youth, had a seemingly insignificant role in the delivery of health information to these youth. Although social networking sites were not dramatically abundant within this youth group, e-mail and cellular phone use was fairly significant. With growing reliance on information technology, all these innovative media should be factored into this age group as well. It is also our strong recommendation to continue working with schools to spread health information to this age group.

Youth Ages 15 to 19 and 20 to 24 Years

These age groups overlapped in several areas, including social networking site usage and method of receiving health information. Although the age group 20 to 24 was concerned more with healthcare and health insurance than that of the 15 to 19 age group, the methods of receiving information were very similar, with the only major difference being in the reliance of the news for gathering information, as distinguished by the 20 to 24 age group.

The importance of cellular phone use, Internet usage, and social networking grows immensely within these age groups, and is an important area to factor into the future of information distribution to these ages. The 15 to 19 age group still relied on obtaining information in schools, and the oldest group, 20 to 24, showed a more independent role toward obtaining information, with an extreme focus on technology.

Although each age group showed varied use of web applications, Internet use, television use, and other methods of obtaining information, the sample data from the research surveys showed an abundant reliance on Internet usage among youth within these age restrictions. It would be recommended to continue to reach out to schools and emphasize education-based information, while also working to implement technology uses.

Text messaging was used frequently across this entire age spectrum. Perhaps weekly "fun facts" could be distributed via text message, or e-mail accounts (which the sample data showed to be of high use) could be sent a concise, easy-to-understand fun fact or message every so often.

Although the data used to come to these conclusions were based on sample data, these samples come from students within the state of Indiana, the exact market for which these health education information concerns are directed. Technology and schools are both highly significant entities in the distribution of health information to youth in Indiana.

Parents/Adults Interacting with Youth

There are a growing number of parents who are staying in touch with their children throughout the day by texting. This may open the communication between parent and child to discuss healthcare issues by sending text messages on different subjects to discuss.

Increasing Impact through Theories of Human Communication

As we worked with the field data from the youth of our sample, we wanted to apply communication theory to help us develop innovative work. The first thing we wanted to do was look at what it means to communicate.

The communication process and the forms of communications are always evolving but we can reference the same basic communication model. Claude Shannon developed a classic model for communication systems that includes an information source, a transmitter, a channel, a receiver, and a destination. This was based on an earlier, secret model of encoding an decoding of encrypted messages Shannon undertook for Bell Laboratories during World War II (Gleick, 2011, pp. 222–223).

Text messaging, e-mailing, and leaving a voice message on someone's cell phone are all considered accomplished ways of sending a message. However, the communication process is not complete without a confirmation from the receiver back to the sender informing the sender that the message was not only received, but also understood. In changing the media and formatting it in a form in which the people want to receive it will help make the information better understood and help to complete the process.

Two Aspects of Communication Theory to Explore

In Sun Tzu's *The Art of War* (1910), he states that most people see all the details of their lives but they cannot see what those details mean in terms of the big picture. As you master position awareness, and mature, you don't see your life as a point but as a path. You see your position in terms of what is changing and what resources are available. You are more aware of your ability to make decisions and your skills in working with others. We need to be looking at the big picture as the world is becoming flatter, in the approach of Thomas Friedman in *The World is Flat* (2007). More than ever, we are in a global community.

Let us now explore two broad aspects: the human communication (or people) aspect and the information technology aspect.

Human Communication: The People Aspect

The communication of people is illustrated from the classic book entitled *Theories of Human Communication* (Littlejohn and Foss, 2008), which shows complex methods in which people respond to one another in order to communicate. The following analytical approach may help us understand the basics.

Classification of Human Communication

Human communication can be broadly classified into two categories: verbal and nonverbal. It is important to study the components of human communication to understand how human communication is classified. The two broad classifications, along with the components are discussed below:

- *Verbal communication.* Humans communicate using language. The language used by humans can be made up of words, phrases, dialects to communicate effectively. Diction refers to the choice of words given to communicate while syntax refers to words or phrases to convey a certain message.
- *Nonverbal communication.* Humans use gestures, body language, writing, gestures, proximity, emotions, and other related components very effectively (*Understanding Communication*, 2009).

Effects of Human Communication

As Littlejohn said, the context of communication from the individual to society affects one another (Littlejohn, 2009, p. 52). The impacts of human communication can be viewed as a layered approach. The different layers of human communication include:

Layer 1—Conversation. Conversation takes place among two or more individuals when they communicate.
Layer 2—Relationship. Relationships happen when conversations among the individuals are fruitful. Relationships can be positive or negative in nature.

Layer 3—Groups. Groups are a result of a positive relationship in human communication. Individuals coming together as groups lay a foundation for an organization.

Layer 4—Organization. Organizations are formed as a result of human communication. Organizations are complex and involve various factors that disrupt communication. This results in complexity. As mentioned by Peters, organizations must learn to thrive on chaos to involve effective human communication (Peters, 1987).

Listening

According to Tom Peters in *Thriving on Chaos* (1987), listening might be one of the most important parts of communication. If you do not listen to what is being said, you will not be able to interpret the message correctly in order to respond.

Communication Persuades People

Aristotle focused on using communication to persuade people more than 2000 years ago. In a time of constant change, persuasive communication tactics are still required.

Persuasion and Group Dynamics

Persuasion also comes into play in group dynamics. The group can motivate the behaviors to interpersonal stimuli, which can then affect individual productivity, thus adding to the group productivity and possibly resulting in bonuses or rewards (Littlejohn & Foss, 2008).

Peters (1987) also says, "A quarter of a century has passed since *In Search of Excellence*, but as the pace of chance accelerates madly, 'a bias for action' is, if possible, more important than ever—and as elusive as ever in sizable organizations."

In *The Wisdom of Teams* (by J.R. Katzenbach and D.K. Smith), it states that one of the differences between a team that performs and one that doesn't is that performing teams discuss, decide, and do real work together (1993, p. 214).

These same persuasion methods are used in the peer-to-peer relationships of youth. This is the reason adolescents "follow the leader" and are sometime easily brainwashed into doing what the leader suggests in order to fit into the group.

Innovation in Media: The Information Technology Aspect

Now consider the technology aspect. In the information-networking model, you can see that information is communicated in much the same way even if it goes over the medium of a technological network.

Internet

The Internet is sometimes referred to as the social and economic fabric, created by people for the sake of human communication and interaction. (Technology and Human Communication, 2002). In fact, Finland is developing public policy that having fast Internet is becoming a legal right (Fast Internet Access). This will be the first country to make such a claim, and if it passes there, others are likely to follow.

Internet 2: The Next Generation

Internet 2 is considered the next level in Internet communication; it is being led by a research and education consortium. Internet 2 operates in the newest dynamic circuit network. (Internet 2, 2009).

Health Departments, Associations, and Affiliates in Other States

Health departments today are coming up with innovative methods to tap these online resources to achieve their objectives. Health departments run interactive campaign-like ads against tobacco and AIDS to get the health messages out in a very effective way. The very popular types of resources used by the health communities are provided as an appendix (Salt Lake Valley Health Department, Salt Lake City, Utah).

Health departments have achieved tremendous success in doing so by:

- Targeting the right audience and understanding the needs of the customers
- Clear objectives as to what is expected from using the social media
- Identifying steps to develop the established social media
- Selecting the right technology to get out the message

"One Small Change" is a social media project launched during Public Health Week in April 2009 by the Salt Lake Valley Health Department (SLVHD). To reach a Salt Lake County Goal—"67% of adults will make one healthy behavior change"—the following simple message was developed: "small changes in behavior can have an impact on health." Building good habits is something that could be performed by youth as well, so that the habit is already established before they become adults.

Innovative Information Media: Three Promising Approaches in Utah

Three promising approaches in Utah include:

1. Utilization of social marketing communication tools (YouTube, Facebook, Twitter, and Flickr) to reach a broad audience.
2. With very limited funding, the campaign was created entirely in-house by staff who designed and created a video using Health Department employees and the Salt Lake County Mayor.
3. The video encourages viewers to make one small health change from a wide array of healthy behaviors, including obesity reduction, injury and cancer prevention, immunizations, environmental health, and many more. Then report that change online using social media.

"One Small Change" has not only reached citizens but has created opportunities for program partnerships with cities, municipalities, and other county agencies to help individuals, families, businesses, and communities create healthier and happier lives.

Data from the first five days of this approach revealed the following:

- Over 1000 YouTube views
- 450 Twitter followers

- 46 Facebook fans
- Numerous TV, radio, and print stories

Directions for Continuing Research

A number of other popular types of social healthcare media are beginning to be explored by public health groups. The following are some promising directions for continuing research:

- Blog: Diabetes Mines, Health Matters, WebMD, NYT health blog
- Microblogs: Livestrong, Stupid cancer
- Podcasts: Johns Hopkins Medical Podcasts, Mayo Clinic
- Social sharing: Flickr, YouTube, IC You
- Forums: Revolution health groups, Google health groups

Youth of today are technology savvy and yet, as we have seen, face significant health challenges. They are finding it desirable that health-related information come to them in small, concise messages that will be easy for them to understand but will transmit across today's media in a fast and effective manner. Developing innovative health information for youth using emerging media applications is a challenging design problem for information and communication scientists. We are encouraged by the observations of Nigel Cross and Kees Dorst, who noted that creative design "seems more to be a matter of developing and refining together both the formulation of the problem and ideas for its solution, with constant iteration of analysis, synthesis and evaluation processes between the two 'spaces'—problem and solution" (cited in Brooks, 2010, p. 51).

We will continue this ongoing research project to further design, develop, and deploy usable and useful information to our research audiences and particularly for youth, whose need for usable and useful health information is more important than ever.

Acknowledgments

An earlier version of this work was presented at the International Telecommunications Education and Research Association, Nashville, Tennessee, and reprinted in the *ITERA 2010 Conference Proceedings*.

We thank Lou Ann Stroup, Chelsey Sigler, and Jay Gillette for their leadership in this Human Factors Institute research, documentation, and writing, as well as our colleagues Vishal Malhotra and Justin Epperly of the Human Factors Institute for their collegiality and input into the development of our work. Jay Gillette is director of the Human Factors Institute, which proposed and sponsored this study under his leadership.

References

Borden, George A. & Stone, John D. (1976). *Human communication: The process of relating*. Menlo Park, CA: Cummings Publishing Company.

Brooks, F. P. (2010). The design of design: Essays from a computer scientist. Upper Saddle River, NJ: Addison-Wesley.

Chesbrough, H. W. (2003). Open innovation: The new imperative for creating and profiting for technology. Cambridge, MA: Harvard Business School Press.

Dexter, M. (2009, August 11). Indiana takes a stand for adolescent health. Retrieved from http://www.in.gov/portal/news_events/41348.htm

Friedman, T. L. (2007). *The world is flat, a brief history of the twenty-first century*. New York, NY: Picador/Farrar, Straus and Giroux.

Gleick, J. (2011). The information: A history, a theory, a flood. New York, NY: Pantheon Books.

Gondim, P. T. (2002). *Understanding communication*. Retrieved from http://www.icc2002.com/understanding_Communication.html

Heath, R. L. & Bryant, J. (2000). *Human communication theory and research: concepts, contexts, and challenges*. Mahwah, NJ: Lawrence Erlbaum Associates.

Hiltz, S. R. & Turoff, M. (1994). *The network nation*: Cambridge, MA: Massachusetts Institute of Technology.

Hesselgrave, D. J. (1991). *Communicating Christ cross culturally*. Grand Rapids, MI: Zondervan Press.

Katzenbach, J. R. & Smith, D. K. (1993). New York, NY: Harper Business.

Kauppila, A. (2007, February 7). Advances in technology affect interpersonal communication. *The Guardian*. Retrieved from http://www.theguadianonline.com/2.9312/advances-in-technology-affect-interpersonal-communication-1.124621

Littlejohn, S. W. & Foss, K. A. (2008). *Theories of human communication*. Belmont, CA: Thomson Wadsworth.

McCloskey, M. (1985). *Tell it often—tell it well*. San Bernardino, CA: Here's Life Publishers.

Meadow, C. A. (2006). *Messages, meanings, and symbols: The communication of information*. Oxford, UK: The Scarecrow Press, Inc.

Miller, K. (2005). *Communication theories: Perspectives, processes, and contexts, 2nd edition*. New York, NY: McGraw-Hill.

Peters, T. (1987). *Thriving on chaos: Handbook for a management revolution.* Schaumburg, IL: Harper Perennial.

Shannon, C. E. (1948). A mathematical theory of communication. *The Bell System Technical Journal,* 27, 379–423. Reissued 1957.

Tannen, D. (1994, August 28). Why don't you say what you mean? *New York Times Magazine.* Retrieved October 19, 2009, from www.anthroprof.org/documents/Docs102/102articles/say9.pdf

Wiio, O. (1985). Information economy and the information society. *Media in Education and Development,* 18(4), 187–91. http://search.ebscohost.com.proxy.bsu.edu

Winslow, M. A. (2002). *Technology and human communication.* Retrieved from http://www.icc2002.com/Technology_and_Human_Communication.html

RE-ENVISIONING THE INDIANAMEDICAID.COM WEBSITE AS A MEMBER-FOCUSED PORTAL

A Case Study on Usability and Technology for Transforming Healthcare Communication

JARED B. LINDER, MS, PMP

Contents

Introduction

In Indiana, the Office of Medicaid Policy and Planning (OMPP), which is a division of the Indiana Family and Social Service Administration (FSSA), administers the state Medicaid program. Medicaid has been expanding significantly both in expenditures as well as in overall members (defined here as recipients of Medicaid services), including an increase of almost 7 percent in total enrollment between year-end 2008 and 2009 (Kaiser Commission, 2010, p. 3). Many of the additional expenditures are, of course, due to the increasing costs of healthcare, even in the wake of funding cuts made to hospitals and providers. However, this expansion is also due to the creation of additional programs to serve more members. Estimates only show these numbers increasing due to healthcare reform, which has been estimated to cost Indiana an additional $3 billion (AP, 2010b) as state programs are anticipated to pick up the tab for new members who become eligible as a result.

Currently, the OMPP manages several varying eligibility packages under the umbrella moniker of the Indiana Health Coverage Programs (IHCP). The IHCP includes not only traditional Medicaid members, who typically qualify for state assistance based upon financial or conditional needs, but also covers school-age children (CHIP), screenings for the elderly applying for admission to long-term care facilities, foster children, and now eligible adults under the Healthy Indiana Plan (HIP). The last of these programs, HIP, includes a new population of healthy adults who meet increased income guidelines (Indiana FSSA, 2009) and who have been previously uninsured for a period of six months or longer, thus opening up affordable healthcare to a previously forgotten segment of Indiana's population. Membership in the IHCP now totals almost one million Hoosiers—or one out of every six people in the state, approximately 16 percent of the total population (State Health Facts, 2009).

Given that healthcare reform has mobilized most in the industry to identify how exactly sweeping changes will affect them, the FSSA has estimated that an additional 500,000 members, an increase of 50 percent, will be added to the IHCP rosters, bringing the total covered population to 1.5 million Hoosiers—or one out of every four people in the state, or 25 percent of Indiana's total population (AP, 2010a).

The results of these changes and the increase in member population are altering the focus of how the OMPP is conducting its activities, and places a strong need on creating outward-facing materials that are information rich and accessible. To most effectively reach out it its members, the OMPP focused its communication outreach efforts on re-envisioning and redeveloping its existing website, www.indianamedicaid.com, including improving its aesthetics,

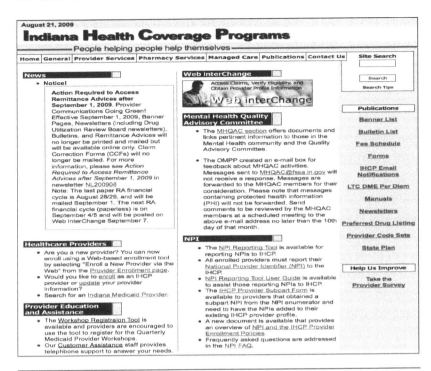

Figure 13.1 Original design of www.IndianaMedicaid.com website.

including a new look and feel, while more importantly focusing its approach on creating information topically focused on subjects relevant to its members.

Previously, the Indiana Medicaid website was more of a provider-focused repository of information, focusing on the tools and information necessary to allow doctors' offices and hospital billing departments to locate program and claims submission guidance. As shown in Figure 13.1, this provider-focused website, although visually cluttered, was rich with information, especially if a visitor was looking for policy updates, newly enacted rules, and other information such as scheduled training and seminar events relating to the business of Medicaid; however, as noted previously, no communication on the existing website was written or organized with the member audience in mind.

This case study outlines the methods and concepts that were applied to transforming the existing Indiana Medicaid website into a vehicle for increased support and communication for its member population through a re-envisioning and redevelopment exercise. In this study, usability analysis involving the OMPP and other stakeholders was conducted to create the new vision for the online presence of Indiana Medicaid to enable the website to serve as a primary resource for its ever-expanding member population.

Re-Envisioning IndianaMedicaid.com

The OMPP's primary vision was to design a website that would be both informative and understandable by its members and to achieve cost and time savings through updated technology using a content management system, which they equated to greater control of the system. The vision was also to create a new home page that would allow users to explore parts of the site based upon their role, whether member or provider. This preliminary thinking envisioned for the creation of a new member website and Indiana Medicaid home page, while— other than changing the existing home page URL—maintaining the integrity and content of the existing website, later to be rebranded as the provider portion of the website.

To redevelop the Indiana Medicaid website to obtain this vision, the OMPP determined that this could not simply be another technology project where a business analyst gathered high-level requirements and turned those over to the technology vendor to create technical requirements for system implementation. To create a stronger communication vehicle and better enhance the brand of Medicaid in Indiana, the OMPP sought the help of a web developer to conduct planning and design activities to develop a solution that best fit into the intended climate (Bolchini, Garzotto, & Sorce, 2009)—meaning that existing technology and web architecture, budget, staff skill set, and intended message all had to be considered.

To assist with achieving this vision, the OMPP began a collaborative project effort among OMPP staff Subject Matter Experts (SMEs); the existing technology vendor that hosted the website; a web design team to identify appropriate solutions, elicit design ideas, and create a usable site; as well as project management staff who helped guide the project scope and timeline. The web developer conducted a usability project over the next several months to elicit both content and design issues from the OMPP SMEs.

In the existing environment, technology would often be seen as an overhead expense. The OMPP typically would contact the existing technology vendor regarding needed website changes, and would go through a change control process that involved analysis of cost, effort, and requirements development as well as following a release schedule. This involved a substantial amount of planning on both sides in order to schedule needed communications appropriately, and also added a burden of continual change control and additional development costs. The goal here was to create an innovative solution that allowed for greater control of content and delivery timing.

All of these proposed concepts allowed for the OMPP to envision a website that would have content and interaction design that spoke to an ever-growing member population, while allowing for ease of change control, page maintenance, and content adjustment.

Analyzing the Current State

To begin the process, the team analyzed the current state environment of the IndianaMedicaid.com website, including the content, aesthetics, structure, and technology utilized (Bolchini, Triacca, & Speroni, 2003). The team also reviewed other web sites in several domains to find best practices and representative samples of what they considered good design. The web developer then produced a site map showing the navigation architecture of the existing website, in order to show the depth and access structures to the current content. The OMPP SMEs in parallel began to envision how new information would be grouped in order to create content for applicable topics.

Creating content for the new website was not as easy as simply taking information from the existing website, as the purpose was to create a site that focused on members, instead of providers, as its target audience. This involved substantial effort on behalf of OMPP staff members to locate and document intended messages in a language and style that would most resonate with target users. Table 13.1 shows how content was then organized in a matrix that allowed for classification and organization of ideas.

The team also reviewed several other websites across industries, but then focused on similar programs from other states to determine if there were best practices or usable examples that the OMPP best liked or wanted to leverage. Examples rating best among OMPP staff utilized clean design with prominent logos and engaging graphics.

Table 13.1 Content Matrix for Member Website

CONTENT ID	PRIMARY	SECONDARY	TERTIARY	QUATERNARY	PURPOSE OF PAGE	CONTENT DIRECTION	KEYWORDS/PHRASES TO INCLUDE IN TEXT
1.0	Member Home Page					Content TBD based on final design.	Indiana Medicaid, Members, residents.
2.0	Am I Eligible?				This section landing page should provide a very broad picture of programs and eligibility.	Discuss in general terms the type of people who are eligible and who have special targeted programs (e.g., pregnant woman, disabled, waivers, etc.); link to these pages in this section. Discuss how DFR is the group who determines eligibility. Encourage people to read the eligibility tool.	Medicaid eligibility, Medicaid qulifications DFR, Department of Family Resources, health insurance, low-income, pregnant woman, Indiana Medicaid eligibility.
2.1		Eligibility Criteria			Helps people understand what factors are considered in Eligibility. Points people to Eligibility Tool and detailed eligibility information (if they want it).	Provide high-level income eligibility tables based on the age (e.g., children can be in a Household earning less than 250% of FPL, Adults in a household earning less than 200% of FPL, Seniors at or below 80% FPL, and indicate other factors that are considered.	Medicaid eligibility criteria, Federal Poverty Level, (FPL), assets, household income, who is eligible, low income, Medicaid income eligibility.

			Indicate that the nitty-gritty detail in a PDF or in specific program eligibility detail pages. Encourage people to use Eligibility Tool.	
2.1.1	Hoosier Healthwise Eligibility	Detailed information for highly functioning potential Members and advocates.	Detailed eligibility information for this program.	Hoosier Healthwise, HHW, eligibility criteria.
2.1.2	Care Select Eligibility	Detailed information for highly functioning potential Members and advocates.	Detailed eligibility information for this program.	Care Select, CS, eligibility criteria, blind, disabled, aged.
2.1.3	M.E.D. Works Eligibility	Detailed information for highly functioning potential Members and advocates.	Detailed eligibility information for this program.	MED Works, eligibility criteria, working while on Medicaid.
2.1.4	Healthy Indiana Plan Eligibility	Detailed information for highly functioning potential Members and advocates.	Detailed eligibility information for this program.	Healthy Indiana Plan, HIP, eligibility criteria, Indiana eligibility.
2.1.5	Traditional Medicaid Eligibility	Detailed information for highly functioning potential Members and advocates.	Detailed eligibility information for this program (unless this is better covered under page 2.5).	Medicare eligibility criteria, dual-eligible.

Also in parallel to these creation and usability assessment activities, a full technical assessment of the existing web architecture and environment was conducted in order to determine any gaps in technical readiness, including hardware and training needs. Based upon this technical analysis, both the web developer and the technology provider worked to make recommendations for what software and hardware components were necessary.

Gap Analysis: Considering the Usability

Upon reviewing with the OMPP all of the proposed requirements from a business perspective, and gathering the samples of other potential website designs, a gap analysis was produced. This gap analysis noted content issues, including where information was either missing or hard to interpret, while also focusing on look-and-feel, navigation, and search engine optimization. Problems for improvement were noted, and recommendations were made to enhance the experience from the existing website. No actual severity ratings (Nielsen, n.d.) or impact assessments were done at this time, as the intention was to create a new design, not to rework the existing site and eliminate its specific problems. Table 13.2 shows some of the identified problems and the appropriate design recommendations.

With these issues noted, the design team achieved buy-in from the OMPP staff to move forward with development by incorporating recommendations into the new system requirements based upon problems noted in the original Indiana Medicaid website.

Table 13.2 Noted Design Problems and Recommendations

PROBLEM	DESIGN RECOMMENDATION
Search engine friendly URLs	Utilize descriptive URLs for page names
Metadata	Add metadata and descriptions to pages
Alt Description tags on images	Use Alt Description tags on all images to ensure accessibility for screen readers
Site map	Create a site map page for ease of information retrieval
Simplified navigation	Reorganize content to eliminate deep navigation paths
Home page simplification	Utilize the home page more as a front door and a branded message rather than as the information repository
Content focus	Focus the site content specifically on the intended audience—in this case, Indiana Medicaid Members

Gap Analysis: Considering the Technology

Like many Medicaid or other state agencies, Indiana relies on a vendor to provide services in relation to its website. The existing website was developed and maintained by an offsite technology vendor that also provides the overall technical infrastructure behind Indiana's Medicaid Management Information System, which pays medical claims and supports the OMPP's other operational functions. The intention was to continue to leverage the existing vendor and infrastructure to house and maintain the new Medicaid website.

To construct a new website, the OMPP surveyed available software and decided that an open-source solution made the most sense. They also opted to pursue a content management system that could be accessed and have content managed by internal staff rather than rely on a model that utilized an organic, custom-built website that needed developer input and interaction to create additional pages and alter or supplement content. This was perceived as a cost-effective solution design that would maximize the value of the new website while adding a new level of control to the stakeholders.

The existing site was constructed utilizing the Microsoft ASP.NET programming language and was hosted on a Microsoft web server using Microsoft SQL Server. Therefore, the design team sought out an open-source content management system that could a function in a similar environment.

Re-Developing IndianaMedicaid.com

To develop the re-envisioned IndianaMedicaid.com website, the team refined objectives into goals and then into specific detailed requirements regarding not only technological needs, but also usability and communication needs. To achieve that end, activities were performed to elicit specific goals of the new site. High-level business and communication needs were elicited and defined through customer interviews with OMPP and external stakeholders, including providers and advocacy groups.

The design team then worked to define in common terms how the specified goals could be mapped to overall labeling and architecture requirements, including topic designation and item grouping. To do this, the team executed a card sort exercise to then help the OMPP realize how specific topics could be organized.

Creating the Future State: Usability

After conducting the analysis of the existing landscape, and understanding what the OMPP was envisioning as possible solutions, the team began to work on creating the future state of IndianaMedicaid.com. Based upon stakeholder conversations including what they wanted to improve regarding the existing website, it was noticeable from the gap analysis that changes should be made across many design dimensions, including content, navigation, graphics, and semiotics (Bolchini, Triacca, & Speroni, 2003). To create maximum impact, this new website was seen as not just simply needing a new color scheme and graphics added to an existing structure, but also a structural reorganization.

To best determine how to organize the new website, the design team took the original vision and objectives and transformed them into goals and strategies that provided concrete guidance on how best to proceed. The OMPP participated in brainstorming sessions that allowed for the creation of strategies and tactics. Two main objectives were noted, and goals then associated with both:

- *Objective One:* Empower members and give them more confidence in the Medicaid system:
  - *Goal:* Members must perceive the system as less complex than it is.
  - *Goal:* Members must feel empowered.

- *Objective Two:* Reduce the administrative cost of providing services:
  - *Goal:* Reduce the number of transitions a member goes through.
  - *Goal:* Increase the number of members who use Medicaid benefits properly.

From this starting point, further examination was conducted to refine these high-level goals into more concrete forms. Table 13.3 shows the details for how an objective was mapped to its necessary goals, strategies, and tactics.

Table 13.3 Objectives Mapping

	OBJECTIVES	GOALS	STRATEGIES	TACTICS
O1	Empower members and give them more confidence in the Medicaid system			
G1.1		System seems less complex than it is		
S1.1.1			Move all member information to a single site	
S1.1.2			Branded programs are de-emphasized, but still available	
T1.1.2.1				Programs treated as "flavors" of Medicaid
T1.1.2.2				Full Program information available on the site
T1.1.2.3				Visitors guided through eligibility info based on individual/family characteristics

Based upon the continual refinement of objectives into tactics, it became clear what business requirements were necessary to achieve the OMPP's goals in redesigning the IndianaMedicaid.com website. While in the requirements development process, it is also critical to note that several items such as e-mail notifications and plan selection wizard tools were determined out of scope for this phase of the project. Table 13.4 displays a sample of gathered requirements.

Once all the high-level content was created, the OMPP then conducted a card sort exercise. A list of relevant terms that had been elicited during the previous requirements phases were used as card sort items; a sample is shown in Table 13.5. The design team created the exercise in Adobe Flash where users could drag and drop content items into appropriate groupings by topic (see Figures 13.2 and 13.3). Users then were asked to name these groupings based upon their interpretation of the content organized within each. The card sort exercise is an industry-recognized method of organizing content pieces into appropriate categories both individually, and as a group, in order to create an agreed-upon grouping of content items (Faiks & Hyland, 2000).

The card sort exercise resulted in the creation of labels and headings that could be used for high-level information groupings. These groupings and labels then became the inputs into developing the navigation structure and information architecture of the member website (Figure 13.4). These new labels demonstrated a focus on actions or tasks in order to signify logical places for users to access desired

Table 13.4 Samples of Requirements

IN-SCOPE REQUIREMENTS
Move all member information to a single site
Branded programs are de-emphasized
Make finding a PMP and other providers easier
Simplify current provider locator
Make grievance procedures obvious
Clearly present Medicaid-covered services

OUT OF SCOPE REQUIREMENTS
Build a wizard to help with plan selection
Provide a translation of notices members get
Provide members a voice in the quality of their service – provider service ratings
E-mail notification or site notification

Table 13.5 Card Sort Examples

MEMBER CARD SORTING ITEMS

Help choosing a Managed Care Plan	Guidelines for using Emergency Room services
Eligibility criteria for Medicaid	Importance of keeping doctor appointments
Requirements of different Medicaid programs	Report a change of address
HIP application	Open enrollment
Care Select application	Approved drugs
Hoosier Healthwise application	Limits for different types of medical services
Traditional Medicaid application	Medicaid waivers
Services that require Prior Authorization	Interim Contact Form
Wellness programs provided by MCOs	Member Responsibility
Grievance procedures	Member Rights
Application instructions	Managed Care explanation
Check status of application	Role of PMP in Managed Care
. . . . .	. . . .

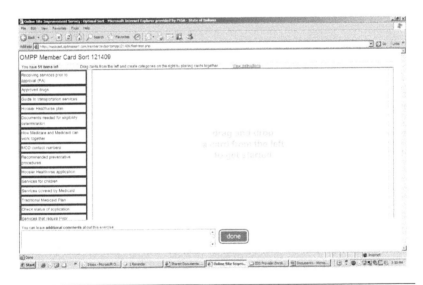

Figure 13.2 Card sort pre-user interaction.

information. Because the audience for this site was already defined as Indiana Medicaid members, task-based groupings presented a more logical method to group the information than using user-based methods (Bolchini & Mylopoulos, 2003). New labels included tasks such as: Am I Eligible?, Apply for Medicaid, Find a Provider, and Contact Us. Content was then organized within these topics to best represent how to achieve those tasks while supporting information reinforced the decisions users could possibly make.

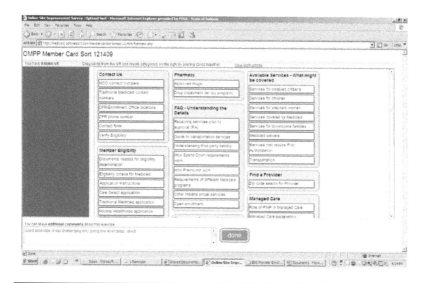

Figure 13.3 Card sort post-user interaction.

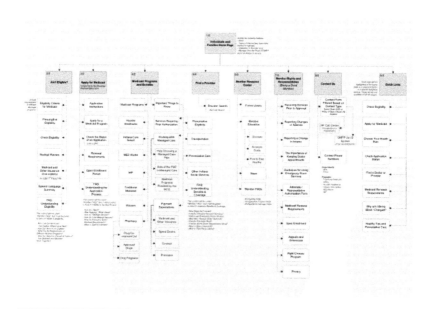

Figure 13.4 Navigation structure and information architecture. (Diagram courtesy of Fusion Alliance.)

In addition to this topic organization, the design team also determined that a consistent frame called Quick Links should also appear on every page on the website. The Quick Links were designed to contain the highest-rated tasks that stakeholders determined would be relevant at any time within the site. Those tasks are also action oriented in their labeling, and include: Apply Now for Medicaid, Check Application Status, and Choose Your Health Plan.

Creating the Future State: Technology

Significant planning was also conducted to ensure that the new website was developed in a manner that the technology vendor could support long-term within the existing technological infrastructure. Originally, the web developer proposed using a content management system that utilized an open-source platform known as Joomla, which primarily utilized Java as its interface language, and ran on an Apache web server and utilized MySQL (Open Source Matters, n.d.).

Although this intended technical design posed many advantages, considerations were given to the technology vendor's existing systems as well as support knowledge and skill-set. This solution design was quickly abandoned in favor of an end-to-end solution that more thoroughly integrated within the existing infrastructure and knowledge base of the existing provider of web services for the OMPP. The existing site was constructed utilizing the Microsoft ASP.NET platform and hosted on a Microsoft web server using Microsoft SQL Server. Therefore, the design team sought out an open-source content management system that could better integrate with the existing environment.

The design team settled on Umbraco, which like Joomla is an open-source content management system meant for web hosting and integration, while more completely integrating within an enterprise-level technology operation similar to this specific technology vendor (Umbraco, n.d.). Due to technical requirements elicited from the technology vendor, and the lack of specific platform needs from the OMPP, this was determined as the solution that most fully integrated into the existing infrastructure while satisfying the stakeholders' needs of communication and transparency. In a traditional case of project give-and-take, the project team found a solution that—although different than originally envisioned—best met the needs of all the stakeholders.

Given that cost is a primary factor within state government, Indiana included, it was integral to find a solution that not only communicated the specific goals and objectives as outlined, but that also cost little to no additional state funds to operate and maintain. Overall, both of these solutions provided a respectable amount of functionality and interoperability; however, in the end, the decision was to use one specific software product over another due to technology considerations rather than cost.

Creating the Future State: Iterating Design Ideas

As design is an iterative process, the visual representation of the new Indiana Medicaid website went through several versions in order not only to capture the appropriate look-and-feel that the OMPP was envisioning, but also to take advantage of the recommendations made during the gap analysis. Preliminary static prototypes were created using tools like Microsoft PowerPoint, Adobe Illustrator, and Adobe Photoshop. These iterations were shared with OMPP staff and design ideas were vetted in order to capture impressions and find a design that best met expectations. Figure 13.5 and Figure 13.6 show two original iterations.

This aesthetic design process occurred concurrently with the creation of navigation, content, and technology exploration. The web designer continued to refine the overall look-and-feel of the website, including altering color schemes and page layout to best accommodate stakeholder satisfaction. The web design team, choosing bold hues both for the background and the pictures within each page, heavily influenced the aesthetic design of the site. Photos were obtained from iStockphoto.com, and represented topically appropriate scenes of families, children, and medical professionals. All the photos are stored within a folder in the content management system and can be selected for use when creating new pages or altering existing pages. Also, on the home page, depending on whether users hover over the member or provider tab to select their destination, the color of the tab as well as the graphics change to also best represent where the user will go. Figures 13.7, 13.8, and 13.9 demonstrate the finished website design.

Figure 13.5   Preliminary PowerPoint prototype.

Figure 13.6   Indiana Medicaid home page wireframe. (Diagram courtesy of Fusion Alliance.)

Figure 13.7   New IndianaMedicaid.com home page. Indiana Medicaid. (2010). Home page. Retrieved from: http://www.indianamedicaid.com.

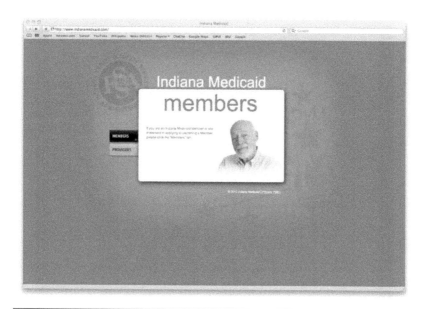

Figure 13.8   IndianaMedicaid.com member tab highlighted. Indiana Medicaid. (2010). Home page. Retrieved from: http://www.indianamedicaid.com.

Figure 13.9 IndianaMedicaid.com new Member landing page. Retrieved from: http://www.indianamedicaid.com.

Reintroducing IndianaMedicaid.com

Original Success

The perceived success of the Indiana Medicaid website was immediate, gauged mainly through the users reacting to the updated look-and-feel, including the revamped color scheme and interface structure. The resulting endeavor created a new home page presenting two distinct access paths, one for Medicaid members and one for users. This new paradigm resonated with viewers of the site. Primarily, in informal interviews the stakeholders were more satisfied with the new site's content and preferred it to the existing site. More thorough interviews will need to be conducted in the future to fully gauge this level of appreciation. But, preliminarily, users—mainly original stakeholders—were more receptive to the new design, up to and including both the new approach and the color scheme.

This success was magnified when users viewed the provider tab of the site, which returned users to the original design, noting the design improvements relating to the color palette and overall organization. No additional user data were collected about this perception of the website because the original intention was to eventually replace the existing website. For purposes of business continuity, the existing site was relegated to being accessible through the provider tab of the new website only—whereas before it was the primary content delivery mechanism of the content desired by the OMPP.

Additional Success

Given the success, as determined by stakeholders, of both the format and the concepts of the new member portion of the website, the OMPP immediately focused attention on creating a new provider website in favor of the preexisting website. As part of this exercise, the web developer conducted a light analysis of the interaction architecture of the provider website and produced a site map of all existing pages. This then allowed for OMPP staff members to utilize the documented architecture as a navigation template to build, order, and structure new pages.

It was always determined that when the web portal for the member website was completed that the web developer would roll off the project, and that the technology vendor and the OMPP would then create a formal plan to develop both the requirements as well as the actual content pages for the new provider portion of the website. Using the guidance of the documented navigation structure, as well as additional user requirements, this provider path of the website was then built within the existing content management system at no further cost to the OMPP and without the ongoing support of the web developer.

Conclusions and Further Recommendations

One of the strongest advantages of developing a website for a government entity within the framework of an open-source platform is the reduction of costs for both up-front procurement and ongoing development (Fitzgerald & Kenny, 2004). Given the integration, installation, and training costs associated with this website, it stands to reason that more research could be done regarding cost savings of using open-source software versus the inherent risks. Other challenges did exist in this case, including lack of developed documentation, support, and training offered by the software provider.

What is already showing positive advantages is the usage of a content management system to manage the site versus using the prior website environment. Giving OMPP staff the ability to create pages using both entered content and graphics using the series of predefined templates will continue to allow for affordable, rapid web page creation and alteration.

This ease of page creation was made possible through thoughtful design and planning; a series of page templates were designed that could be used in various situations and altered by showing and hiding specific content sections to create variety, including the creation of a sample architecture structure of how pages would be organized within the new site. This was one advantage of using project management and planning principles within the project, where costs and resources were defined early in the project to define the development piece was in scope for the web developer.

The creation and development of the new Indiana Medicaid website is a good first step in providing a solid foundation for the OMPP to communicate its policies and messages on the web, from reinforcing the intended messages to providing an accessible platform with the utilized technology. Starting from this foundation, the OMPP can utilize other projects to help continue to craft and refine their message as well as provide for a pleasurable user experience for all members and other site visitors. This can be accomplished by undertaking usability studies using proven methods (Nielsen, 2002; Redish, 2007).

Other states can also benefit by looking to IndianaMedicaid.com as a model example of how to undertake a collaborative development effort to re-envision and redevelop a website that has the ability to speak to its growing member population through common language, ease of information retrieval, and the low cost of using a content management system to manage a website.

Given the significant amount of research done regarding usability (Krug, 2000; Leavitt & Shneiderman, 2006), it stands to reason that further study should be given to the usability of the new Indiana Medicaid website to evaluate the effectiveness and success of this project. An analysis of heuristic guidelines (Nielsen, 2005) including conducting expert review and scenario-based walkthroughs can be employed by designers to gauge the effectiveness of the finished product (Nielsen, 1994). This is a well-known method that can help locate and fix other problems noted within websites. Also, the OMPP could solicit feedback, whether informally or in a usability study, from members and other users of the site to determine user impressions.

By applying common-sense approaches to modern web development, as well as a bit of flare for design, the OMPP has been able to conduct a project to develop and deploy a website built around its predefined goals and objectives. Although this is of course not the first website—governmental, healthcare based, or otherwise—to be analyzed or redesigned using commonly accepted practice methodologies (Gant & Gant, 2002; Tat-Kei Ho, 2002), it certainly was the first time that the OMPP mobilized to undertake such an endeavor. This attempt to create a new task- and message-focused member website is hopefully construed positively by members and users of the site, given that the OMPP worked to create a communication mechanism that was cost-effective, focused, informative, and relevant for all of Indiana's members and providers now and in the future.

References

AP (Associated Press) (2010a, April 26). How will overhaul affect Indiana's Medicaid enrollment? *The Indianapolis Star*. Retrieved from http://www.indystar.com/article/20100426/LOCAL/4260321

AP (Associated Press) (2010b, October 26). New estimate drops health plan's cost to Indiana. *The Indianapolis Star*. Retrieved from http://www.indystar.com/apps/pbcs.dll/article?AID=2010101026022

Bolchini, D., Garzotto, F., & Sorce, F. (2009). Does branding need web usability? A value-oriented empirical study. *Human-Computer Interaction—INTERACT 2009*, 5727, 652–665. DOI: 10.1007/978-3-642-03658-3_70.

Bolchini, D. & Mylopoulos, J. (2003). From task-oriented to goal-oriented web requirements analysis. *Web Information Systems Engineering 2003*, 166–175. DOI: 10.1109/WISE.2003.1254480

Bolchini, D., Triacca, L., & Speroni, M. (2003). MiLE: A reuse-oriented usability evaluation method for the web. *Proceedings of the International Conference on Human-Computer Interaction HCII 2003*.

Faiks, N. & Hyland, N. (2000). Gaining user insight: A case study illustrating the card sort technique. *College & Research Libraries*, 61(4), 349–357.

Fitzgerald, B. & Kenny, T. (2004). Developing an information systems infrastructure with open source software. *IEEE Software*, 21(1), 50–55. DOI:10.1109/MS.2004.1259216.

Gant, J. & Gant, D. (2002). Web portal functionality and state government e-service. *System Sciences, 2002, HICSS. Proceedings of the 35th Annual Hawaii International Conference on*, pp. 1627–1636. DOI: 10.1109/HICSS.2002.994073.

Indiana FSSA (Family and Social Services Administration) (2009). *Am I eligible?* Retrieved from http://www.in.gov/fssa/hip/2333.htm

Kaiser Commission on Medicaid and the Uninsured (2010). Publication 8050-02, Medicaid Enrollment: December 2009 Data Snapshot. Retrieved from http://www.kff.org/medicaid/upload/8050-02.pdf

Krug, S. (2000). Don't make me think! A common sense approach to web usability. Indianapolis, IN: Macmillan USA.

Leavitt, M. O. & Shneiderman, B. (2006). Research-Based Web Design & Usability Guidelines. Washington, D.C.: U.S. Department of Health and Human Services.

Nielsen, J. (n.d.). Severity Ratings for Usability Problems. Retrieved from http://www.useit.com/papers/heuristic/severityrating.html

Nielsen, J. (2002). The usability engineering life cycle. *Computer,* 25(3), 12–22. DOI: 10.1109/2.121503.

Nielsen, J. (1994). Heuristic evaluation. In *Usability inspection methods.* New York, NY: John Wiley & Sons, Inc.

Nielsen, J. (2005) Ten Usability Heuristics. Retrieved from http://www.useit.com/papers/heuristic/heuristic_list.html

Open Source Matters. (n.d.). Joomla! Technical Requirements. Retrieved from http://www.joomla.org/technical-requirements.html

Redish, J. (2007). Expanding usability testing to evaluate complex systems. *Journal of Usability Studies,* 2(3), 102–111.

State Health Facts. (2009). Indiana: Trends in Medicaid Enrollment (in thousands), December 2009 (data file). Retrieved from http://www.statehealthfacts.org/profileind.jsp?cmprgn=1&cat=4&rgn=16&ind=795&sub=52

Tat-Kei Ho, A. (2002). Reinventing local governments and the e-government initiative. *Public Administration Review,* 62(4), 434–444, DOI: 10.1111/0033-3352.00197.

Umbraco. (n.d.). Integrate.NET Controls. Retrieved from http://umbraco.org/get-started/next-step-guide/developers/integrate-net-controls

Appendix: Glossary of Health Care Terms from IBM

AAFP: American Academy of Family Physicians. AAFP is the national association of family doctors. The mission of the AAFP is to improve the health of members, families, and communities by serving the needs of members with professionalism and creativity.

ACH: Automated Clearinghouse. A financial entity that acts an intermediary for electronic funds transfers.

AP: Associated Physicians (Provider).

BRS: Business Requirements Specification.

BSS: Business Support Services. A component of CSDP.

BTO: Business Transformation Office.

CBS: Composite Business Service. A CBS is a pre-built business accelerator for the innovation and transformation of core processes. In general, a CBS is a loosely coupled collection of IT services that, when taken together, address a business issue. Example: Provider Claims Suite.

CH: Clearinghouse.

Clearinghouse: An entity that acts as an intermediary between a provider and a payer. Typical clearinghouse services include translation (to and from HIPAA format), claims error detection, and receipt/transfer of funds from a payer into a provider's accounts.

COB: Coordination of Benefits. A process for determining the respective responsibilities of two or more health plans that have some financial responsibility for a medical claim.

CPA: Claims Payment Summary. A single document that indicates the financial obligations of the payer and member.

CSDP: Common Services Delivery Platform.

EDI: Electronic Data Interchange. A protocol for transmission and receipt of electronic data between two entities (e.g., a payer and a provider).

EHR: Electronic Health Record.

EOB: Explanation of Benefits. A document supplied by the payer to the provider and member indicating financial details of a claim. Includes status (approved/denied), physician charges, charges permitted (adjusted charges), amount covered by payer, member responsibilities, accumulators (deductibles and out-of-pocket), reason codes if denied.

Epic: A Practice Management System (PMS).

FSA: Flexible Spending Account (see Health Fund).

GBS: Global Business Services, IBM's primary consulting organization.

GTS: Global Technology Services.

HDHP: High Deductible Health Plan. An HDHP requires a high deductible before the health insurance starts. The benefit of an HDHP is that it offers significant premium savings over low- or zero-deductible health plans. HDHPs are often used in combination with HSAs.

Health Fund: An account whose purpose is to pay for unreimbursed healthcare expenses such as co-pays, deductibles, out-of-pocket expenses, and non-covered health-related items. Four types of Health Funds are HSA, FSA, HRA, and RRA. Each has unique characteristics such as who is eligible, who can contribute, funding options, tax benefits, and reimbursement procedures.

HIPAA: Health Insurance Portability and Accountability Act.

HIPAA messages: See below. Order shown is based on applicability to HTS and pairings of inquiry and response. "Provider" is shown as one party to each transaction, although an intermediary such as a clearinghouse could operate on behalf of a provider:

270: Eligibility and Benefits Inquiry (provider to payer)

271: Eligibility and Benefits Response (payer to provider)

837: Healthcare Claims Submission (and COB) (provider to payer)

835: Healthcare Claim Payment Advice (payer to provider) A standard 835 message must be tied to a corresponding financial transaction

835 Prime: Similar to 835 except that a financial transaction does not need to be tied to the 835

820: Payment Order / Remittance Advice (payer to provider)

276: Claims Status Inquiry (provider to payer)

277: Claims Status Response, Claim Request for Additional Information (payer to provider)

275: Additional Information to Support a Health Care Claim (includes claim attachments) (provider to payer)

278: Referral certification/Referral authorization (both Request and Response)

HRA: Health Reimbursement Arrangement (*see* Health Fund).

HSA: Health Savings Account (*see* Health Fund).

HTS: Healthcare Transaction Services.

KPIs: Key Performance Indicators. Business metrics that are tracked and reported on which indicate the overall success of the business process.

MBPS: Managed Business Process Services.

McKesson: A Practice Management System (PMS).

ODS: Operational Data Store. HTS will maintain a permanent ODS for member data.

Payer: A health insurance company. Payers receive claims and send remittances to the submitter (typically a provider).

PCS: Provider Claims Suite.

PMS: Practice Management Systems. A PMS is the core software solution for operation of a physician's office, clinic, or hospital. Epic is an example of a PMS.

POS: Point of Service. Examples: physician's offices, clinics, hospitals.

Provider: An entity that is a supplier of healthcare services (e.g., physicians office, hospital, clinic). Providers submit claims for their services to payers.

Provider Claims Suite: A WBSF Composite Business Service. Business functions include:

Claims File and Response

Online Claims Entry

Claims Status

Claims Correction

RA: Remittance Advice. Information sent from a payer to a provider indicating payment has been made.

RRA: Retiree Reimbursement Arrangement (*see* Health Fund).

RTA: Real Time Adjudication.

Superbill: A standardized form that includes patient name and other identifying information, payer identification, and codes for diagnosis, visits, services performed, and provider fees charged. Input to a HIPAA 837 Claims Submission message.

Index